THE PHILOSOPHY OF THE BEATS

THE PHILOSOPHY OF
THE BEATS

Edited by
SHARIN N. ELKHOLY

 UNIVERSITY PRESS OF KENTUCKY

Copyright © 2012 by The University Press of Kentucky

Scholarly publisher for the Commonwealth,
serving Bellarmine University, Berea College, Centre College of Kentucky,
Eastern Kentucky University, The Filson Historical Society, Georgetown College,
Kentucky Historical Society, Kentucky State University, Morehead State
University, Murray State University, Northern Kentucky University, Transylvania
University, University of Kentucky, University of Louisville, and Western
Kentucky University.

Editorial and Sales Offices: The University Press of Kentucky
663 South Limestone Street, Lexington, Kentucky 40508-4008
www.kentuckypress.com

16 15 14 13 12   5 4 3 2 1

Library of Congress Cataloging-in-Publication Data

The philosophy of the beats / edited by Sharin N. Elkholy.
    p. cm.
  Includes bibliographical references and index.
  ISBN 978-0-8131-3580-9 (hardcover : alk. paper)
  ISBN 978-0-8131-3582-3 (ebook)
  1. Beat generation. 2. American literature—20th century—History and
criticism. I. Elkholy, Sharin N.
  PS228.B6P49 2012
  810.9'0054—dc23   2012000006

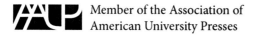 Member of the Association of
American University Presses

CONTENTS

INTRODUCTION

Sharin N. Elkholy

The great historian of ideas Arthur O. Lovejoy once wrote: "The word 'romantic' has come to mean so many things that, by itself, it means nothing. It has ceased to perform the function of a verbal sign."[1] One could say the same about the word "Beat." "Beat" encompasses such an array of meanings and contexts—cultural, social, literary, political, and philosophical—that an exact definition of the term is hard to establish. Still, we might follow Lovejoy's trajectory. He notes that the term "Romantic" is best defined by the set of German thinkers, poets, and authors who first used it to describe not only their literary and aesthetic styles, but also their styles of life. Likewise, we may define "Beat" and its several cognates, "beatnik," "beat-i-tude," "beat generation," "beat," by the group of writers who, similarly, utilized the term to describe both their literary styles and styles of life. Since the word "Beat" refers to both a literary movement and a lifestyle, it may be helpful to use the term Beat with an uppercase *B* to describe the writers grouped under the genre of Beat, either willfully or not, and beat with a lowercase *b* to describe the lifestyle and sentiments expressed by Beat authors and adopted by those known as beat to create perhaps the most enduring American subculture to date.

The best-known Beat writers are Jack Kerouac, Allen Ginsberg, and William S. Burroughs. Kerouac, Ginsberg, and Burroughs met near Columbia University in New York City in the early 1940s. John Clellon Holmes, Gregory Corso, and LeRoi Jones (Amiri Baraka) were also among their ranks, along with the street hustler Herbert Huncke and Neal Cassady, who served to inspire the above writers. Ann Charters traces the original source of the term "beat" to jazz musicians and hustlers in post–World War II New York, who used it to characterize the lifestyles of the down-and-out, poor, exhausted, and beat-up.[2] Burroughs first heard the term used by Huncke and brought it to the attention of Kerouac and Ginsberg. Years later (1948) in conversation with Holmes, Kerouac adopted the term "beat" to explain certain attitudes, gestures, and lifestyles belonging to those who embodied "a weariness with all the forms, all the conventions of the world."[3] These folks would come to be known as "hipsters," or simply "beat," those "who *really* know where we are."[4]

Thus the term "Beat" primarily serves to group together the above set of New York writers who self-consciously chose the word to identify their writings. But, as stated above, "beat" also captures diverse but related impulses and sentiments. These sentiments and styles, to be discussed below, were shared outside of New York by another set of West Coast writers and poets who, often begrudgingly, found their works grouped together as Beat. The most well-known of these writers are Gary Snyder, Philip Whalen, Michael McClure, Lawrence Ferlinghetti, Diane di Prima, Joanne Kyger, Bob Kaufman, and Ken Kesey.

In *The Philosophy of the Beats,* leading scholars in the field of Beat studies and philosophy provide cutting-edge analysis of beat style—literary, personal, and political—by drawing on philosophical theories and frameworks to recast the themes explored in Beat writings in light of their philosophical relevance. Each essay introduces its Beat subject and the philosophical figure and theory that will be used to discuss the work of the Beat writer. It then develops the Beat work from the new philosophical perspective, and, likewise, uses Beat writings and life forms to illuminate leading philosophical ideas and concepts. Writers explored in this volume include Kerouac, Ginsberg, Burroughs, Holmes, Snyder, Kaufman, Kyger, di Prima, Baraka, Charles Bukowski, and Beat filmmaker Peter Whitehead. From critical race theory, feminist theory, film theory, deconstruction, and environmentalism, to phenomenology, contemporary French philosophy, political philosophy, existentialism, Descartes, and Eastern philosophies, *The Philosophy of the Beats* explores the significance of the Beats through a range of philosophical perspectives while engaging the questions, concerns, influences and contributions of Beat writers for the contemporary reader.

In various ways, Beat writers introduced Americans and their readers around the world to new beginnings, new mythologies, and new frameworks for self-understanding through the spontaneous and dynamic modes of expression that came to mark both the Beat literary style and the beat way of life. The Beats captured an American ethos of intensity, vitality, excess, and enthusiasm. Kerouac depicts this high energy in a well-known passage from his breakthrough novel *On the Road* (1957): "The only people for me are the mad ones, the ones who are mad to live, mad to talk, mad to be saved, desirous of everything at the same time, the ones who never yawn or say a commonplace thing, but burn, burn, burn like fabulous yellow roman candles exploding like spiders across the stars and in the middle you see the blue centerlight pop and everybody goes 'Awww!'"[5]

Beat writers commonly voiced a disaffiliation with the American mainstream, its conservative values and measures of success. In opposition to the materialism and prevailing standards that defined happiness as securing a place for oneself within the higher echelons of Corporate America, the Beats promoted a turning inward. Snyder writes: "Better to live simply, be poor, and have the time to wander and write and *dig* (meaning to penetrate and absorb and enjoy) what was going on in the world."[6] Beat writers were more likely to support independent publishing and poetic legitimation outside of academic channels. Their commitment to collaborative work was intense. Tirelessly encouraging, inspiring, and promoting each other's work so freely and generously, they gave the term "collaboration" a special meaning. The Beats initiated a radical break with the old formalistic forms of expression, introducing a new relation to power and language, particularly the poetic voicing of personal experience and the articulation of positions of marginality. Beat poets took their art to the streets, on the road, performing in alleyways, coffee shops, bars, and galleries—often with jazz music accompanying a reading. At the Six Gallery in San Francisco in October 1955, Ginsberg read his poem "Howl." This poem resonated with many youth and gained the Beats national and worldwide attention. Obscenity violations further added to the poem's popularity and the notoriety of what would come to be called the beat generation.

> I saw the best minds of my generation destroyed by madness, starving hysterical naked, . . .
> . . . .
> who threw their watches off the roof to cast their ballot for Eternity outside of Time, & alarm clocks fell on their heads every day for the next decade[7]

Still, while beat mannerisms, practices, and mythologies caught on and served to inspire a generation of artists and disaffected youth, they were not without their critics. New York Beat writers in particular turned to the underworld of the thief, the hustler, the hobo, and the addict for their inspiration. They looked toward an African American cultural world, jazz musicians, bebop, and saw in that world's style of improvisation and spontaneity an affirmation of life and dynamism worth emulating. Turning to the oppressed and the downtrodden, they carved out a subculture parallel to those lived by marginalized Americans. Significantly, however, unlike the marginalized, who are cast out of society, many Beat writers and beats cast themselves out of society, choosing a form of self-marginalization in explicitly rejecting the mainstream. Notoriously, Beat writers were also known for their experimentalism with sexual practices, hetero- and homosexual, and with heavy drug use.

Robert Brustein, in "The Cult of Unthink," describes a beat as someone who is culturally and socially detached, and who revels in the criminal world and in self-abandon: "He is concerned chiefly with indulging his own feelings, glorifying his own impulses, securing his own 'cool' kicks."[8] The lust for life that Kerouac describes in *On the Road,* Brustein interprets as uncommitted and undirected physical energy that has no end: "It is no accident that Kerouac's characters are constantly seeking new kicks outside the pale of everyday experience: the experience of everyday life never touches them. In that speeding car, only objects move . . . while the characters stand immobile. Never learning or developing, they remain perpetually hungry until the inevitable disenchantment sets in."[9] Interestingly, Brustein's critique of Beat writers and beats echoes Kierkegaard's critique of the German Romantic writers and their young followers. Kierkegaard characterized Romantics as embarking upon an indiscriminate, purposeless, and unquenchable striving and yearning for experience as such, and emotional experience in particular. This striving, he argued, failed to have any roots in the "real" world and therefore absolved the Romantic of any sense of responsibility and commitment to others or to society at large.

But Holmes understands a beat's detachment from the mainstream differently: as "passive resistance to the Square society in which he lives."[10] The Beats diagnosed the ills of modern life to be primarily spiritual. Even Burroughs, who was most attuned to the workings of power and political forms of manipulation, suggested alternative modes of perception and experience to combat what he dubbed the invading "virus" of social control that sought to destroy vitality and dull the mind. Perhaps to their credit, Beat writers and beat sympathizers did not generally engage their critics directly in debate, or feel the need to defend their lifestyles. Holmes writes:

"If you can't see it [the world] in the way they do, you can't understand the way they act."[11] While often being on the "GO" is characteristic of many Beat writers, Holmes also describes this distinguishing feature of mobility not as a flight from existence, but rather as a search for meaning and firm beliefs by which to live.[12]

Sandwiched between the classical and modern, the Romantics made an indelible mark on the nineteenth century, which may arguably be called the century of Romanticism. The Beats share the distinction of defining a generation—establishing the boundaries of an enduring American literary movement and subculture, influencing the hippies, the 1960s generation, the punk movement, and even the grunge scene. Perhaps it would not be too far-fetched to define the twentieth century and beyond as beat. While most Beat writers were not political in any conventional sense, beat sensibilities guide the transformative developments in progressive political thought, inspiring the ecology movement, new age spirituality, indigenous rights, minority and women's rights, and gay liberation. Inspired by their many travels and living substantive amounts of time abroad, in North Africa, Mexico, Asia, and Europe, Beat writers help us to conceptualize the possibility of an emerging global cosmopolitanism. By approaching Beat literature through philosophical lenses and frameworks, the writers of *The Philosophy of the Beats* hope to highlight the relevance of Beat ideas and Beat writings for the modern reader.

Notes

1. Arthur O. Lovejoy, "On The Discrimination Of Romanticisms," *Modern Language Association of America* 39, no. 2 (June 1924): 232.

2. Ann Charters, introduction to *The Portable Beat Reader*, ed. Charters (New York: Penguin, 1992), xvii.

3. Ibid., xix.

4. Ibid.

5. Jack Kerouac, *On The Road* (Penguin: New York, 1999), 5.

6. Gary Snyder, "Notes on the Beat Generation," in *Beat Down to Your Soul: What Was the Beat Generation?*, ed. Ann Charters (New York: Penguin, 2001), 519.

7. Allen Ginsberg, *Howl and Other Poems* (San Francisco: City Lights, 2001), 16.

8. Robert Brustein, "The Cult of Unthink," in *Beat Down to Your Soul: What Was the Beat Generation?*, ed. Ann Charters (New York: Penguin, 2001), 50.

9. Ibid., 52.

10. John Clellon Holmes, "This Is the Beat Generation," in *Beat Down to Your Soul: What Was the Beat Generation?,* ed. Ann Charters (New York: Penguin, 2001), 235.

11. Ibid., 232.

12. Ibid.

I

THE BEATS

Creating a Subculture

The Philosophy and Non-Philosophy of Potato Salad

F. Scott Scribner

Howl. Howl for Carl Solomon, "who threw potato salad at CCNY lecturers on Dadaism."[1] Ginsberg said it well. Well, yes. The philosopher and his shadow. As Nietzsche knew, philosophy requires a double. The Beats, too. If Ginsberg, Kerouac, and Burroughs achieved literary renown for their raw expression of lived experience, it was by means of a kind of literary stunt-double, a vicarious codependence that would make their art possible at all. You see, Burroughs found his authentic junkie in Herbert Huncke, Kerouac had his vagabonding Neal Cassady, and Ginsberg reached out to his muse of insanity in the figure of Carl Solomon and his potato salad. The pursuit of lived-reality, like the holy grail of truth itself, demands expression and in doing so, sets up a double structure that cannot be readily contained, but rather tends to proliferate. So, yes. The Beats had their doubles. But to what extent could the Beats be thought of as a kind of double for philosophy? A double's double? And to what extent is this double an essential structure for self-contestation?

Like a self-help program, philosophy claims to have been trying to rid itself of its most secret self ever since Plato suggested, with sly irony, that poets be banished from the Republic. The worst thing one could do then would be to "out" philosophy as mere literature, to name it in an act of disparagement that would somehow affirm the purity and sanctity of its accuser.[2] But this trajectory, historically, has moved in only one direction. After all, the victors do tend to write history; and intellectual history is no different: it is written by those with the more acute and determinate conceptual mastery. As a consequence, philosophy runs roughshod over literature; while the Beats, in turn, give voice, as their own voice, to an experience they themselves may have never had. However, it may well be worth asking about the trajectory of this relationship in the other direction. In other words, philosophy may need the Beats, as literature, but do the Beats need philosophy?

The so-called beat generation sought a "supreme reality" through performative and experiential acts of defiance that defined a lifestyle, if not a philosophy. From Carl Solomon's potato salad toss at a lecturer on Dadaism, to Ginsburg's dalliances in crime, to the widespread experimentation in drugs, this essay asks the metaphilosophical question of whether the lifestyle of the Beats can be said to be a philosophy at all. A defining paradox of philosophy as a discipline is that it remains a site of contestation.[3] The paradox, then, is that to contest the tradition is, ironically, the only authentic way to participate within it. Contestation is the very certificate of philosophical authenticity; and the Beats clearly took part in this willful contestation. Through a meditation on the discursive limits of the discipline of philosophy itself, as a microcosm of the very motor of Western culture, this essay looks at the intimate dynamic between tradition and defiance, philosophy and non-philosophy, to assess the extent to which the experiential and performative acts of the beat generation can be said to be recoupable by the tradition and thus can be said to be a philosophy at all.

Howl's Double Inscription

The extended title of Ginsberg's poem, "Howl for Carl Solomon," expresses, or better, confesses the failure of expression, the limit of even the Beats' rupture with literary form, and its consequent dependence upon its inexpressible other. Carl Solomon, immortalized in Ginsberg's "Howl," is perhaps best known for throwing potato salad at a Dada lecture. But what else is one to do when words get in the way; when reason threatens to colonize the very subject it presents; when thought threatens to deny the disorderly vitality of life? While the potato-salad event was real, like Dada itself, it marks the resurgence of the unconscious, undermining and erasing the force of reason and its will to order insofar as it has overstepped its limits. Solomon's own muse, after all, was Antonin Artaud, and his founding inspiration was Artaud's performance of poetry as a scream.

It's worth considering the subtle difference of inflection between Ginsberg's "Howl" and Artaud's performance of poetry as a scream. The howl and the scream seem to mark two sides of the same liminal event. If "Howl" works to constitute meaning through expression of the formerly inexpressible, Artaud's performance, like Solomon's potato salad, works at the very limit of expression to undo sedimented meaning in which performative action undercuts cognitive expression. But it's really all a matter of perspective, this working and unworking. From the perspective of the poetic howl or even a visceral scream, philosophy works to constitute conceptual meaning, whereas from the perspective of philosophy, the performative work of howling or screaming is decidedly an unworking, an erosion of sedimented meaning. For instance, Ginsberg's "Howl" then could be understood to situate itself at the nexus of this bivalent dynamic of working and unworking, between philosophy's conceptual frame and the non-philosophy of the event of Carl Solomon's potato salad.

"Carl Solomon! I'm with you in Rockland, where you're madder than I am." The refrain that dominates the third section of "Howl"—"I'm with you at Rockland"—not only affirms an intellectual and artistic solidarity, but references the very first start of their friendship.[4] It was at a New York State mental hospital that Ginsberg first met Solomon. Ginsberg was there, as an alternative to jail, for some petty thefts; Solomon was there for more evident reasons. It was likely Carl Solomon whom Ginsberg had in mind when he penned the very first line of "Howl" as well: "I saw the best minds of my generation destroyed by madness, starving hysterical naked."[5] The potato-salad line continues, "and subsequently presented themselves on the granite steps of the madhouse with shaven heads and harlequin speech of suicide, demanding instantaneous lobotomy."[6] This instantaneous lobotomy is both a call for decapitation of the domination of an instrumentalized reason and rationality's only response—and a repressive one at that—to the threat of noncompliance that madness represents. Both philosophy and Beat poetry seek to embrace this difficult realm making and unmaking, the very site of self-contestation. The analogy ought to be clear: philosophy is to the Beats, what the Beats—or, Ginsberg, at least—are to Carl Solomon. If the Beats, or poetry more generally, stand as an inarticulate creative and perhaps primal source that philosophy works to bring to cognitive and conceptual clarity, then Solomon represents a likely source for Ginsberg. In considering Plato's inability to banish poetry from the Republic, however, it may well be worth considering whether philosophy is separable from poetry, whether Ginsberg is separable from Solomon, or whether the dyad itself—perhaps even the Beats and philosophy—names an inexpressible duplicitous entity that is irrevocably and simply a site of self-contestation, a dynamic that thrives in the process of its own contest.

Self-Contestation: Philosophy and Non-Philosophy

Philosophy embodies the seeming contradiction of self-contestation—biographically, historically, and thematically. The Platonic dialogue the *Crito* makes clear philosophy's biographical self-contestation.[7] After Socrates is put on trial and sentenced to death, friends arrive at his cell and offer to break him out of jail and help him escape. He refuses, explaining to them that his role, and by extension philosophy's role, is to be a "straddler" of tradition. His role is not to violate tradition and break the law, but rather to keep one leg within tradition and one leg without by vigorously questioning tradition, all the while remaining respectful of what tradition has given to him. In order to be true to himself, Socrates shows us (at least as retold by Plato) that philosophy begins in an act of self-contestation. Philosophy is at odds with itself. Its role as gadfly is to question tradition without violating it.

This relation between philosophy and its other is also visible in the history of philosophy's own emergence. Philosophy arose out of the Homeric oral tradition, but was constituted in and through the discrete linear cognition made possible by the literary technology of writing.[8] Philosophy emerged through the constitution of this unique logos made possible by writing, yet Socrates would seem to renounce both origins. Although philosophy emerged in an overturning of the oral tradition in view of a thinking made possible by the technology of writing, Socrates left no written documents and appears to have been committed to an oral style of pedagogy known as the Socratic method. And despite his celebration of the power of philosophy made possible by the technology of writing, he was deeply suspicious of the techniques of rhetoric and its instrumentalizing the logos.

Philosophy's relation to non-philosophy, or, in other words, the site of its own self-contestation, is seen nowhere clearer than in Plato's *Republic*. As is well known, Plato's concern with distinguishing truth from imitation leads him initially to banish the artists and poets from the Republic. Some of the greatest dangers would be posed by the unchecked imitation of slaves, madmen, and women, representing, respectively, the loss of autonomy, instability, and hysteria.[9] Plato eventually concedes that although he might attempt to ban the poets, he cannot eradicate the imitative mimesis essential to education and, in particular, essential to the education of the guardians. Of course, as Plato is well aware, the Socratic method and his own rhetorical prowess implicate him, and by extension philosophy as whole, in those very aspects he feigns to banish. Philosophy, in part, remains an act of self-contestation by virtue of philosophy's own uneasy relation with its other(s).

Self-Contestation and the History of Madness

Philosophy's strange bifurcation, its relation with its "other," as non-philosophy, establishes its own task as a dynamic process that continuously works to articulate and give voice to what is not yet expressible; its cognitive powers are constantly working to give voice to a kind of madness beyond it. Of course, the question is whether anyone can ever speak for another: Can philosophy ever give voice to poetry, to the Beats—or Ginsberg to Solomon? Or is speaking for another just a kind of silencing through speech? Such interrogatives critically question whether self-contestation is even possible—whether it is real, or merely feigned.

Plato's own attempt to secure philosophic truth through the eradication of imitation in *The Republic* is taken up by Descartes, through his own concern in "The Meditations," by means of securing truth through the methodic exclusion of madness. As the contemporary French philosophers Jacques Derrida and Michel Foucault make clear, Plato was likely much more aware than Descartes of philosophy's relation to non-philosophy, and the manner in which sense is bound to non-sense, and truth to madness. In his book *Madness and Civilization,* Foucault works to offer an alternative archaeology of history that aspires to articulate an insanity itself beyond the colonializing discourse of reason, embodied, for instance, in the psychological sciences, in order to let madness speak. Foucault writes: "The language of psychiatry, which is a monologue of reason on madness, could be established only on the basis of such a silence. I have not tried to write the history of that language but, rather, the archeology of that silence."[10] Now it's tempting to desire the authenticity of this silence. To dismiss philosophy in favor of the Beats. Or, better still, to forget Ginsberg, as a mere appropriation, and embrace Solomon's potato salad firsthand in its mute, frivolous density. After all, why not just "scream" with Artaud? It's worth noting that Derrida, in his work "Cogito and the History of Madness," critically takes Foucault to task for the "unfeasibility of his book" in "letting madness speak for itself."[11] In other words, for Derrida, "the maddest aspect of his project" is Foucault's attempted "determination to bypass reason."[12] Like the work of philosophy itself, the genius of Ginsberg is in his work as a mediator or translator between two worlds: he brings the universality of expressive discourse to the mute silence of Solomon's potato salad. It is an homage to both worlds, even if, like the best of translations, it is unavoidably a betrayal. Ironically, when Derrida remarks of Foucault that "the misfortune of the mad . . . is that their best spokesmen are those who betray them best," he is suggesting that the worst betrayal of all is, out of fear of the inevitable interpretative betrayal of giving them any voice, to condemn them to the so-called authenticity of utter silence.[13]

Does the Subaltern Speak?

We have spoken as if Solomon were mute, truly mad.[14] Yet what are we to make of the fact that Solomon himself, like Ginsberg, wrote and published? In the late 1960s, Solomon published a series of notes, poems, and essays entitled *Mishaps, Perhaps.*[15] His best-known piece, however, is his account of shock-therapy treatment used in asylums—of which he had firsthand experience: "Report from the Asylum: Afterthoughts of a Shock Patient."[16] Do we really need Foucault, or even Ginsberg for that matter, if the "mad" can speak for themselves? Can Carl Solomon be both the figure of "madness," of so-called authentic experience, and the voice that brings it to rational expression, without also thereby reinscribing a kind of double, the double of self-contestation within himself? Ginsberg at least seems to express his own uneasiness in this role of writer/spokesperson in yet another verse in "Howl." He writes, "I'm with you in Rockland, where we are great writers on the same dreadful typewriter." The contrast in this verse is striking. Ginsberg affirms their intellectual affinity on the order of "madness" with the expression, "I'm with you in Rockland," yet the typewriter acts almost as an object of disidentification. Yet on what order does this disidentification take place? What is even more strange is that in the midst of this disidentification with this "dreadful typewriter," Ginsberg reaffirms their identificatory unity as "great writers." At first glance, the typewriter seems to stand as a kind of symbolic institutional mandate, a compulsion to speech and the demands of the universality of reason. Yet what does it mean to be a writer who refuses or disidentifies with the typewriter? It is a will to expressivity that aspires to remain truer to the purity of the event than to the institutional demands of specific conventionally ordered forms of expression—like that of the typewriter. It may well be the very difference between the Beats and philosophy, that insidious double of self-contestation that seems to reinscribe itself everywhere and at every moment.

In the same way we saw the distinction between raw experience and its written expression manifest itself—even in the figure of Solomon—so, too, the notion of expression is saved from itself through a double self-contestatory gesture in which the "actual" expression of "great writers" is separated off through disidentification from its institutional expression in the figure of the typewriter. In the same way that authentic experience is preserved in the figure of Solomon as an emblem of madness, so, too, does the typewriter, as a kind of philosophical straw man, make possible the preservation of the authentic expression of "great writers." All of these doubling and nested frames of self-contestation make the task of preserving the delicate balance between experience and its expression a dangerous event in which one is always positioning—perhaps as the very task of the artist—for a kind of redemptive safety. Yet like the emblem of the philosophy and the Beats' dyad, Ginsberg and Solomon each face their own respective dangers. If for Solomon it is the danger of the mute expressivelessness of madness, for Ginsberg the danger is the typewriter—an institutionally mandated expression without authentic experience. Thus Ginsberg can exclaim, with particular worry for Solomon's unique weakness and proclivities for danger, "ah, Carl, while you are not safe I am not safe, and now you're really in the total animal soup of time—."[17]

In the same way that philosophy needs the unworking of non-philosophy, by calling it back to experience to reconsider sedimented concepts, so, too, does non-philosophy need philosophy to give it voice.[18] If the poet-voice of Ginsberg then represents an experiential touchstone of language for philosophy, philosophy, in turn, provides Ginsberg with a conceptual counterweight necessary to bring Solomon's silence to speech. Philosophy may be the high fortress of reason, but it is a necessary one at that. In reference to Foucault's talk of madness, Derrida writes: "The perception that seeks to grasp them . . . in their wild state, necessarily belongs to a world that has already captured them. The liberty of madness can be understood only from the high fortress that holds madness prisoner."[19] The notion of freedom represented through the madness in Beat poetry is not madness per se, but a literary trope that is already conceptually and philosophically determined. And it's not only OK, but essential that we are unhappy with that. Caught between, on the one hand, the utter silence of madness and, on the other, the burden of an overdetermined conceptual sedimentation, the very dynamic of philosophy's self-contestation emerges out of its relation with non-philosophy, and it is a touchstone to which it must forever return for it will always amount to little more than an uneasy failure.

Notes

1. Allen Ginsberg, *Howl and Other Poems* (San Francisco: City Lights, 1956), 18.

2. This same dynamic is clear today in which aspects of analytic philosophy work to solidify the status of their own style of philosophy as scientific through (in what Nietzsche might refer to as a reactive gesture) a disparagement of other styles of philosophy as mere literature. Of course, Plato knew better. And like thinkers like Derrida today, he worked to embrace the complex, contested, and tenuous nature of philosophy's own emerging status.

3. While some might try to argue that such a sweeping claim—that philosophy is always a site of contestation—is surely not without exception, it is an assertion that is largely and arguably true. For instance, even those philosophers like the Scholastics who would seem to seem to be averse to agitation (Aquinas, for instance), I would argue, have nevertheless taken a position of contestation to the extent that they are working to expand and contest philosophy's own disciplinary limits within the realm of religious vocation. The model of overturning the status quo is, of course, much clearer in major figures from Plato to Descartes to Kant to Nietzsche.

4. Ginsberg, *Howl and Other Poems,* 18.

5. Ibid., 9.

6. Ibid., 18.

7. I use the word "self-contestation" because, although one could speak of philosophy in the more abstract terms of inner contradiction, it is my view that real philosophy is always undertaken—as a struggle—in the first person.

8. See Walter Ong, *Orality and Literacy: The Technologization of the Word* (London: Routledge, 1982).

9. Philippe Lacoue-Labarthe, *Typography: Mimesis, Philosophy, Politics,* ed. Christopher Fynsk (Cambridge: Harvard University Press, 1989), 129.

10. Cited in Jacques Derrida, *Writing and Difference,* trans. Alan Bass (Chicago: University of Chicago Press, 1978), 34.

11. Ibid., 33.

12. Ibid., 34.

13. Ibid., 36.

14. The subheading is inspired by Gayatri Chakravorty Spivak's well-known article "Does the Subaltern Speak?," in *Marxism and the Interpretation of Culture,* ed. C. Nelson and L. Grossberg, 271–313 (Basingstoke, U.K.: Macmillan, 1988).

15. Carl Solomon, *Mishaps, Perhaps,* ed. Mary Beach (San Francisco: City Lights, 1966).

16. Ibid.

17. Ginsberg, *Howl and Other Poems,* 19.

18. In his essay "Philosophy and Non-Philosophy since Hegel," Merleau-Ponty also identifies non-philosophy with the immediate of experience he names "the chiasm" (Maurice Merleau-Ponty, "Philosophy and Non-Philosophy since Hegel," in *Non-Philosophy since Merleau-Ponty,* ed. Hugh J. Silverman, 9–83 [New York: Routledge, 1988]).

19. Derrida, *Writing and Difference,* 37.

LAUGH OF THE REVOLUTIONARY

Diane di Prima, French Feminist Philosophy, and the Contemporary Cult of the Beat Heroine

Roseanne Giannini Quinn

> Woman must put herself into the text—as into the world and into history—
> by her own movement.
>
> —Hélène Cixous, "The Laugh of the Medusa"

The Beat literary movement can safely be described as masculinist. To wit, Jack Kerouac infamously describes female writers of his day as "girls" who "say nothing and wear black."[1] It is no wonder then that, similar to the ways in which they were often dismissed by the men in the movement, the female Beats have gone decades without getting their scholarly due. In particular, Diane di Prima, writer of more than thirty books, whose work has been translated into at least thirteen languages, has not yet had a book of literary criticism devoted to her substantial contribution to American letters and to radical social and political theory. Some of her most recognized titles include *This Kind of Bird Flies Backward* (1958); *Memoirs of a Beatnik* (1969); *Revolutionary Letters* (1971, rereleased with additional new poems in 2007); the serial poem *Loba* (1973; 1976; 1977; 1978; 1998); *Pieces of a Song: Selected Poems* (2001); and the first volume of her autobiography, entitled *Recollections of My Life as a Woman: The New York Years* (2001). Over the last two decades, the critical attention that has been paid to her the most consistently has come from Italian American literary critics who write of her as a foremother to today's Italian American women writers within and outside of a Beat context.[2]

In this essay, I wish to situate di Prima within a larger feminist and Beat context in two ways: first by looking briefly at the current state of di Prima herself as being a still-living San Francisco Beat-poet feminist icon; and second, by examining her radical poetics, primarily via an analysis of her long poem *Loba* (2008) and *Memoirs of a Beatnik* (1969). To this end, I will employ a theoretical framework derived from the French feminist philosopher Hélène Cixous, whose call for women to "write the body" is exemplified in di Prima's writing and in her life. Even as di Prima herself eschews her literary investment in the Beat movement today, she publicly interacts with young writers who clearly come to see her out of Beat nostalgia, and to some extent, I argue, revere her as a figure of popular culture rather than as a deeply serious social philosopher and innovative feminist poet. Throughout my analysis, I foreground the importance of di Prima's decades-long social critiques of war, capitalism, and patriarchal violence that, when set alongside Cixous's conceptualizations of the "true texts of women—female-sexed texts"—may contribute to our much-needed expansion of the importance of women to the Beat movement and to a broader understanding of their literary and cultural legacies.[3]

In a recent interview with Diane di Prima by Jackson Ellis in the online magazine *verbicide,* as di Prima is reminiscing about her friendships with quintessential Beat William Burroughs and Black Mountain poet Charles Olson, she pauses and says: "If you're a woman, you have the disadvantage [that] you're a woman and nobody pays attention to you."[4] Certainly, the gendered ignoring of female Beat poets has a continuous history. Just take a trip to the Beat Museum in the North Beach section of San Francisco. The location of the women's room is up a flight of stairs and tucked in tiny area; stepping into it can be described and experienced as walking into a small closet. If you judge appreciation by square footage, this display is decidedly underwhelming. One of its most noticeable features, not surprisingly perhaps, is the moody black-and-white photograph of di Prima in her straight-haired youth—no updated picture—as if she and her work no longer exist.

Recently, however, this real and symbolic legacy shrinking seems to be more at odds with the current attention being paid to her. Most crucially, di Prima was named the fifth poet laureate of San Francisco in May 2009, with the official inauguration on February 24, 2010 (following Lawrence Ferlinghetti, Janice Mirikatani, devorah major, and Beat veteran Jack Hirschum). An important phenomenon emerged leading up to the poet laureate proclamation by Mayor Gavin Newsom and that was the vocal and organized support of di Prima by young working poets in the San Francisco Bay Area, who lobbied the award committee of the Friends of the San Francisco Public

Library via Internet websites, bookstores, and personal blogs for the selection of di Prima. This grassroots public outcry has been accompanied by the reverent attendance by younger generations of writers at her events. From the beginning of the announcement, she has taken her duties very seriously, making public appearances throughout the city at locations ranging from small neighborhood library branches and independent bookstores to larger community venues such as the Mission Cultural Center, where her inauguration celebration took place. It could be argued, I suppose, that finally di Prima has gotten her due and we can all rest easier that, at last, her place as the current grande dame of Beat Women is secured. Except . . .

After one such appearance, in which di Parma was reading and in conversation with the Italian American writer Rachel Guido deVries at the bookstore Bird and Beckett in San Francisco, I approached di Prima and cautiously informed her that I was working on an essay about her work for a book called *The Philosophy of the Beats*. Without hesitation, she tilted her head back in delighted laughter and replied, "Do the Beats have a philosophy?" Of course, I have thought a lot about her response, and I confess have been a bit haunted by it. Its immediacy signaled that there were several meanings at play in her reaction. Perhaps I thought that these would become obvious to me over time. First, what she said, I do think I understood. How can we impose just one philosophical position or influence on the Beats? Surely, there are so many. More important, though, was the layer of *laughter* itself—her initial reaction. What am I supposed to make of this?, I wondered. This mode of derision, it seemed to me at the time—and still seems to me now, upon reflection—I had experienced before.

Many in my shared U.S. second-wave feminist generation were first introduced to the French philosopher Hélène Cixous via the academic periodical *Signs: The Journal of Women in Culture and Society*. Her astonishing essay entitled "The Laugh of the Medusa" first appeared in the United States in the summer 1976 issue of *Signs*. Translated by Keith Cohen and Paula Cohen, it was based on the first published version *"Le rire de la mêduse"* in 1975. Cixous, author of more than seventy works spanning multiple genres, is arguably most widely known for her critical work on the deconstructionist Jacques Derrida. She has also, however, written vital monographs on the Russian poet Marina Tsvetaera and the avant-garde prose author Clarice Lispector. Though formally retired, Cixous is currently a visiting scholar at Cornell University through 2014 and continues to teach via the Collège international de philosophie in Paris, the free and open institution cofounded by Derrida and others in 1983.[5] To many U.S. feminists, influenced by the existentialist philosopher and first-wave feminist foremother Simone de Beauvoir and her *The Second Sex* (1949), this period of time exposed North American academic feminists to what would become known—in a recognizably broad canonized stroke—as "French feminist theory": specifically, the English translations of the works of Cixous; the Belgian feminist philosopher Luce Irigaray and her *Speculum of the Other Woman* (1974) and *This Sex Which Is Not One* (1977); and the Bulgarian-French semiotician Julia Kristeva and her *Desire in Language: A Semiotic Approach to Literature and Art* (1980).

While this influential trio of French feminist philosophers was producing such critical works as these throughout the 1970s, Diane di Prima was producing, in serial form, her long poem entitled *Loba*. As Peter Covino writes in "Innovation, Interdisciplinarity, and Cultural Exchange in Italian American Poetry," "di Prima's poetics is predicated on a sense of urgency and unconventional narrative strategies."[6] Considered to be a feminist poetic tour de force, and often referred to as the female version of Allen Ginsberg's *Howl*, *Loba*'s innovation rests in the unconventionality of having an epic poem voiced by a she-wolf goddess.[7] More important, perhaps, is di Prima's own directive as to how to move through the series. Before the opening page, there is a note: "The author reserves the right to juggle, re-arrange, cut, osterize, re-cycle parts of the poem in future editions. As the Loba wishes, as the Goddess dictates."[8] The secret handshake begins where di Prima sets forth a way of writing that destabilizes conventional ways of reading. We should not get too comfortable with any ideas of "master" narrative here. We should anticipate that the pulse of the work can change its beat, if you will. Di Prima's she-wolf reserves the right to howl, not just as muse, but as mother.

In *Loba*'s opening section, "AVE," the speaker addresses "O lost moon sisters," where women wander city streets, through desert grass, above the seashore looking for solace from each other. Within the poem, di Prima establishes what would be her steadfast feminist aesthetic—that her literary art would not sacrifice revealing the material realities of women's lives:

> pregnant you wander
> barefoot you wander
> battered by drunk men you wander
>   you kill on steel tables
>   you birth in black beds
>   fetus you tore out stiffens in snow[9]

Di Prima's insistence on materiality does share tendencies with male Beats. As Blossom Kirschenbaum notes, "Her diction resembles that of other Beat poets in inclusion of argot from jazz musicians, narcotics users, prostitutes—those who gamble with life, live marginally, evade the law or claim alliance to a higher law, and connive to gratify socially disapproved desires."[10] That is a helpful connection, but one that is not gendered enough. As has been explored extensively, much of the male Beat culture was experienced as homosocial masculinity, whether or not the writers were straight or gay. In di Prima's poetic oeuvre, as if in response, it is primarily women who are riffing; the ones beaten or outlawed; and, more importantly, the ones who either retain or regain agency. At the end of the poem, the she-wolf leads the speaker toward community, communion, incantation:

> you are the mirror image and my sister
> you disappear like smoke on misty hills
> you lead me thru dream forest on horseback
> large gypsy mother, I lean my head on your back
> I am you
> and I must become you
> I have been you
> And I must become you
> I am always you
> I must become you[11]

The animist female archetype is also visited in Cixous's "Laugh of the Medusa." Overall, the work is a chronicle of what is known as "*l'écriture féminine,*" or feminine writing. Cixous explains, "This practice can never be theorized, enclosed, coded—which doesn't mean that it doesn't exist."[12] The corollary being that it does not mean that in seeking to understand Cixous's framework, critical theorists cannot try to resist overcodification themselves. Like di Prima's she-wolf in *Loba,* the reconceptualized Medusa, wrested away from patriarchal myth, represents or is representative of what results when, per Cixous's call, "women must write through their bodies."[13] This corporeal idea/ideal metaphor is quite prevalent during and post second-wave feminism. Think of the influential collection of writing by women of color *This Bridge Called My Back,* where Gloria Anzaldúa memorably encourages Latinas, "*Don't let the censor snuff out the spark, nor the gags muffle your voice. Put your shit on the paper*" (italics in original).[14]

The embodied self on the page is a distinctly feminist act/action amid cultural histories where women are overwhelmingly and customarily written out of the story or only written in via the crudeness of misogyny. Philosophically speaking, Cixous's approach to *l'écriture feminine* is a way to organize the production of knowledge and thought that *resists* a system of knowledge and thought that by its very nature contains, restrains, represses, and oppresses women specifically (and men as well as its by-product). In *White Ink: Interviews on Sex, Text and Politics,* published more than thirty years after "Laugh of the Medusa," Cixous says, "I would situate myself in a space which tends toward poetry a little and towards philosophy a little: where poetry tends toward the philosophical."[15] When women write through the body, the space that opens up becomes potentially boundless, and "feminist invention" is the revolutionary result.[16] The infinite promise of the poetic line is intertwined with women's right to thought, and feeling, and to creating art. In turn, the old myths and laws and traditions that have constituted men's and women's ways of being, a philosophy of gender hierarchy put in practice throughout time, place, and institution can be replaced in order, as Cixous writes, "for history to change its meaning."[17]

When Medusa is laughing, she is laughing at men's folly for thinking that they could get away with this—unchallenged and forever. Cixous upends Cartesian conveniences of mind and body with the wild and uncontained embodiment that is Medusa. In the article "The Laughing Medusa," Meiling Cheng writes: "[Medusa's] body melds together multiple creatures across the species lines, including woman (her face), snake (her hair), bird (her wings), and fish (her scaly neck). . . . This cranial convergence of many heads transmutes into the Cixousian style of beginning again and again, as she strives to do away with the logic of sequential argument."[18] In one section of *Loba,* di Prima ends the short poem "The Loba Recovers the Memory of a Mare" with the line, "just out of reach."[19] The mimetic impulse to render female reality through the representation of the Medusa or the Loba is mediated via the manner of representation. As Cixous privileges a discourse of untamed analogy, di Prima asserts a poetics just beyond the line itself. Boundlessness of form follows the function of feminist content for both of them. More than a decade after the publication of her book, di Prima muses: "Now when people say 'What is *Loba* about?' I'm able to say it's about the feralness of the core of women, of the feminine in everything. In everyone."[20]

Throughout the years, the meanings attached to di Prima's own arguably feral sexuality have been explored mainly by feminist literary critics.[21]

Beginning with her now infamous prose work *Memoirs of a Beatnik,* originally published in 1969, di Prima has put the right to have a sexuality at the forefront of her feminist discourse. Those outside a feminist perspective have mostly ignored this undeniably crucial aspect of her work. In a recent interview by the poet David Hadbawnik of the Beat and San Francisco Renaissance poet David Meltzer, he states of *Memoirs of a Beatnik,* "It's a very interesting book, but I think it's done as much to box her in people's minds as a Beat."[22] In response, Meltzer explains: "It's this tendency to one-dimensionalize anything that might seem problematic. I've always considered the Beat Generation as a dissident movement, a kind of resistance movement, anti-materialist, pro–civil rights, early poetic ecology, a whole bunch of things, and that it came out of a very complex postwar American culture."[23] I find this exchange fascinating in its typicality related to discussions of di Prima's work in general via gendered lines. Nowhere in their discussion do the words "woman," "feminist," or "female sexuality" appear. This is just one example of the "one-dimensionalizing" of di Prima's corpus by those who continue to define her legacy.

Memoirs of a Beatnik continues to be read and taught, for example, in women's studies classrooms, as an early example from the women's movement of, in current parlance, a sex-positive narrative. Di Prima sleeps with men and women, quite happily, and with vigorous energy. Despite profound Italian cultural dictates, she also does this outside of marriage with not a single familiar model to the contrary. The fact that she dares to *write* about her sexuality is in many ways even more astonishing. Di Prima explains, "No one of my thirty-four aunts or uncles had ever been heard to complain of their sex life or marriage—it would have been an inconceivable breach of etiquette."[24]

In one particularly amusing chapter entitled "Some Ways to Make a Living," di Prima begins to pose for a photographer named Mr. Gay Faye. After they begin their first photo-shoot, Mr. Faye pauses to complain that the work was becoming difficult because Diane had too much hair. He asks her to consider shaving off her pubic hair. Di Prima describes: "I got a prickly, itchy feeling between my legs at the very thought, and I frowned—what I hoped was thoughtfully." She tells Mr. Fay: "'I don't know,' I said. 'Depends how much work there is.' 'Certainly not,' is what I was thinking. 'Life is hard enough.'"[25] Further in the chapter, di Prima receives another gig with the photographer and part-time pornographer Duncan Sinclair. He offers her job as his amanuensis in addition to posing for him. Sinclair has one requirement, as di Prima explains: "the only stipulation being that I work—type, answer the phone, etc.—entirely in the nude. I declined, because as I explained to him, I figured that I was making more than enough money and didn't want to tie myself up with a regular job."[26] She is living this life in the West Village of New York where she would have been considered one of the "'new Bohemians' (the word 'beatnik' had not yet been coined)."[27] Di Prima is very funny throughout this book, a humor that is completely tied to her position as pre-beatnik girl among boys.[28]

In *Memoirs*, di Prima uses explicit, descriptive sexual language throughout the text. There are so many cocks and balls, pussies and buttocks that their appearances take on an almost disembodied quality that can also be quite funny. Cixous would no doubt welcome di Prima's fulfilling bisexuality. In "The Laugh of the Medusa," Cixous defines bisexuality compellingly as the "multiplication of the effects of the inscription of desire."[29] In other words, colloquially, it is the more the merrier for women who choose this broader mode of sexual expression. More seriously, bisexuality represents the possibility that "the old single-grooved mother tongue [can] reverberate with more than one language."[30] Cixous explains: "We've been made victims of the old fool's game: each one will love the other sex. I'll give you your body and you'll give me mine," which she calls "the system of couples and opposition."[31]

Neither Cixous nor di Prima is a practical or philosophical gender separatist. Both theorize their own versions of feminine writing as manifestations of desire—accessible for both men and women but only outside of heteronormative convention. Cixous exclaims: "Isn't it evident that the penis gets around in my texts, that I give it a place and appeal? Of course I do. I want it all."[32] In this vein, Cixous spends a considerable amount of her time engaged in opposition to Freudian binaries of possession and lack in order to render them bogus. She writes, "We are in no way obliged to . . . reinstate again and again the religion of the father. Because we don't want that. We don't fawn around the supreme hole. We have no womanly reason to pledge allegiance to the negative."[33] Her similar response to the Lacanian extension of psychoanalysis to language resonates with parallel evocative humor. Cixous declares, "The woman who still allows herself to be threatened by the big dick, who's still impressed by the commotion of the phallic stance, who still leads a loyal master to the beat of the drum: that's the woman of yesterday."[34]

She calls for both women and men to dam the familial Oedipal stream once and for all. In an extended section on countering the well-known misogynist psychoanalytic paradigm of "penis envy," Cixous utters a collective call, writing, "Let us defetishize."[35] In this section, Cixous tries to strip away the notion that women's desire to experience motherhood comes from the unconscious place of trying to create a phallus (through the creation of a nuclear family unit) since she can't embody one herself. Here, as in many areas of her writing, Cixous speaks plainly: "Either you want a kid or you don't."[36] This refreshing approach not simply to Freud but to motherhood seems to apply to Diane di Prima herself. Choosing to have five children from multiple partners, di Prima has for decades transgressed any boundary of conventional motherhood that could encode her. In my mind, this kind of birth and motherhood is evoked in these lines from the section "Another Part of Loba":

> beginnings
> just out of reach.
> Spilt milke
> from a crystal
> pitcher.[37]

The image also is evocative of the figure of the she-wolf herself. Long associated with the birth of Rome, the she-wolf of Roman mythology suckled the infants Romulus and Remus after they had been abandoned by their father, Mars, and sent floating down the Tiber River. Many works of writers and fine artists, of course, have memorialized this myth, perhaps including the abstract expressionist painter Jackson Pollack. Of his postsurrealist painting *She-Wolf* (1943), Pollack commented, "Any attempt on my part to say something about it, to attempt an explanation of the inexplicable, could only destroy it."[38] Painted in profile of swirling black and white, her body, overlaid and surrounded by figure and line, resembles cave hieroglyph. It looks as if there is language there, ancient and important, but of what? It appears, perhaps, that the she-wolf is prepared to walk straight across and off of the canvas; the frame will not contain her. Di Prima, a painter herself, comments on her she-wolf:

> She does not leave in her going, she arrives
> continuously
>   no epiphany
>
> only Presence[39]

In Verena Andermatt Conley's well-known study *Hélène Cixous: Writing the Feminine,* in a series of interviews, she quotes Cixous's further explanation of *écriture féminine* as embodying liberated structures "which are not delimited texts with neat borders, with chapters, with beginnings, endings, etc., and which will be a little disquieting because you do not feel the arrest, the edge (the *arrêt* or the *arêt*)."[40] Like Pollack and di Prima, the requirement of the philosopher critic is to *resist* the need for the edge, or the finished line, or the finish line in the painting or the poem or the essay.

However, di Prima does not title her book "she-wolf." She uses the Spanish word, of course, and also opens the section "Book I" with a song excerpt from the Tlingit indigenous peoples of the Northwest Coast of North America, "It would be very pleasant to die with a wolf woman."[41] The Tlingit, still flourishing in Alaska, for example, are known for their animistic crested totem poles in which the wolf remains one of the prominent symbols of matriarchal lineage.[42] Clearly, di Prima is drawing from many myths, cosmologies, philosophies in *Loba.* Perhaps, there is none more present than the Mexican "*la loba,*" or bone woman, collector of wolf bones who represents the reverse cycle of life from grandmother to mother to laughing maiden. "And when a ray of the sun, or the moon, strikes the wolf at just the right time and place, it turns into a woman, a laughing woman, who you may see running toward the horizon."[43]

In "Castration or Decapitation?," Cixous takes on the children's story of "Little Red Riding Hood," whom she calls jokingly the "little clitoris." In an extended section on the story, Cixous interrogates this particular fairy tale as a male psychoanalytic captivity narrative where Little Red must be punished for doing "what women should never do, travels through her own forest."[44] In so doing, our heroine is wrested away from the power of female legacy, the grandmother, whose very person is stolen by, yes, the Big Bad Wolf. Cixous writes: "We know that lying in wait for us somewhere in some big bed is a Big Bad Wolf. . . . So, between two houses, between two beds, she is laid, ever caught in her chain of metaphors, metaphors that organize culture."[45] At the end of this essay, Cixous makes an important move in her thinking about how to reconstitute culture, noting: "Writing in the feminine is passing on what is cut out by the Symbolic, the voice of the mother, passing on what is most archaic. . . . So the movement, the movement of the text, doesn't trace a straight line. I see it as an outpouring."[46] This way of thinking is so evident in di Prima, including her making primary Native American cultural values as a cornerstone of *Loba.* As Paula Gunn Allen writes in the section "Grandmother of the Sun, Grandmother of the Night," in *The Woman Who Owned the Shadows:* "'When you've seen for generations how everything, everyone you love dies so hard, you laugh. A lot. At everything,' she said. . . . She talked, her thoughts ran in circles. Which couldn't be helped. Indians lived in circles, did not care for lines that broken went nowhere. For her the sun was a clock, a calendar, like her body. . . . She thought in accretions, concretions. Like pearls grow. Like crystals. Like the earth."[47] Certainly, other Beats in addition to di Prima display profound interest if not devotion to non-Western forms of thought and philosophy including shamanism, Zen Buddhism, and meditative states of consciousness. When viewed through Cixous as well, both multicultural understanding and cultural transformation are grounded female imperatives. Cixous concludes: "Culturally speaking, women have wept a great deal, but once the tears are shed, there will be endless laughter instead. Laughter that breaks out, overflows, a humor no one would expect to find in women—which is nonetheless surely their greatest strength.[48] Feminist revolution comes first by recognizing the absurd hilarity in what women have had to endure to survive in the first place and to create in the second.

And, this sentiment can also be communicated much more soberly without anything being funny at all. In di Prima's book *Revolutionary Letters,* she describes "Ancient History":

> The women are lying down
> In front of the bulldozers
> Sent to destroy
> The last of the olive groves.[49]

To place di Prima in the history of the Beats today is to centralize her. Brenda Knight has recently written, "More than any other woman of the Beat, di Prima has taken her place alongside the men as the epitome of Beat brilliance."[50] I would not want to hierarchize di Prima in that way, just thinking of Joanne Kyger and Anne Waldman, but I do appreciate the effort to have us acknowledge her place with justified reverence. For decades, di Prima has taught workshops in her home and in her community to women: across age, ability, race, ethnicity, prosody, name, place. She has offered sliding-scale fees and no fees. She has mentored, cajoled, and made better women who are prominent writers and women who write to survive in order to live the beat of another day. Besides her own body of work, that perhaps will be di

Prima's greatest legacy: teacher of women, a she-wolf herself. You can call this lived philosophy.

Currently, there is an Internet petition posted by the youngest of Diane di Prima's children to name a street after her in San Francisco, close to where she lived when *Loba* was first published. Rudi di Prima posts: "We should easily be able to accomplish this and honor the name of a woman who has worked tirelessly in the name of Poetry, Freedom (political, sexual, social . . .), Healing in San Francisco."[51] This would be a fitting tribute—especially if we stepped off of the edge of the street's sidewalk and kept right on going.

Notes

I would like to thank the Cecil H. Green Library at Stanford University for allowing me visiting research access to their collections.

1. Ronna C. Johnson and Maria Damon, "Recapturing the Skipped Beats," *Chronicle of Higher Education,* October 1, 1991, B4, B6.

2. Mary Jo Bona, *By the Breadth of Their Mouths: Narratives of Resistance in Italian Americana* (Albany: State University of New York Press, 2010), 147.

3. Hélène Cixous, "The Laugh of the Medusa," trans. Keith Cohen and Paula Cohen, *Signs: Journal of Women in Culture and Society* 1, no. 4 (1976): 877.

4. Jackson Ellis, "Interview: Diane di Prima," *verbicide,* July 29, 2010, 2.

5. Daniel Aloi, "A. D. White Professor-at-Large Hélène Cixous to Visit," *Chronicle Online* (Ithaca, N.Y.: Cornell University Press, 2010), www.chronicle.cornell.edu.

6. Peter Covino. "Innovation, Interdisciplinarity, and Cultural Exchange in Italian American Poetry," in *Teaching Italian American Literature, Film, and Popular Culture,* ed. Edvige Giunta and Kathleen Zamboni McCormick (New York: Modern Language Association of America, 2010), 107.

7. Johnson and Damon, "Recapturing the Skipped Beats," B6.

8. Diane di Prima, *Loba* (New York: Penguin, 1998), 1.

9. Ibid., 4.

10. Blossom S. Kirschenbaum, "Diane di Prima Extending *La Famiglia,*" *Melus* 14, no. 3–4 (1987): 64.

11. Di Prima, *Loba,* 5–6.

12. Cixous, "The Laugh of the Medusa," 863.

13. Ibid., 896.

14. Gloria Anzaldúa, "Speaking in Tongues: A Letter to 3rd World Women Writers," in *This Bridge Called My Back: Writings by Radical Women of Color,* 2nd ed., ed. Cherríe Moraga and Gloria Anzaldúa (New York: Kitchen Table: Women of Color Press, 1981), 173.

15. Hélène Cixous, *White Ink: Interviews on Sex, Text and Politics*, ed. Susan Sellers (New York: Columbia University Press, 2008), 18.

16. Ibid., 150.

17. Cixous, "Laugh of the Medusa," 885.

18. Meiling Cheng, "The Laughing Medusa," in *Feminaissance*, ed. Christine Wertheim (Los Angeles: Les Figues Press, 2010), 66.

19. Di Prima, *Loba*, 125.

20. Diane di Prima, "The Tapestry of Possibility," *Whole Earth* (Fall 1999): 20.

21. Brenda Knight, *Women of the Beat Generation: The Writers, Artists, and Muses at the Heart of a Revolution* (Berkeley, Calif.: Conari, 1996), 2.

22. David Hadbawnik, "Interview with David Meltzer—Diane di Prima Feature," *Big Bridge* webzine, March 2010, www.bigbridge.org.

23. Ibid.

24. Diane di Prima, *Memoirs of a Beatnik* (New York: Olympia, 1969), 48.

25. Ibid., 76.

26. Ibid., 77.

27. Ibid., 111.

28. Ibid., 110.

29. Cixous, "Laugh of the Medusa," 884.

30. Ibid., 885.

31. Ibid., 885, 887.

32. Ibid., 890–91.

33. Ibid., 884.

34. Ibid., 892.

35. Ibid., 890.

36. Ibid., 890.

37. Di Prima, *Loba*, 218.

38. Alexander B. Herman and John Paoletti, "Re-reading Jackson Pollack's *She-Wolf*," *Artibus et Historiae* 25, no. 50 (2004): 139.

39. Di Prima, *Loba*, 242.

40. Verena Andermatt Conley, *Hélène Cixous: Writing the Feminine* (Lincoln: University of Nebraska Press, 1984), 137.

41. Di Prima, *Loba*, 7.

42. Thomas F. Thorton, *Being and Place among the Tlingit* (Seattle: University of Washington Press, 2007), 31–32.

43. David Leeming and Jack Page, *Goddess: Myths of the Female Divine* (Oxford: Oxford University Press, 1994), 173–74.

44. Hélène Cixous, "Castration or Decapitation?," trans. Annette Kuhn, *Signs: Journal of Women in Culture and Society* 7, no. 1 (1981): 44.

45. Ibid., 44.

46. Ibid., 54.

47. Paula Gunn Allen, *The Woman Who Owned the Shadows* (San Francisco: Spinsters/Aunt Lute, 1983), 185.

48. Cixous, "Castration," 55.

49. Diane di Prima, *Revolutionary Letters* (San Francisco: Last Gasp, 2007), 139.

50. Brenda Knight, "San Francisco Poet Laureate Can Teach Us All to Write," *San Francisco Examiner*, March 3, 2010, www.examiner.com.

51. Rudi di Prima, "Petition to Rename Rose Alley Diane di Prima St.," Care12: Petitionsite, www.petitionsite.com.

Beat U-topos or Taking Utopia on the Road

The Case of Jack Kerouac

Christopher Adamo

> We were leaving confusion and nonsense behind and performing our one and noble function of the time, move.
>
> —Jack Kerouac, On the Road

As Russell Jacoby details in *Picture Imperfect,* utopian thought has come under suspicion in the twentieth century. The political actualization of Marxism in the form of Soviet communism gave many twentieth-century thinkers pause, horrified and puzzled that a state apparently or allegedly inspired by Marx's vision of a society without economic class or political coercion could so quickly show itself to be ruthlessly totalitarian and dictatorial. Philosophers as diverse Hannah Arendt, Isaiah Berlin, and Karl Popper, reflecting upon the Marxist historical and philosophical impulses of the nineteenth century, concluded that utopian thinking akin to that of Marx's work—but certainly not limited to his work alone—once actualized inclines toward political totalitarianism.[1] To put this position in different terms, these thinkers assert utopian thought to be incompatible with political liberalism.

To the extent that such classical utopian visions were collective, the Beats, including Kerouac, align with this anti-utopian sentiment, suspicious that any collective (political) answer to the question, "How are we to live?" threatens to rob man of his individuality, freedom, and dignity—key values of political liberalism. For the Beats, however, this question becomes all the more pressing given the lack of any satisfactory collective answer, given our being "condemned," as Sartre put it, to answer it individually. In this light, the Beats channeled their utopian impulses toward the individual life as it could be lived, the best possible individual human life, a life concerned with politics, the collective, only to the extent that it frustrates or promotes the pursuit of experiments in such a life. For Kerouac specifically, only the injunction not to harm others places limits on such individual experiments. Such a principle finds support not only in the basic tenets of Buddhism, which Kerouac fully embraces, but also in a basic tenet of political liberalism, John Stuart Mill's harm principle. In particular, this fusion of political liberalism with Buddhist philosophy finds expression in Kerouac's own cross-continental travels, as well as in the hobos who find their way into his narratives, Mississippi Gene and the St. Theresa Bum.

But can utopian thought, generally rooted in ideas of collective communities, be compatible with political liberalism and its ethos of individualism? What new form, literary or otherwise, must utopian thought take so as to remain compatible with political liberalism without ceasing to be, at minimum, iconoclastic, if not, in some sense, programmatic? My most general contention is that both the work and praxis of the Beats engages the tension between utopian thought rooted in collectives, and political liberalism rooted in individualism. Specifically, I propose Jack Kerouac's *On the Road* as an exemplar of utopian thought that remains compatible with both the lineage of utopian thought and the basic tenets of political liberalism. My analysis of this work follows a brief sketch of both political liberalism and the trajectory of utopian literature since Thomas More.

Political Liberalism

The basic principles of political liberalism originate with the social contract theories of Thomas Hobbes (*Leviathan*) and John Locke (*Two Treatises of Government*). Despite their vast differences, both Locke and Hobbes assert that man's natural condition by right is one of liberty. Individuals organize themselves into collectives (states) in order to better protect their liberty and the results of its exercise (e.g., property) from the usurpation of others. The political collective aims to safeguard each individual's liberty to do as one pleases so far as such action does not impede the exercise of liberty by any other. Any ceding of individual liberty to the collective (e.g., one's right to exact retributive justice against someone who has interfered with the exercise or results of one's liberty) secures its political legitimacy only in the name of protecting the exercise of personal liberty.

John Stuart Mill captures this basic principle of political liberalism in *On Liberty*: "The sole end for which mankind are warranted, individually or collectively, in interfering with the liberty of action of any of their number is self-protection. . . . The only purpose for which power can be rightfully exercised over any member of a civilized community, against his will, is to prevent harm to others."[2] This principle, known as the harm principle, proscribes, albeit ambiguously, the limits within which the collective can utilize its power to constrain or dictate the actions of any one of its members. This principle enshrines the sanctity of the liberty of thought, the liberty of lifestyle, and the liberty of association. It is the liberty of lifestyle that will be of chief concern here. Mill devotes considerable energy in *On Liberty* to demonstrating both the practical and the intrinsic worth of liberty of lifestyle—individuality: "As it is useful that while mankind are imperfect there should be different opinions, so is it that there should be different experiments of living; that free scope should be given to varieties of character, short of injury to others. . . . Where not a person's own character but the traditions or customs of other people are the rule of conduct, there is wanting one of the principal ingredients of human happiness, and quite the chief ingredient of individual and social progress."[3] Freedom and a variety of situations are necessary conditions of human development and progress because these conditions "render people unlike one another."[4] "Europe," Mill writes, "is . . . wholly indebted to [a] plurality of paths for its progressive and many-sided development."[5] In short, the end results of political liberty are plurality and individuality, which both possess intrinsic value and remain essential catalysts for continued human development.

A Brief History of Utopian Thought

From its initial use by Thomas More, the term "utopia" revels in ambivalence, meaning literally, "no place" (*u-topos*) but alluding also to a "happy-place" (*eu-topos*). Mimicking the style of New World travelogues, utopian writers of the age of exploration established their utopias on remote islands hitherto undiscovered by Europeans. These utopias were isolated city-states from which Europeans could learn a thing or two about the manner in which political, social, even religious institutions ought to be organized so as to maximize justice, stability, and collective contentment. The ideal city outlined by Socrates in Plato's *Republic* is also, retrospectively, regarded as a seminal piece of utopian thought since Thomas More drew inspiration from it and frequently alluded to Plato's *Republic* in his own *Utopia*.

During the nineteenth century, the socially critical and ironic tone of utopian literature came to be overshadowed by a more explicitly programmatic tone. The rise of industry promised both to alleviate humanity of one of its most onerous social burdens—coerced labor—while simultaneously overcoming one of the chief sources of conflict between men—scarcity. The ascendency of greater political inclusiveness but also, as important, the various claims of philosophers to have deciphered the key to historical progress endowed Europeans with a new sense of control over their personal and political future. Armed with the knowledge of history's hitherto secret logic, one (so it was thought) could actually hasten the coming of perpetual peace (Kant), or the stateless state (Marx)—a world without war, without want, without political or economic coercion. Hence the increased production of what Russell Jacoby has called "blueprint utopias," imaginative productions that lean much more toward concrete proposals for revolutionizing existing unjust and/or inefficient practices and institutions than toward mere mocking criticism of current practices and institutions. In addition, as the portion of the globe untouched by European institutions had shrunk down to virtually nothing, these utopian communities grew to occupy not merely islands, but entire continents, and finally, by 1905 in H. G. Wells's *A Modern Utopia,* the entire globe.[6]

Classical Utopian Thought and Political Liberalism

Many twentieth-century thinkers claim that such a programmatic brand of utopianism intellectually inspired, if not enabled, the political atrocities and dictatorships of this past century by licensing the sacrifice of individual liberty and dignity for a collective good. This position is anticipated and reflected in twentieth-century literature with the rise of the anti-utopian and dystopian works of Aldous Huxley, George Orwell, Ayn Rand, and Yevgeny Zamyatin, among others. *Brave New World, 1984, Anthem,* and *We* all present radically reformed societies gone horribly wrong; and all, in their own way, concur that where they have gone wrong is in the loss of freedom, liberty, and individuality.

Gorman Beauchamp notes that despite the diversity of the details, until the twentieth century almost all utopian works prioritize political stability. The logic is simple. If the utopian state captures the best possible organization of society, then any subsequent change in the society can only be for the worse. Thus, Beauchamp summarizes: "Utopian theorists . . . reject the conflict model of society—one in which the state regulates and adjudicates among competing interests—in favor of an equilibrium model—one in which social life is so perfectly regulated that no further systematic change is desirable or possible."[7] Such a telos by nature would be inimical to the cultivation of diverse lifestyles inasmuch as Mill is correct about the connection between experiments in living and social progress. There can no longer be any further progress resulting from individual experiments in living, only regress, since the utopian vision, once fully actualized, is the best of all possible worlds. Gorman Beauchamp summarizes the conflict between political liberalism and utopian thinking: "The former [political liberalism] celebrates pluralism, diversity, individual, even conflict in . . . 'the marketplace of ideas'; the latter [utopian thinking] desires uniformity, harmony, conformity and statis."[8]

E. L. Chertkova additionally underscores another common assumption among classical utopian thought that precludes plurality. In Plato's *Republic,* insight into theoretical truth legitimates the rule of the philosopher king; the implication is that *truth* ought to be the basis of political praxis.[9] Whether the knowledge be of the elusive Good, God's will, or the inner logic of history, the underlying principle is that those with such knowledge are in a better position to detail and implement how society ought to be organized to maximize the well-being, or "good," of all. In other words, the raison d'être of the state is not so much to protect individual liberty as it is to promote the collective Good. The logic of such a position becomes clear: if the role of the state is to promote the collective Good (claimed to be *known* as *the* Good), the good of the individual, as she personally conceives of it, can be compromised in the name of the collective Good. Chertkova echoes the observations of both Isaiah Berlin and Karl Popper, who, in their own ways, claim that there can be no such rational knowledge of the nature of the Good, the very claim to knowledge upon which utopian thinkers (and totalitarian states) base the rationale of their utopian designs. The collective must only manage conflict, as value-neutrally as possible, as tensions inevitably arise from each individual's pursuit of his or her own chosen personal Good among the plurality of legitimate possibilities.

Kerouac, Political Liberalism, and the Utopian Imagination

At first blush, the work of Jack Kerouac would seem to have little to do with utopian literature or utopianism. To the extent that traditional utopian productions have been detailed descriptions of political, economic, and social institutions, quite clearly little Kerouac wrote fits such a description, though we may be inclined to invoke the loosely knit community of "rucksack wanderers" envisioned by Japhy Ryder in *The Dharma Bums.*[10] In addition, to my knowledge, Kerouac uses the term "utopia" only once in his novels—in *Desolation Angels:* "Dostoevsky said 'Give man his Utopia and he will deliberately destroy it with a grin' and I was determined with the same grin to disprove Dostoevsky!"[11] The passage itself raises all the modern ambiguities of the term "utopia," as the type of "utopia" Dostoyevsky has in mind in the quoted passage is precisely the overly programmatic utopias that threatened man's liberty, dignity, and integrity; and it is hardly the case that Kerouac understood his work as an attempt to show that a person could be happy in such a regimented, scientifically planned and micromanaged society.

Should the lack of any detailed description or meditation on political and social institutions disqualify Kerouac's work from the canon of utopian literature? Before such principled exclusion, it would be well to consider the following observations. First, by John Clellon Holmes: "Everywhere the Beat Generation seems occupied with the feverish production of answers . . . to a single question: how are we to live? And if this is not immediately recognizable in leather-jacketed motorcyclists and hipsters 'digging the street,' it is because we assume that only answers that recognize man as a collective animal have any validity; and do not realize that this generation cannot conceive of the question in any but personal terms."[12] At bottom, the classical utopian writers address this central philosophical question—"How ought we to live?" Whether their work is primarily critical and iconoclastic, using the imaginative utopias to suggest that we are not living the way we ought, or whether their work is primarily programmatic, using the imaginative utopia to proscribe how we ought to live, their work provides collective—not personal—answers to this central question.

Certainly the description of an ideal personal life, as opposed to the ideal city, changes the literary form the utopian vision must take. But ironically, an additional reason this form must change is precisely because the hegemonic grip of the present society has virtually foreclosed setting a spatial political utopia anywhere on this planet. Arguably this moment is signaled most clearly in the celebrated utopian works of the late nineteenth century, *Looking Backwards* and *News from Nowhere,* where the protagonists no longer travel through space, but through time, in order to reach the utopian society (Boston and London of the twenty-first century, respectively). And, as noted, H. G. Wells's *A Modern Utopia* (1905) presents us with a global utopia situated on a doppelgänger Earth to which the protagonists have been mysteriously transported.[13]

For these reasons, the literary critic Northrop Frye, as early as the 1960s, already makes clear: "If there is to be a revival of utopian imagination in the near future, it cannot return to the old-style spatial utopias. New utopias would have to derive their form from the shifting and dissolving movement of society that is gradually replacing the fixed locations of life. They would not be rational cities evolved by a philosopher's dialectic: they would be rooted in the body as well as the mind, in the unconscious as well as the conscious, in forests and deserts as well as in highways and buildings, in bed as well as the symposium."[14] What is fascinating here is Frye's claim that the utopia can no longer be of place, despite, or maybe true to, its etymology—"no-place." Speaking more specifically, the place of utopia can no longer be the polis, the state, the "place" of politics. Thus works of the utopian imagination can no longer be limited to those that fit the traditional literary format of a travelogue providing detailed descriptions of social, collective institutions and practices.

On the Road

Jack Kerouac's celebrated *On the Road* makes for an interesting case study in this light. Its narrator, Sal Paradise, seeks his personal answer to this basic question—How is he to live?—by heading west, and later south, by going "on the road." *On the Road* reads as a travelogue and hence, in its form, echoes that of the utopian works from the age of exploration. However, while the protagonists in traditional utopian novels happen upon the utopia accidently, Sal Paradise deliberately sets out on the road to find his personal answer.

An additional difference is that the focus quickly shifts from places (the West, Mexico) to persons and their lifestyles. Certainly, Dean Moriarty's lifestyle is romanticized in *On the Road,* though, ultimately, Sal becomes disenchanted with his friend. But Dean's lifestyle is not the only lifestyle romanticized. Sal's first cross-continental trip brings him into contact with the lifestyle of hoboism, which, unlike Dean's lifestyle, is never repudiated in *On the Road.* What both Dean and Mississippi Gene of *On the Road* (or the St. Teresa Bum in *Dharma Bums*) embody is personal liberty taken to its extreme, captured in *On the Road* by the idealizing of a condition normally associated with transition from place to place, being "on the road."

Hence, the implication is that personal liberty, the cardinal value of political liberalism, is best found and lived by being, literally, of no-place (*u-topos*), of being in constant movement.

Certainly the central character of *On the Road* is Dean Moriarty. Analysis of Sal's search and transformation in *On the Road* frequently focuses upon his relationship with Dean.[15] It is with "the coming of Dean Moriarty" that Sal's "life on the road" begins.[16] Sal is taken by Dean's persona for a number of reasons: "He reminded me of some long-lost brother" (10); already Dean sparks nostalgia for a time now past: "the sight of his suffering bony face . . . made me remember my boyhood in those dye-dumps and swim-holes and riversides of Paterson and the Passaic" (10). Simultaneously, Dean stirs up visions of the West, to which Sal had "often dreamed of going" (3), and Dean appears as "a sideburned hero of the snowy West" (5). It is a place to which Sal has yet to travel and hence can still mythologize. It is this association with the West that also has Dean sticking out like a sore thumb when among Sal's "New York friends," who are "in the negative, nightmare position of putting down society and giving the tired bookish or political or psychoanalytical reasons" (10); by contrast, "Dean raced with society, eager for bread and love"; even his criminality "was a wild yea-saying overburst of American joy; it was the Western, the west wind, an ode from the Plains" (10).

Sal sets off spurred by the visions of the West that Dean's speech and manner inflames within him. Since, for Sal, Dean's persona is fused with place—the West—one could argue that Sal still views "utopia" as place—the West. However, the allure of the West is that it produces men such as Dean and the Nebraska farmer Sal encounters in a diner between Omaha and Grand Island, Nebraska: "He [the Nebraska farmer] didn't have a care in the world and had the hugest regard for everybody. I said to myself, Wham, listen to that man laugh. That's the West, here I am in the West" (21).

Thus, the mythic West is represented by persons and not vice-versa. In terms of place, the cities of the West disappoint. For instance, upon arriving at Council Bluffs: "I looked out. All winter I'd been reading of the great wagon parties that held council there before hitting the Oregon and Santa Fe trails; and of course now it was only cute suburban cottages of one damn kind and another, all laid out in the dismal gray dawn" (19). Most instructive is Sal's reaction to the Wild West festival in Cheyenne: "I was amazed, and at the same time I felt it was ridiculous: in my first shot at the West I was seeing to what absurd devices it had fallen to keep its proud tradition" (33). Sal quickly discovers that much of the mythic West has vanished and seems to live on only in such persons as Dean, the Nebraska farmer, and the hobos he meets like Mississippi Gene.

It should be noted that Sal narrates with the knowledge of the end of his travels with Dean: "Although my aunt warned me that he would get me into trouble, I could hear a new call and see a new horizon, and believe it at my young age; and a little bit of trouble or even Dean's eventual rejection of me as a buddy, putting me down, as he later would, on starving sidewalks and sickbeds—what did it matter?" (10–11). This passage references the end of the second journey, when Sal is left with Marylou in San Francisco while Dean patches things up with Camille; it also references the end of the fourth and last journey when Dean, once obtaining divorce papers, leaves a sick Sal behind in Mexico City. The careful reader should then find it no surprise that Sal's final pronouncement on Dean is that he is a "rat" (303). It should additionally be noted that, as Paul Maher Jr. has indicated, from its inception in 1948, Kerouac's vision for his road novel was of a quest that would end in some degree of disenchantment.[17]

But the disillusionment with Dean ought not to lead one to conclude that Sal no longer feels the lure of the road and that *On the Road* therefore ends with "a return to middle-class conformity," as Allan Johnston has recently argued.[18] Much of Sal's personal transformation occurs during the first cross-continental trip, during which he didn't speak with Dean "for more than five minutes the whole time [in Denver]" (59). This transformation occurs through Sal's brief encounter with Mississippi Gene.

What distinguishes Dean Moriarty's travels from those of Mississippi Gene? As Allan Johnston rightly notes, Sal's disenchantment with Dean comes from "his gradual recognition that Moriarty has to use people—and use up people—to keep going."[19] In other words, Dean's lifestyle inevitably harms others (e.g., Camille, Marylou, Sal himself) and is thus in conflict with J. S. Mill's harm principle. But Dean's lifestyle is not the only manner one can live perpetually on the go. By contrast with Dean, Mississippi Gene travels with a charge, who Sal describes as "a sixteen-year-old blond kid, also in hobo rags" (25). As the ride rolls through Nebraska, Sal regards Mississippi Gene with clear admiration: "Every now and then Gene leaned out of his Buddhistic trance over the rushing dark plains and said something tenderly in the boy's ear. The boy nodded. Gene was taking care of him, his moods and his fears. . . . They had no cigarettes. I squandered my pack on them, I loved them so. They were grateful and gracious" (30). Sal also discovers to his delight and amazement that the hobos have a sort of community that transcends belonging to a political space. "Ogden," Gene explains, "is the place where most of the boys pass thu and always meet there" (28). On a lark, Sal asks Gene about a Big Slim Hazard, whose story (football star at LSU turned merchant marine turned hobo by choice) echoes Kerouac's personal history and, of course, Gene knows him, though by the moniker Louisiana Slim. Sal's enthusiastic response: "Damn!" (29). Mississippi Gene leaves enough of an impression upon Sal that he recalls with fondness Big Slim Hazard and Mississippi Gene while in New Orleans (147).

It is of interest here that, as demonstrated by Robert Holton, the Beats responded to the impending cultural homogeneity of the American 1950s by developing a sense of community detached from any specific place. Rather than a spatial, political identity, belonging to the Beat community was a matter of social differentiation—of having certain musical tastes, employing a certain language, frequenting certain establishments.[20] Perhaps for Sal, and perhaps for Kerouac himself, the loose-knit community of hobos provided the lure of a sense of community and belonging without any permanent attachment to specific persons or places that would compromise one's personal liberty.

The influence the hobo lifestyle has upon Sal becomes quickly evident. After the trip to Crystal City, Sal senses his "moments in Denver were coming to an end" (57). The banter of hobos, overheard during a dull afternoon with Rita "made me want to get back on that road" (57). It is not Dean that sets him on the road here; Dean remains in Denver. Nor does Sal seem concerned with the job Remi Boncoeur promised for him in San Francisco. It is the chatter of *hobos* that makes him want to get *back on that road,* apparently irrespective of the destination: "I heard the Denver and Rio Grande locomotive howling off to the mountains. I wanted to pursue my star further" (57).

On the Road provides a foretaste of Kerouac's romanticizing of hoboism in his nonfiction, while lamenting its disappearance in "The Vanishing American Hobo." Kerouac praises the hobo in this essay and his "idealistic lope to freedom and the hills of holy silence and holy privacy. . . . There's nothing more noble than to put up with a few inconveniences like snakes and dust for the sake of absolute freedom."[21] Kerouac also notes that "in America there has always been . . . a definite special idea of footwalking freedom."[22] The hobo is defined by "having nothing to do with a community."[23] Certainly Kerouac's roll call of "hobos" stretches lexical extension of the term; Kerouac includes, for instance, Teddy Roosevelt and Albert Einstein in his roll call of great hobos, suggesting that the term applies equally to an independence of thought as an independence from place.[24]

This theme reappears, of course, in the *Dharma Bums,* in Japhy Ryder's vision of the rucksack wanderers referenced above. Here, though, we note an increased concern with harming no one, a contrast between Dean of *On the Road* and Japhy of *Dharma Bums.* Japhy's vision has a tinge of the negative in it insofar as it is a rejection of a burgeoning consumerist lifestyle. Ray Smith finds some solace in the vision of a couch-potato, junk-consuming America, pointing out that "the people watching television, the millions and millions of the One Eye: they're not hurting anyone."[25] And though space does not permit full analysis here, in *Desolation Angels,* this principle of both continual movement and of endeavoring to do no harm is captured in the trope of "passing through."

Thus one of the central tenets of Buddhism emphasized by Kerouac in his life and work—a vow to hurt no living thing—can be situated in the context with the crucial limit to personal liberty set by J. S. Mill—one is at liberty to do and act as one wishes so long as those actions do not bring harm to others. Certainly its application to all living things transmutes the principle from one of political theory to one of spiritual matters; my only point is that such a principle, in Kerouac's view, could easily be rendered consistent with an idealized vision of America and the political principles of liberty and individualism America stands for, though, as Kerouac perceived, these were in danger of being eviscerated within the burgeoning consumer and corporate culture of the 1950s.

In sum, in his life and work Kerouac radicalized the central tenet of political liberalism—personal liberty—expressed both in the freedom of movement and in the harm principle, to endeavor to exercise one's liberty to the fullest extent possible without doing harm to others. The extent to which Kerouac in his own life succeeded in this is certainly debatable; and certainly his celebrity compromised the personal liberty he had worked so hard to protect (perhaps for the sake of his art). The reasons why Kerouac himself gave up his hoboism seem wide-ranging: a commitment to care for his mother once his work became commercially successful; the increasing difficulties of such journeys;[26] the physical strain Kerouac's fame and impending alcoholism took.[27] I do not find grounds, however, that Kerouac abandoned his personal hoboism because he refuted the ideals he saw in hoboism. Certainly one can debate whether Kerouac meant such a lifestyle as described in his fiction and essays to be programmatic, or whether Kerouac mainly meant such advocacy to be iconoclastic. Certainly one can argue that Kerouac, by romanticizing the lifestyle of the hobo, deflects needed attention from serious social and economic problems of which transience is a symptom.[28] However, it cannot be debated that Kerouac's utopian vision of such persons as Mississippi Gene, of Japhy Ryder and St. Teresa Bum continues to inspire almost three generations of readers with a personal vision of the good life, a life lived "on the road," a life of "passing through" that infuses the key principles and values of an increasingly utilitarian political liberalism with a deeper spiritual significance.

Notes

1. Russell Jacoby, *Picture Imperfect: Utopian Thought for an Anti-Utopian Age* (New York: Columbia University Press, 2005), see esp. chaps. 1 and 2. In chapter 1, Jacoby articulates three reasons for the ascendency of anti-utopianism; in chapter 2, Jacoby summarizes and evaluates the arguments of prominent philosophers associated with anti-utopianism, including, but not limited to, Isaiah Berlin, Karl Popper, and Hannah Arendt.

2. John Stuart Mill, *On Liberty* (Indianapolis: Hackett, 1978), 9.

3. Ibid., 54.

4. Ibid., 70.

5. Ibid., 69.

6. For a more detailed summary of the history of utopian literature, and speculation upon its future, see Krishan Kumar, "Utopia on the Map of the World," *Hedgehog Review* 10, no. 1 (2008): 7–18.

7. Gorman Beauchamp, "Changing Times in Utopia," *Philosophy and Literature* 22, no. 1 (1998): 219–30.

8. Ibid., 224.

9. E. L. Chertkova, "The Metamorphoses of Utopian Consciousness," *Russian Studies in Philosophy* 46, no. 2 (Fall 2007): 6–24.

10. Jack Kerouac, *The Dharma Bums* (New York: Penguin, 1976), 97.

11. Jack Kerouac, *Desolation Angels* (New York: Riverhead, 1995), 255.

12. John Clellon Holmes, "The Philosophy of the Beat Generation," in *Nothing More to Declare* (New York: Dutton, 1967), 119.

13. One of the most recent of the old-style spatial utopias, Aldous Huxley's *Island* (1962) eulogizes the disappearance of such spatial and political utopias. At the close of the novel, the utopian island, Pala, is occupied by a colonizing military force desirous of Pala's natural resources, and hence, the fragile, isolated utopia is forcibly swept up into global politics and economics the society had worked so hard to avoid in order to preserve its distinctive way of life.

14. Northrop Frye, "Varieties of Literary Utopias," in *Utopias and Utopian Thought,* ed. Frank E. Manuel. (Boston: Houghton Mifflin, 1966), 25–49.

15. See, for example, George Dardess, "The Delicate Dynamics of Friendship," in *The Beats: Essays in Criticism,* ed. Lee Bartlett (Jefferson, N.C.: McFarland, 1981), 127–32; Allan Johnston, "Consumption, Addiction, Vision, Energy: Political Economies and Utopian Visions in the Writings of the Beat Generation," *College Literature* 32, no. 2 (2005): 103–26; Steve Wilson, "'Buddha Writing': The Author and the Search for Authenticity in Jack Kerouac's *On the Road* and *The Subterraneans,*" *Midwest Quarterly* 40, no. 3 (1999): 302–15; and George Mouratidis, "'Into the Heart of Things': Neal Cassady and the Search for the Authentic," in *On the Road: The Original Scroll,* by Jack Kerouac, ed. Howard Cunnell (New York: Penguin, 2007), 69–81.

16. Jack Kerouac, *On the Road* (New York: Penguin, 1976), 3. Subsequent references to this work are to this edition and appear parenthetically in the essay text.

17. Paul Maher Jr., *Jack Kerouac's American Journey: The Real Life Odyssey of "On the Road"* (Cambridge, Mass.: Thunder Mouth, 2007), 110.

18. Allan Johnston, "Consumption, Addiction, Vision, Energy: Political Economies and Utopian Visions in the Writings of the Beat Generation," *College Literature* 32, no. 2 (2005): 103–26.

19. Ibid., 117.

20. Robert Holton, "'The Sordid Hipsters of America': Beat Culture and the Folds of Heterogeneity," in *Reconstructing the Beats,* ed. Jennie Skerl (New York: Palgrave Macmillan, 2004), 11–26.

21. Jack Kerouac, "The Vanishing American Hobo," in *Lonesome Traveler* (New York: Grove, 1988), 172–73.

22. Ibid., 173.

23. Ibid., 176.

24. Ibid., 175–76.

25. Kerouac, *Dharma Bums,* 104.

26. See Jack Kerouac, *Big Sur* (New York: Penguin, 1992), 44–48; and Kerouac, "The Vanishing American Hobo," 181.

27. These speculations are indebted to my study of two Kerouac biographies: Ann Charters, *Kerouac: A Biography* (San Francisco: Straight Arrow, 1973); and Gerald Nicosia, *Memory Babe: A Critical Biography of Jack Kerouac* (New York: Grove, 1983).

28. And for these reasons it is unfortunate that even in the nonfiction "The Vanishing American Hobo," Kerouac does not maintain a distinction between an elective transience (hoboism) and a nonelective transience (homelessness). Even the distinction Kerouac begins to draw, but does not seem to observe in the piece, between hobos and bums rests more on whether the hobo has lost his pride: "Sometimes hobos were inconsiderate, but not always, but when they were, they no longer held their pride, they became bums—" (177).

BEING-AT-HOME

Gary Snyder and the Poetics of Place

Josh Michael Hayes

> Nature is not a place to visit, it is *home.*
> —Gary Snyder, *The Practice of the Wild*

What does it mean to be at home in a place? Is the home a psychic space we project upon the places we inhabit, or does it possess a specific geographical location that defines our identity as human beings? Moreover, can we ever really be at home? These are all questions that might be uniquely attributed to the poetry and prose of Gary Snyder as a participant in the Beat Generation. While Snyder has acknowledged that he does not easily identify with the popular cultural history of this generation, I hope to provide a series of preliminary gestures that might at least lessen Snyder's uneasy relation to the Beats. First, I shall begin by investigating the poetic significance of "being-at-home" in his own practice as a Zen Buddhist and as a student of primitive cultures. Second, I will turn to how this sense of place is reflected in his concrete ethical and political commitments, specifically his avowed pragmatism as an environmentalist. I will conclude with his reflections upon language that warrant a radical paradigm shift in how we might begin to speak about the "nature" of place.

The poetic significance of "being-at-home" throughout Snyder's writings is intimately tied to his earliest reflections upon the Beats. How does Snyder find himself in relation to the Beats, particularly if he is historically considered to be among the first and last representatives of this generation? What does "being-at-home" mean for Snyder and what does it mean for the Beats? In an early article entitled "Notes on the Beat Generation," published in 1960 in the Japanese journal *Chuo-koron*, Snyder presents his first candid

assessment of the international significance of the Beats: "The beat generation is particularly interesting because it is not an intellectual movement,
but a creative one: people who have cut their ties with respectable society
in order to live an independent way of life writing poems, painting pictures,
making mistakes, and taking chances—but finding no room for apathy or
discouragement. They are going somewhere."[1] While Snyder identifies with
their distinctive brand of antibourgeois intellectualism as "some of the only
truly proletarian literature in recent history" (Snyder 1995, 10), it is much
more difficult to assess whether the other aspects of Snyder's personal biography as a poet, teacher, scholar, and public intellectual resonate with the
spirit of that generation. If one is to attempt to characterize Snyder's creative
contributions to the Beats, it would surely include his embrace of an intellectual cosmopolitanism responsible for bringing the Eastern tradition of
Zen Buddhism into conversation with the American literary scene. Yet such
a cosmopolitanism is already at work within the values of the beat generation itself: "In a way one can see the beat generation as another aspect of the
perpetual 'third force' that has been moving through history with its own
values of community, love, and freedom. It can be linked with the ancient
Essene communities, primitive Christianity, Gnostic communities, and the
free-spirit heresies of the Middle Ages; with Islamic Sufism, early Chinese
Taoism, and both Zen and Shin Buddhism" (Snyder 1995, 12). Snyder's
earliest prose devoted to the phenomenon of the Beats also includes his
resistance to being classified according to the more pervasive characteristics of the label. In a subsequent essay entitled "The New Wind," Snyder
advertently identifies himself as belonging not to the beat generation per se,
but to an independent group of poets who share some affiliation with the
San Francisco Poetry Renaissance, a series of loosely organized readings,
publications, and meetings during the late 1950s and early 1960s. Following
Don Allen's preface to the *New American Poetry,* Snyder lists the American
literary scene of his generation according to five classes: (1) The poets who
first associated with *Origen* magazine and *Black Mountain Review;* (2) the
San Francisco Poetry Renaissance; (3) the Beats, specifically Jack Kerouac,
Allen Ginsberg, Gregory Corso, and Peter Orlovsky; (4) New York poets;
and (5) the last group, "a sort of miscellaneous collection of independent
characters who cannot be fitted into any other class and who all have individual styles" (Snyder 1995, 17). Therefore, Snyder's distinctive contribution as a poet to the philosophy of the Beats, if there is such a philosophy,
remains an open question.

First, there is the obvious difficulty of presenting a coherent philosophy of the Beats since the most iconic figures of that generation, namely Jack Kerouac and Allen Ginsberg, are notorious for defying simple labels. John Clellon Holmes's landmark 1958 essay "The Philosophy of the Beat Generation" (Holmes 2001), presents the Beats broadly enough as seekers on a spiritual path attempting to overcome the intellectual despair and moral chaos of their generation. Echoing Kerouac, Holmes writes that "if they seemed to trespass most boundaries, legal and moral, it was only in the hope of finding a belief on the other side. The Beat Generation . . . is basically a religious generation" (Holmes 2001, 229). If Kerouac's novel *On the Road*, epitomizes this spiritual quest, it cannot be easily defined according to the boundaries of traditional religious experience. Indeed, such a quest reflects the distinctive identity of each individual of that generation. When Jack Kerouac was asked in an interview to whom he prayed, his reply reflects an intensely personal approach to religion: "I pray to my little brother, who died, and to my father, and to Buddha, and to Jesus Christ, and to the Virgin Mary . . . I pray to those five people" (Holmes 2001, 237). Like Kerouac, Snyder's own spiritual quest reflects the myriad activities that have come to shape his personal identity, including working as a seaman, logger, and forest lookout and keenly studying such seemingly divergent discourses as the anthropology of Native American lore, Zen Buddhism, and the deep ecology movement. Snyder's vocation as a poet is itself rooted in a spiritual intimacy with the natural world that one might identify with the perspective of previous American Transcendentalists, like Emerson, Thoreau, and Whitman. However, Snyder's spiritual quest is best illustrated by his uncanny ability to blend these naturalist themes with an intellectual cosmopolitanism. While Snyder has consistently resisted the temptation to equate himself with the fictional character Japhy in Jack Kerouac's novel *Dharma Bums,* the parallel is quite striking for presenting a personality endowed with an immense degree of intellectual enthusiasm for a diverse range of topics under the sun:

> I'll do a new long poem called "Rivers and Mountains without End" and just write it on and on a scroll and unfold on and on with new surprises and always what went before forgotten, see, like a river, or like one of them real long Chinese silk paintings that show two little men hiking in an endless landscape of gnarled old trees and mountains so high they merge with the fog in the upper silk void.

I'll spend three thousand years writing it, it'll be packed full of information on soil conservation, the Tennessee Valley Authority, astronomy, geology, Hsuan Tsung's travels, Chinese painting theory, reforestation, Oceanic ecology, and food chains. (Kerouac 1958, 157)[2]

Throughout *Dharma Bums,* Japhy is portrayed as a learned yet carefree student of the Zen Buddhist tradition who eagerly departs for Japan at the conclusion of the novel. The character of Japhy clearly mirrors Snyder's own personal biography and his relationship with Jack Kerouac, yet there is another more profound aspect of Snyder's personality that is sincerely invested in understanding and discerning the natural rhythms of a place. It might seem sensible to contrast Snyder's contributions as a poet with the wayfaring spirit of the beat generation by returning to his abiding respect for a sense of place. However, the incessant spiritual quest embodied by the narrator, Sal Paradise, in Kerouac's *On the Road* shares a certain affiliation with the place-based nature of Snyder's own poetry and prose. Kerouac's own sense of place is not identified with a geographical location as much as it is with a state of mind. In a 1982 retrospective devoted to the San Francisco Poetry Renaissance, Snyder remarks that California represents "a long tradition of political radicalism, including early environmental activism, IWW labor organizing, and anarchopacifism" (Davidson 1989, 11). While the political strands of Snyder's sense of place are apparent in his poetry and prose, there exists another layer to Snyder's reflections about place that is clearly indebted to his own travels abroad.

After his long stay in Japan from 1959 to 1965, Snyder has exhibited both an intellectual and geographical sense of "rootedness" and a keen awareness of the virtues of the hearth: "Still—and this is very important to remember—being inhibitory, being place-based, has never meant that one didn't travel from time to time, going on trading ventures or taking livestock to summer grazing. Such working wanderers have always known they had a home-base on earth, and could prove it at any campfire or party by singing their own songs."[3] Importantly, Snyder's sense of "being-at-home," while implying that one culturally identifies with a place, also occupies another layer of the palimpsest by equating one's physical surroundings with our home base here on earth. Thus, while one identifies with a specific geographical location, the geographical always extends to the geological. We are both locally and globally rooted. While this plural identity might present a challenge to Snyder, his writings reflect a commonsense approach to the political themes of cosmopolitanism and liberal pluralism that resonate with the uniquely American tradition of pragmatism: "Just as when I went to Japan I found out who I really was . . . an American pragmatist" (Davidson 1989, 100). The hearth or the home figures prominently in Snyder's writings as not merely a space for taking practical actions in all matters personal and political, but ultimately as a space of creativity where poetry and prose might begin to flourish. The art of poetry flourishes only when one finds oneself embedded in the very fabric of a place. While one stereotype of the Beats insistently proclaims the virtues of Kerouac's "spiritual seekers" always on the road, Snyder cleverly provides a new conception of place that questions our tendency to think in terms of such binary oppositions. In an essay entitled "Blue Mountains Constantly Walking" (Snyder 1990), Snyder equates being-at-home with being homeless in his description of a poem from the early Chinese Tang poet Han-shan: "'Homeless' is here coming to mean 'being-at-home in the whole universe.' In a similar way, self-determining people who have not lost the wholeness of their place can see the households and their regional mountains or woods as within the same sphere" (Snyder 1990, 104). This condition entails not only a kind of self-reliance upon the rhythms of the natural world, but also a spontaneous receptivity to respond to whatever "turns up on the doorstep." Living in step with nature has never been far from Snyder's poetry and prose. One might even claim that his writings originate from his own place, Kitkit-dizze, which he has inhabited for more than forty years on San Juan Ridge in the Sierra Nevada foothills.

Snyder's essay "The Place, the Region, and the Commons" (Snyder 1990) proposes an understanding of place as an experience that gradually deepens as one develops through time. The essay begins with a line by the founder of the Soto school of Zen Buddhism, Dōgen, "When you find your place where you are, practice occurs" (Snyder 1990, 25). One grows into a place and gradually recognizes that by inhabiting a place, we become what we are. However, inhabiting a place does not entail that one spends their entire lifetime in the same place. Travel presents a special significance to place and effectively assists us in better knowing our own place. In traveling to and from the heart of a place that is the home, our sense of place develops a kind of fluidity: "Yet even a place has a kind of fluidity: it passes through space and time—'ceremonial time' in John Hanson Mitchell's phrase. A place will have been grasslands, then conifers, then beech and elm. . . . But each is only for a while, and that will be just another set of lines on the palimpsest" (Snyder 1990, 27). Just as places undergo not only seasonal and geographical transitions, so do humans undergo a similar set of transitions from birth to death. While the fluidity of a place may be understood in psychic or even unconscious terms, the metaphors employed are predominantly physical or geographical in origin. The physical identity of a place converges with our own psychic identity so that there no longer remains a strict division between them: "We live in a universe 'one turn' in which, it is widely felt, all are one and at the same time, all are many. The extra rooster and I were subject and object until one evening we became one" (Snyder 1995, 47). If we extend this metaphor to a sense of place, Snyder's poetry reflects the unity between a person and a place yet also respects this difference. While it is the task of the philosopher to investigate the difference between both kinds of identity, the poet functions much more like a yogi in her connection with nature, "an experimenter, whose work brings forth a different sort of discourse, one of deep hearing and doing" (Snyder 1995, 49). Snyder traces the work of the yogin to a set of disciplines (breathing, meditation, chant-ing, dietary practices) that run counter to the Occidental tradition so that the yogic becomes identified with the shamanic: "The shaman speaks for wild animals, the spirits of plants, the spirits of mountains, of watersheds. He or she sings for them. They sing through him. This capacity has been achieved via sensibilities and disciplines. In the shaman's world, wilderness and unconscious become analogous: she who knows and is at ease in one will be at home in the other" (Snyder 1995, 50).

Snyder's earliest writings have been at home with this shamanic ten-dency. In his 1951 senior thesis at Reed College, "He Who Hunted Birds in His Father's Village," published under the same title in 1979, one already glimpses a distinctive aspect of this shamanism, a kind of creative sponta-neity present in the oral performance of a poem: "What I'd emphasize now, even more than I did when I wrote it, is the primacy of performance: in the dark room, around the fire, children and old people, hearing and joying together in the words, the acting and the images. It's there that the shiver of awe and delight occurs, not in any dry analysis of archetypes or motifs—or the abstractions of the structuralist" (Snyder 1979, xi). This document fore-shadows an important theme of the Beats. The primacy of a performance expressed in those primitive rituals that began the San Francisco Poetry Renaissance—which has since become part of the whole phenomenon known as the "beat generation" (Snyder 1995, 8). Snyder fondly recalls how a motley band of poets gathered on a cold October evening in 1955 with their court jester, Jack Kerouac, "beating tunes on empty bottles" to inaugurate a night of poetry: "What we had discovered, or rediscovered, was that imagination has a free and spontaneous life of its own, that it can be trusted, that what flows from a spontaneous mind is poetry" (Snyder 1995, 8–9).[4] Snyder is perhaps the only Beat poet who has consistently returned to the primitive production of poetry as a natural process. The spontaneous imagination like a natural spring perpetually renews itself through the movement of production by making the old new again. This kind of poetry that constantly returns to the primitive reflects the most authentic dimension of human experience: "Poetry must sing or speak from authentic experience. Of all the streams of civilized tradition with roots in the Paleolithic, poetry is one of the few that can claim an unchanged function and relevance which will outlast most of the activities that surround us today" (Snyder 1957, 118).[5]

Snyder's 1974 collection of poems entitled *Turtle Island* illustrates this concern with making the primitive new again so that we might come to rediscover our own sense of place in the natural world. It is the responsibility of a given culture to appropriate a given historical situation by making it one's own. There is a need to recover the primitive so that it still speaks to us today to address our own contemporary concerns: "Such poetries will be created by us as we reinhabit this land with people who know they belong to it; for whom 'primitive' is not a word that means past, but primary and future" (Snyder 1977, 42–43). This intimate relation between poetry and dwelling also resonates with the claim of the German philosopher Martin Heidegger that "poetically man dwells." Heidegger develops the implications for such a turn of phrase by beginning his essay of the same title with a series of questions that deserve special attention: "If need be, we can imagine that poets do on occasion dwell poetically. But how is 'man'—and this means every man and all the time—supposed to dwell poetically? Does not all dwelling remain incompatible with the poetic?" (Snyder 1990, 69).[6] The term "dwelling" throughout Heidegger's writing essentially refers to the nature of human existence or how we find ourselves as being finitely situated in a world. Heidegger claims that poetry is what really lets us dwell. It is only through poetry that we come to build and thus to make our dwelling. Snyder's poetry exhibits this same concern for poetry as making possible a space for dwelling. The poets bear the burden of reestablishing our lost bond with the primitive by singing not about society, but about nature and the primordiality of place. This retrieval entails that we transcend the entrapments of the modern ego and begin to recognize the relative impermanence of all things.

The theme of impermanence resonates throughout Snyder's poetry and prose and is particularly prevalent in his commentaries upon Zen Buddhism: "The marks of Buddhist teaching are impermanence, no self, the inevitability of suffering, connectedness, emptiness, the vastness of mind, and a way to realization. A poem, like a life, is a brief presentation, a uniqueness in the oneness, a complete expression, and a gift" (Synder 1995, 115). Poetry reflects a certain humility by calling our attention to the profoundly ordinary. It is this same reverence for the ordinary that we find in Heidegger's essay "The Thinker as Poet," specifically his regard for the "splendor of the simple." Such a splendor is revealed in Heidegger's description of a farmhouse in the Black Forest: "Here the self-sufficiency of the power to let earth and heaven, divinities and mortals enter in simple oneness into things, ordered the house. A craft which, itself, sprung from dwelling, still uses its tools and frames as things, built the farmhouse" (Heidegger 1971, 160). Just as the time of poetry exists as a finite phenomenon of orality expressed around the hearth, nature itself follows a similar trajectory of impermanence in coming to be and passing away. Snyder describes this impermanence as a kind of wildness by playing upon the Chinese word for "wild," "ye," which basically means "open country": "The world is nature, and in the long run inevitably wild, because the wild, as the process and essence of nature, is also an ordering of impermanence" (Snyder 1990, 5). While nature and the wild can be interpreted in terms of their impermanence, the human species all too easily lives under the illusion of permanence. By reversing Thoreau's proclamation, "Give me a wildness no civilization can endure," Snyder compels us to imagine a civilization that wildness can endure: "Wildness is not just the preservation of the world, it is the world. . . . We need a civilization that can live fully and creatively together with wildness. We must start growing it right here in the New World" (Snyder 1990, 6).

Snyder's turn to wild nature as necessary for the preservation of the world also importantly reflects Heidegger's claim that the earth preserves the world. While the earth constitutes a place and space for human dwelling, the world might be characterized as always already grounded in and delimited by this dwelling: "The world is the self-disclosing openness of the broad paths of the simple and essential decisions in the destiny of a historical people. The earth is the spontaneous forthcoming of that which is continually self-secluding and to that extent sheltering and concealing. World and earth are essentially different from one another and yet are never separated. The world grounds itself on the earth, and the earth juts itself through world. But the relation between world and earth does not wither away into the empty unit of opposites unconcerned with one another. The world, in resting upon the earth, strives to surmount it. As self-opening, it cannot endure anything closed. The earth, however, as sheltering and concealing, tends to draw the world into itself and keep it there" (Heidegger 1971, 174). Like Heidegger, Snyder recognizes that this play between earth and world is fundamentally a reflection of the order of impermanence that grounds reality itself. By reminding ourselves of this impermanence, we can begin to develop a new etiquette of freedom that defies the constraints of modern subjectivism: "To be truly free one must take on the basic conditions as they are—painful, impermanent, open, and imperfect—and then be grateful for impermanence and the freedom it grants us" (Snyder 1990, 5). The freedom accorded by the recognition of our own impermanence might enable an ethos fundamentally guided by the imperative to save the wildness of the world. Such a sparing and preserving is concordant with a historically informed, albeit primitive sensitivity toward inhabiting the land: "Saving does not only snatch something from a danger. To save really means to set something free into its own presencing" (Heidegger 1971, 150).

Snyder's writings have always expressed a pervasive concern with the welfare of the natural environment. From his earliest works of poetry to his later prose, Snyder's approach to resolving many of the pressing environmental concerns confronting us today displays an uncanny sense of the natural history of a place. Snyder describes this "bioregional" approach as a sensitivity toward the dynamic properties of each region: "Bioregionalism calls for commitment to this continent place by place, in terms of geographical regions and watersheds. It calls us to see our country in terms of its landforms, plant life, weather patterns, and seasonal changes—its whole natural history before the net of political jurisdictions was cast over it" (Snyder 1995, 246–47). Snyder proposes a set of concrete political goals for the preservation of a bioregion beginning with the transformation of existing "historical" names and boundaries so that one might cultivate an awareness of one's surroundings that reflects the existing geography. Such a radical transformation requires redrawing the surface of the planet so that we can be at home in our given landscape: "As sure as impermanence, the nations of the world will eventually be more sensitively defined and the lineaments of the blue earth will begin to reshape the politics" (Snyder 1990, 43). From renaming northern California the "Shasta Bioregion" to reflect the rivers that flow downward to the San Francisco Bay and upward to the Sacramento and San Joaquin Rivers to renaming America "Turtle Island," the name given to this continent by Native American mythology, one could begin to develop a more informed sense of the biodiversity that one is meant to defend. Snyder criticizes the millions of Americans who live in a land that they do not "know." There is a certain cognitive dissonance present when we speak about the United States, Canada, and Mexico as political entities, even a homelessness that departs from any sense of rootedness, "Home—deeply, spiritually—must be here. Calling this place 'America' is to name it after a stranger" (Snyder 1990, 40).

Snyder's bioregionalism ultimately reflects a communal sense of stewardship whereby one shows a sense of solidarity with a place: "With this kind of consciousness people turn up at the hearings and in front of trucks and bulldozers to defend the land. Showing solidarity with a region! Bioregionalism is the entry of place into the dialectic of history—we are not limiting our analysis of difference to class. And there are 'classes' that Marx overlooked—the animals, rivers, and grasses are now entering history" (Snyder 1990, 41). Snyder encourages us to think of these classes as not occupying a specific place per se, but as forces of energy. To speak about classes would thereby require attention to their constantly changing and evolving nature. Snyder is keenly aware of the biological and geological processes that must be taken into account if we are to accord nature a distinct political status: "A worldwide purification of mind is called for: the exercise of seeing the surface of the planet for what it is—by nature" (Snyder 1990, 41). For such a worldview to succeed, it must be practiced predominantly at the local level. To echo the sentiment of Max Cafard, author of "The Surre(gion)alist Manifesto": "We have no country, we live in the country. We are off the Interstate. The Region is against the Regime. Regions are anarchic" (Snyder 1990, 44).

While Snyder's anarchism is another attribute of the radical politics of the Beats, Snyder's politics are also consistently tempered by a pragmatic respect for the existing structures necessary to effect political change. In his landmark essay "Four Changes" (Snyder 1974), Snyder takes on what he sees as the four most pressing environmental issues: population, pollution, consumption, and personal transformation. Beginning with the issue of population, Snyder claims that we should strive to cut in half the global population. Social and political action must be taken by first alerting the governments and leaders of the world to the severity of the problem by encouraging legalization of abortion and voluntary sterilization. To attain a low and steady birth rate, Snyder recommends that we more vigorously explore alternative family structures, such as group and polyandrous marriage, and encourage adoption. Snyder also turns to the excessive amount of pollution that continually threatens and harms the environment. While the banning of DDT and other pesticides is necessary and recycling has become an effective habit for many industrialized countries in the First World, what is most needed at the global scale is a reduction in the level of air pollution. Snyder encourages a culture of walking and an adoption of the mantra "Don't waste" to become the ethos for present and future generations. We are so devoted to the myth of global capitalism that we frequently do not consider how life could be different without such a paradigm: "People fear small society and the critique of the State. It is difficult to see, when one has been raised under it, that it is the State itself that is inherently greedy, destabilizing, entropic, disorderly, and illegitimate" (Snyder 1990, 41). Reflecting his own living situation at Kitkitdizze, Snyder embraces communal living whereby one engages in a cooperative community of creating and sharing by engaging in the virtues of simplicity and mindfulness.

Transformative change depends upon practices that tread lightly upon the earth and a constant awareness of our own egoism. Such a personal transformation might essentially function to remind us of our primitive connection with wild nature: "Wildness is the state of complete awareness. That's why we need it" (Snyder 1995, 41). While technology has succeeded in bringing us together, it has also caused a decrease in interhuman contact that has taken us away from our primitive roots. How can we successfully return to the primitive without fully denouncing the advantages of technology? Since technology frees us from many of the obligations previously accorded to past generations, this relative freedom could be utilized to reflect upon our own impermanence: "We have these advantages to set off the obvious disadvantages of being screwed up as we are—which gives us a fair chance to penetrate some of the riddles of ourselves and the universe, and to go beyond the idea of 'human survival' or the 'survival of the biosphere' and to draw our strength that at the heart of things is some kind of serene and ecstatic process that is beyond qualities and beyond birth and death" (Snyder 1990, 45).

For Snyder, the human species at this moment in history requires not merely a transformation of personal and political boundaries, but linguistic boundaries. In a conversation with the linguist Ron Scollon, who has worked for many years with the Athapaskan family of languages, Snyder remarks that we must learn to think about language as essentially belonging to our own biological nature: "Human beings are a wild species (our breeding has never been controlled for the purpose of any specific yield), and would you agree that language is also wild? The basic structures are not domesticated or cultivated. They belong to the wild side of the mind" (Snyder 1990, 70). To cultivate this natural bias, Snyder recommends that we must first begin to speak about nature differently. As a student of cultural anthropology, Snyder reminds us of the dangers of our anthropocentric egotism when we attempt to "humanize" nature as a political entity with a distinctive set of rights. While we are indeed responsible for the welfare of the planet, nature cannot simply be qualified so narrowly in either strictly political or even cultural terms.

Snyder's essay "Tawny Grammar" (Snyder 1990) discusses how we might come to speak about nature as having its own language. Snyder borrows the phrase "tawny grammar" from Thoreau to express our forgetfulness about our own human nature: "This vast, savage howling mother of ours, Nature, lying all around, with such beauty, and such affection for her child as the leopard. . . . The Spaniards have a good term to express this wild and dusky knowledge, *Gramatica parda,* tawny grammar, a kind of mother wit derived from that same leopard to which I have referred" (Snyder 1990, 76). While grammar is traditionally understood as the description of the structure of language and the system of rules that govern it, the root of the word "grammar" means "to scratch" (*gerebhh* or *grebhh*). Here Snyder recalls an insightful story about the origin of writing in the early Chinese tradition: "In very early China diviners heated tortoise shells over flames till it cracked and then read meanings from the design of these cracks. It's a Chinese idea that writing started from copying these tracks. Every form of writing relates to natural minerals. . . . Lifting a brush, a burin, a pen, or a stylus is like releasing a bite or lifting a claw" (Snyder 1990, 66). Snyder's story about the origins of writing reveals an understanding of language that transcends the human and must otherwise be presented as a gift of nature.

If we begin to understand language as an organic phenomenon, then one might begin to speak of an ecology of language. Most importantly, writing should remain distinct from speech since the speech indicates an original event of nature: "Grammar comes from the *gramma techne,* 'woven scratches.' But it is quite clear that the primary existence of language ('tongue') is in the event, the utterance. Language is not a carving, it's a curl of breath, a breeze in the pines" (Snyder 1990, 69). The natural event of language brings to the fore a radical difference between oral and written transmission throughout cultures. While "books have become our grandparents" in the civilized world, the elders of the primitive world transmitted culture by means of stories containing those natural utterances that still resonate with us today. This emphasis upon orality is especially important for Snyder's oeuvre when he speaks about poetry as a phenomenon of our own primitive nature. Snyder develops this theme in yet another direction by claiming that language is myriad in its natural tendencies of oral expression. We possess not only a grammar, but multiple grammars that reflect an order already manifest in nature: "The grammar not only of language, but of culture and civilization itself, is of the same order as this mossy little forest creek, this desert cobble" (Snyder 1990, 76).

An ecology of language might entail that we begin to consider different systems of language in terms of how they participate in the nature of our own region. Language would first and foremost have to reflect a sense of place where a local culture is always embedded in the deeper web of the natural world: "Some historians would say that 'thinkers' are behind the ideas and mythologies that people live by. I think it also goes back to maize, reindeer, squash, sweet potatoes, and rice. And their songs" (Snyder 1990, 61). Unfortunately, we live by the illusion that things are otherwise if we continue to believe that language is a uniquely human construct. On the contrary, Snyder's reflections on language remind us that language is an organic phenomenon that makes a natural appeal to us. In fact, we are just as responsible for heeding its primitive call as those poets inhabiting North Beach once did. Such a responsibility is always rooted in our connection to a place. We cannot sever language from how we find ourselves "being-at-home" in this *place in space*. Returning to the words of the Zen Buddhist philosopher Dōgen: "To carry yourself forward and experience myriad things is delusion. But myriad things coming forth and experiencing *themselves* is awakening" (Snyder 1990, 76).

Notes

1. Gary Snyder, "Notes on the Beat Generation" and "The New Wind," in Snyder 1995, 13. Snyder ironically composed both pieces during his first extended stay in Japan between 1959 and 1965 while studying under the Zen master Oda Sessa Roshi. Snyder

proclaims in an afterword to the essay that his audience is not the authors and critics of the American poetry, but the "urban intelligentsia. These folks were existentialist Marxists, with a French symbolist aesthetic—an imported mindscape, incompletely assimilated into the just beginning Japanese industrial renaissance and rising affluence. These pieces reflect the downright joy I felt over the new American poetry. They were first published in *English in American Poetry* 2, no. 1 (Fall 1984)" (Snyder 1995, 18).

2. "Japhy Rider was a kid from eastern Oregon brought up in a log cabin deep in the woods with his father and mother and sister, from the beginning a woods boy, an ax man, farmer, interested in animals and Indian lore so that when he finally got to college by hook or crook he was already well equipped for his early studies in anthropology and later in Indian myth and in the actual texts of Indian mythology. Finally he learned Chinese and Japanese and became an Oriental scholar and discovered the greatest Dharma Bums of them all, the Zen lunatics of China and Japan" (Kerouac 1958, 9).

3. Gary Snyder, "The Place, the Region, and the Commons," in Snyder 1990, 26.

4. Indeed, such a spontaneity of imagination originating with poetry must be essentially characterized as a natural phenomenon. Here, the Greek term for poetry (*poiesis*) at once connotes a kind of producing and making which occurs not only through the imagination of the poet but ultimately as an activity of nature (*physis*).

5. "Poets, as few others, must live close to the world that primitive [people] . . . are in; the world, in its nakedness, which is fundamental for all of us—birth, love, death; the sheer fact of being alive" (Snyder 1957, 118).

6. Heidegger is also clearly aware of the power of language as that which appeals to us: "To reflect on language means—to reach the speaking of language in such a way that this speaking takes place as that which grants an abode for the being of mortals" (Heidegger, 1971, 192). Such a granting of an abode entails that language comes to us, we do not come to language. "Man speaks only as he responds to language" (Heidegger 1971, 210).

References

Davidson, Michael. 1989. *The San Francisco Poetry Renaissance*. Cambridge: Cambridge University Press.

Heidegger, Martin. 1971. *Poetry, Language, Thought*. Translated by Albert Hofstadter. New York: Harper and Row.

Holmes, John Clellon. 2001. "The Philosophy of the Beat Generation." In *Beat Down to Your Soul*, edited by Ann Charters. New York: Penguin.

Kerouac, Jack. 1958. *Dharma Bums*. New York: Viking.

Snyder, Gary. 1957. *Earth House Hold: Technical Notes and Queries to Fellow Dharma Revolutionaries*. New York: New Directions.

_____. 1974. *Turtle Island*. New York: New Directions.

_____. 1977. *The Old Ways: Six Essays.* San Francisco: City Lights.

_____. 1979. *He Who Hunted Birds in His Father's Village: The Dimensions of a Haida Myth.* Bolinas: Grey Fox Press.

_____. 1990. *The Practice of the Wild.* San Francisco: North Point.

_____. 1995. *A Place in Space: Ethics, Aesthetics, and Watersheds.* Berkeley: Counterpoint.

II

BEAT IDENTITIES

Selfhood and Experimentation

FROM SELF-ALIENATION TO POSTHUMANISM

The Transmigration of the Burroughsian Subject

Micheal Sean Bolton

The connections between William S. Burroughs's narrative and stylistic innovations and postmodern theory have been well established in Burroughs criticism. Many critics recognize that his disintegrations of conventional prose effectively reflect postmodernism's concern with societal as well as artistic fragmentation. Less frequently considered, though, are the implications of Burroughs's reconception of the subject for understanding the plight of subjectivity in postmodernity. Postmodernism views subjects as fractured beyond reintegration, and representations of postmodern subjects in literature are often marked by psychosis, disconnectedness, and self-alienation. The subjects in Burroughs's novels seem to particularly exemplify this condition of self-alienation. "Burroughs's ultimate vision of subjectivity," as Timothy Murphy observes, "presents it as an aggregate of irreconcilable fragments . . . whose ends (in both the narrative and intentional senses) are in conflict."[1] Specifically, Burroughs's subjects feature profound internal fragmentation brought about by the "Other Half," a parasitical entity that doubles and opposes its human host, resulting in a split subject perpetually in conflict with itself. Disintegrated through parasitical invasion, Burroughs's subjects seem paradigmatic of postmodernism's nonsubjects: individuals who, through profound self-division, lack either the autonomy or the agency that conventionally define subjectivity.

However, to read Burroughs's subjects as irreparably fragmented and impotent beings is to miss an important innovation in his treatment of subjectivity. Throughout his experimental novels, his subjects are rendered not as victims of psychosis and estrangement but as practitioners of multiplicity and hybridity. Rather than suffering in its state of psychic fragmentation, the Burroughsian subject instead employs a process of self-alienation to achieve a detached and decentered condition that prefigures the discursive subjectivities of theorists such as Jacques Lacan and Jacques Derrida. Through this process of self-alienation, Burroughs's subjects ultimately pass beyond a state of postmodern disintegration into a state of being that anticipates N. Katherine Hayles's posthuman subjectivity: no longer the body-bound, unitary subjects of humanism, but subjects extended into and integrated with their technologized environments.[2]

Traditional notions of alienation—such as those of Hegel, Marx, and Nietzsche[3]—require a viable subject who can experience estrangement from his/her society. Postmodernity, according to many, offers no such humanist subject, discernible in itself and separable from its social and cultural realm. In fact, many postmodern theorists follow Jean Baudrillard in asserting that "we are no longer a part of the drama of alienation" at all.[4] These theorists insist that, in the postmodern world, subjectivity has become so irretrievably fragmented that "there is no longer a subject to be alienated."[5] However, this position begs the question as to why feelings of alienation persist, even in postmodernity. Although the extreme fragmentation accompanying the postmodern condition may well entail the loss of the unitary subject, this loss does not discount either subjectivity or subjects' feelings of alienation. Inasmuch as alienation continues to be a condition of the postmodern subject, notions of the alienation of the subject need to be reassessed. The Burroughsian subject provides an exemplary case for such reassessment.

As early as his first experimental novel, *Naked Lunch* (1959), Burroughs anticipates the emergence of an alternative subject who is not simply fragmented but is moreover decentralized and dispersed: "I was standing outside myself trying to stop those hangings with ghost fingers. . . . I am a ghost wanting what every ghost wants—a body."[6] This character, The Vigilante, is not fragmented so much as dis-located, a "schizo" character positioned both in and out of a body wherein "no organ is constant as regards either function or position."[7] Even the body's fragments are unstable and dislocated. Such fractured and dislocated figures occur throughout Burroughs's novels and evoke a profound sense of alienation. In some cases, alienation derives from the monstrousness of hybrid forms such as Fish People or Lemur People, fantastic animal-human composites alienated from human society due to states of perpetual transformation and dislocation. But most often Burroughs's subjects appear mundanely human; they are estranged and disconnected due more to internal divisions than to any externally visible differences. They fail to connect with their surroundings because they cannot adequately connect with themselves. The resulting subject is not just alienated but "is alien in its very constitution."[8] For characters such as Agent K9, Clem Snide, and Kim Carsons, these conditions of self-division and detachment elevate their human subjectivities and can be advantageous to their programs of resistance to control structures.

This notion of self-division takes on particular importance in assessing the postmodern condition of the subject. The emphasis of alienation shifts from the subject's estrangement from society to an estrangement from his/her sense of self through increasing feelings of internal fragmentation and disintegration. Burroughs's characters, while certainly social outcasts of one form or another, are most notable for just such internal divisions. Rather than resulting in the dissolution of the self or in psychosis, the divisions within these characters offer a means of resisting the systems of oppression and control that threaten to destroy or, more often, consume the possibility of autonomous subjects. "Under no pressure to maintain the perimeters of a defensive ego," such characters are "free to *think*."[9]

For Burroughs, disintegration rather than unity represents the possibility of freedom of the self. Stable, fixed identities allow for oppression by societal power structures since the subject that can be defined can be subjugated. Consequently, his characters never settle into distinct identities. Whereas conventional autonomy includes a continuity of identity based on the integrity of a character and the coherence of his/her perceptions, Burroughs does not allow characters to maintain any fixed identity or perspective by which to establish such continuity. For him, autonomy derives not from continuity but from multiplicity of identity. For example, one character may function as a multitude of different identities: "Salvador Hassan O'Leary, alias The Shoe Store Kid, alias Wrong Way Marv, alias Afterbirth Leary, alias Slunky Pete, alias Placenta Juan, alias K. Y. Ahmed, alias El Chinche, alias El Culito, etc., etc. for fifteen solid pages of dossier."[10] More than mere aliases referring to a single subject, these extensive alter egos can appear separately as distinct personas in the narrative or, as above, be combined within a single character. This flux of identity is vital to the character's freedom.

Such multiplicities of naming are essential, as a fixed name translates to a fixed identity: "I was looking for a name. My mind was sorting through names, discarding at once F. L.—Fuzz Lover, B. W.—Born Wrong, N.C.B.C.—Nice Cat But Chicken; putting aside to reconsider, narrowing, sifting, feeling for *the name, the answer*."[11] The equation of *the name* with *the answer* figures a name as something to be gained that exists prior to and apart from its discovery. A name, in this view, can be incorrect, and the failure to find the right name indicates a lack of identity without which one is not whole. Burroughs, however, warns against the dangers of this line of thought. Through naming, rather than becoming complete, an individual becomes a "fixed image . . . a ME that cannot be allowed to change."[12] He further explains: "The IS of identity always carries the assignment of permanent condition. To stay that way. All naming calling presupposes the IS of identity."[13] As a result, an individual can be commodified through his/her name: "That name must be paid for. You have not paid. My name is not yours to use."[14] Name, here, resembles Derrida's notion of "signature," which (however problematically) stands as an assertion of ownership. In order to avoid such commodification, and to maintain autonomy, one's identity must be fluid and one's names must be multiple and exchangeable.

This multiplicity of identity operates internally as well as externally. For Burroughs, all subjects are divided, split between the individual as host and the parasitic word virus that inhabits and controls its host. "The human form is a product of viral infection," writes Christopher Land, "and is perpetuated by the neurotic subvocalizations that are symptoms of this infection and which produce identity."[15] Land argues that, ironically, the human identity of Burroughs's characters results from the "self-continuity" provided by the "expressly non-human" internal monologue conducted by the word virus.[16] However, the monologue he refers to is actually a dialogue, and the subject produced from it is not continuous but split. Burroughs clarifies the issue: "Why do you talk to yourself all the time?—Are you talking to yourself?— Isn't there someone or something else there when you talk?"[17] All internal thought, including the individual's self-awareness, carries on as a dialogue between the subject host and the parasitic word virus. Lacan refers to the division created by this internal dialogue as a divided or split subject, which is composed of the individual and its linguistically structured unconscious. Like Burroughs, he argues that this division represents a necessary characteristic of the subject: "There is no subject without, somewhere, *aphanasis* of the subject, and it is in this alienation, in this fundamental division, that the dialectic of the subject is established."[18] In this view, self-alienation represents a necessary process in the development of the subject, and not the dissolution of the subject as proposed by postmodernism.[19]

Both Burroughs and Lacan affirm language as the source of the subject's fundamental division and self-alienation. Lacan proposes the "Other" as the locus of speech, or language, "in which is constituted the I who speaks to him who hears."[20] Lacan further insists: "Language is not immaterial. It is a subtle body, but body it is. Words are trapped in all the corporeal images that captivate the subject."[21] Burroughs similarly conflates image and word in his notion of the word virus: "Word begets image and image *is* virus."[22] And, as with Lacan, he views the word/image as the source of subjectivity: "Word And Image write the message that is you on colorless sheets determine all flesh."[23] Burroughs's word virus constitutes what he names the "Other Half": "The 'Other Half' is the word. The 'Other Half' is an organism. Word is an organism."[24] Both Lacan's "Other" and Burroughs's "Other Half" produce the subject as a discursive subject, a subject constructed of and by language, a notion common to postmodern thought. The discursive subject as split subject is, then, a product of the internal and self-reflexive dialogue implicit in language. A dialogue in which, according to Lacan, "speech always subjectively includes its own reply."[25]

On first look, the "Other Half" seems to be the very sort of binary, inside/outside opposition to which Burroughs opposes his narratives. Burroughs does, in fact, represent it as one half of a dyad, writing: "The body is two halves stuck together like a mold—That is, it consists of *two* organisms—See 'the Other Half' invisible."[26] Its equation to the word virus appears to solidify its role as enslaver and finally murderer of the host subject. Burroughs explains that "the 'Other Half' is 'You' next time around—born when you die—that is when 'the Other Half' kills you and takes over."[27] At the surface, the host and the "Other Half" appear to exist in an irresolvable state of conflict with one another, irreparably fragmenting the subject. However, upon closer scrutiny, the relationship between the subject and the "Other Half" reveals itself to be far more integrated.

Burroughs's paradigm for this sort of self-contained duality can be found in the figure of Mr. Bradley Mr. Martin. Bradley and Martin appear at times as separate individuals in the novels; however, they/he are/is most frequently rendered as the single character, Mr. Bradley Mr. Martin, "thought to be the leader of the mob—the nova mob."[28] In an episode from *Nova Express,* his character begins as the separate figures of Bradley and Martin, but quickly blurs into one: "Martin fished in the evening with Bradley who slept in the bunk next to his or in his bunk back and forth changing bodies in the blue silence."[29] Not only do the "two" exchange bodies and, in a sense, identities, but they also blend into one another as "in the bunk next to his" becomes "in his bunk." The two occurrences of the "his" pronoun may refer to either of the two separate albeit indistinguishable characters, Bradley or Martin, or to both as the singular Mr. Bradley Mr. Martin. Furthermore, the character of Mr. Bradley Mr. Martin displays a multiplicity beyond mere duplicity. Just as Burroughs's other characters feature multiple aliases and identities, "'Mr Bradley Mr Martin' [is] also known as 'Mr and Mrs D' also known as 'the Ugly Spirit.'"[30] Even the exemplar of duality manages to transcend his own binary nature. His multiplicity functions, as it does with Burroughs's other characters, to establish a metonymic relationship between identities that suggests interconnection and interdependence rather than distinction.

Lacan provides this explanation for the interdependence of subject and other: "What I seek in speech is the response of the other. What constitutes me as subject is my question. In order to be recognized by the other, I utter what was only in view of what will be. In order to find him, I call him by a name that he must assume or refuse in order to reply to me."[31] Burroughs, characteristically, complicates this relationship in such a way as to deny the implied binary: "I am alone but not what you call 'lonely'—Loneliness is a product of dual mammalian structure—'Loneliness,' 'love,' 'friendship,' all the rest of it—I am not two—I am *one*—But to maintain my state of oneness I need twoness in other life forms—Other must talk so that I can remain silent—if another becomes one then I am two—That makes two ones makes two and I am no longer one—."[32]

Here the subject and the other blur, become indistinguishable even as they separate. There simply are no stable subject positions, even in opposition.

Burroughs's subjects cannot be determined even in relation to a central albeit unconscious "Other," but only as fragmented and constantly shifting sets of relationships. In Burroughs's words, "in the beginning there was no Iam . . stale smoke of dreams it was Iam . . haunted your morning and will you other stale morning smell of other Iam . . no Iam there . . no one . . silences."[33] Iam, the being of the subject, cannot be located, only conceived as ephemera, the "smoke of dreams." Derrida similarly recognizes that "the center could not be thought in the form of a present-being, that the center had no natural site, that it was not a fixed locus but a function, a sort of non-locus in which an infinite number of sign-substitutions came into play."[34] The center or defining essence of the subject, for Burroughs as for Derrida, is always marked by the absence of "the original or transcendental signified, [which] is never absolutely present outside a system of differences."[35]

The autonomy of the Burroughsian subject, as noted earlier, does not emerge from the self-continuity that an unalterable, absolute presence—a transcendental signified—provides. Rather, autonomy results from the multiplicity of the subject, the sort of multiplicity indicated by Derrida's "system of differences." One might conclude that such systems of differences provide the contexts within which such subjects and their identifying signs are determined. But for Derrida, neither contexts nor signs are determinate of one another. Contexts are not merely sets of circumstances surrounding and creating meaning from outside. And signs do not provide fixed central positions around which contexts are constructed. As Derrida argues, "Context is always, and always has been, at work *within* the place, and not only *around* it."[36] In other words, the possibility of the occurrence of a sign within a given context always exists, and is in fact a feature of the context, even prior to the existence of the context. This possibility results from the iterability of signs.

Derrida posits two simultaneously occurring marks within each singular occurrence of a sign: "one mark inside and the other outside the deconstructed system."[37] The mark, though often seemingly synonymous with the sign, works less as a linguistic object from which texts are constructed than as a feature of the structure of language—not the sign, but an operant within the sign. In other words, one aspect of the mark operates outside any given context to establish the identity of the sign across contexts and one operates within context to create the possibility of breaking from contexts and to establish the iterability of the sign. This double-structured mark resembles Burroughs's Penny Arcade peep-show viewer who appears inside the peep-show film that he is, at the same moment, observing from outside: "The narrative sequences are preceded by the title on the screen then I am in the film. . . . The structuralized peep show may intersperse the narrative and then I am back in front of the screen and moving in and out of it."[38] Both the Derridean mark and the peep-show viewer function in apparently dual roles simultaneously, allowing for a sort of continuity of the sign/subject as it moves between contexts while also distinguishing its operations on either side of the "screen."

The mark functioning outside the deconstructed system implies the presence of an originary and unalterable sign. Indeed, "a certain self-identity of this element (mark, sign, etc.) is required to permit its recognition and repetition."[39] However, it also represents the potential for violent exclusion or "othering." For Burroughs, this state of inflexible identity created by pure repetition results in exclusionary and divisive violence, which he character-izes as the "Human Virus," and which is ultimately committed by the subject against itself. The condition of self-alienation, then, stems from a misrecog-nition of the unalterable identities of both the subject and its "Other Half" as "a ME that cannot be allowed to change."[40]

Liberation from this condition must be found in the second function of the sign, the mark functioning inside context. Derrida proposes that "a written sign carries with it a force that breaks with its context, that is, with the collectivity of presences organizing the moment of its inscription."[41] This force of rupture, the function of the mark inside, represents the possibility of difference within context and, so, the possibility of transcending the bina-ries created by the mark outside. The violence instituted by the mark inside is that of the rupture from and the graft into context, an inclusionary vio-lence as opposed to the mark outside's violence of distinction and exclusion.

These two aspects of the mark should not, however, be viewed as oppos-ing referents dividing the sign, but as complementary functions that nego-tiate between signs and their contexts. Thus, "the mark is neither present nor absent,"[42] only perceptible by its operations. Burroughs anticipates this notion of the Derridean mark as early as *The Soft Machine,* postulating a third entity that serves to transcend the binary of subject and other, as "the third that walks beside you."[43] Robin Lydenberg also recognizes in the novels "the 'eruptive emergence' of a third term which cannot be absorbed into a binary structure and which, in fact, confounds and disperses it," and notes its similarity to "Derrida's notions of 'supplement,' 'difference,' and 'trace.'"[44] However, viewing the third element in this way limits it to a purely decon-structive function: "to dwell within and explode the dual structure."[45] Con-ceptualizing the operation of the third as equivalent to that of the mark, on the other hand, adds another more constructive dimension. Burroughs insists: "You don't need any 'Other Half'—Why not take the middle line? ... The Other Half will be born inside feeling both halves of the body."[46] The third arises as that which at once "dwells within" and surrounds the sub-ject. It can contain and *feel* both parts of the binary; and, subsequently, can recast the duality of the split subject as the multiplicity of the hybrid subject.

The best representation of the hybrid subject in Burroughs is Joe the Dead, a character who not only controls the other characters in the last two novels, but contains them as well. He first appears in *The Place of Dead Roads* as a minor character and mentor to the novel's main character, Kim Carsons, whom he trains to "become invisible."[47] However, in *Western Lands,* Joe is revealed to be the puppet master behind Burroughs's menagerie of characters. More accurately, as Murphy notes, he is the old writer William Seward Hall, "the forger who controls the writer-warrior Joe the Dead and, through Joe, all the recurring characters from the earlier novels."[48] But, more than controller and controlled, Hall and Joe actually become interchangeable by the novel's end as the old writer takes on the name "Joe."[49] In much the same way, Joe contains and can be exchanged with the characters he controls. After literally killing Kim Carsons by shooting him, Joe also sheds his own Kim persona with a sound "like a snake shedding its skin."[50] Burroughs writes, "Joe understood Kim so well that he could afford to dispense with him as a part of himself not useful or relevant at the present time."[51] Kim is not only a character that Joe has written—as William Hall[52]—and can discard, but is a part of Joe's own hybrid subjectivity and "a source of excruciating pain" of which Joe must divest himself.[53]

Joe's hybridity also becomes projected outward as his mission "to alter the human equation" through "hybridization and mutation."[54] He pursues the creation of biological hybridization with the aim of "totally subverting the present natural order" by "break[ing] down the lines that Mother Nature, in her ripe wisdom, has established between species . . . to invite biologic and social chaos."[55] His agenda reflects the function of the third element, which acts to liberate subjects from the trappings of duality by re-creating them as multiple and hybrid. Joe both embodies (if such a thing is possible) and carries out the function of the third. For both, it is the case that they *are* what they *do*.

The notion of the third is borrowed from T. S. Eliot's *The Wasteland:* "When I count, there are only you and I together / But when I look ahead up the white road / There is always another one walking beside you."[56] As with the mark, the third entity is an absent presence. In Derrida's words, "It is *there,* but out there, *beyond,* within repetition, but eluding us there."[57] Burroughs reinforces the point, writing, "Empty is the third who walks beside you."[58] The emptiness of the third is not simply that of a vacant form, but a lack of any discernible form at all. Speaking of the force of rupture enacted by the mark, Derrida similarly observes, "It is never known in itself, 'as such,' but only in its 'effects' and its effects are 'incomparable,' they do not lend themselves to any conceptual generalization."[59] Like the Derridean mark, the third entity can only be observed through its effects and most often appears in Burroughs's works as a cloud, a wind, a vapor, or a dream figure. The figure of the third appears in these ethereal forms throughout the novels, as the following passage demonstrates: "Pieces of cloud drifted through someone walking—Mountain wind around his body trailing sweat drew him into other body alterations, sky blue through viscera of the other."[60]

Each image evokes fluidity and formlessness, and each displays the power to disrupt absolute conditions and to transcend the binary of subject and other. The third entity always already exists within the hybrid self, operating as a constant negotiation between subject and other "to traduce or transfigure and reduce a man's pulsating multiplicity to untranslatable inchoate word for latent consensus of 'otherness.'"[61] It represents the always (non)present possibility for transcendence of apparent dualities.

For Burroughs, this multiplicity is exemplified by the ancient Egyptian concept of the seven souls that inhabit and comprise the subject: "Ren, the Secret Name . . . Sekem: Energy, Power, Light . . . Khu, the Guardian Angel . . . Ba, the Heart . . . Ka, the Double . . . Khaibit, the Shadow, Memory . . . Sekhu, the Remains."[62] These souls exist as individual entities, in some sense distinct from the subject, but are not subjects in themselves. Upon the death of the subject the first three souls "go back to Heaven for another vessel" and "the four remaining souls must take their chances with the subject in the Land of the Dead."[63] Some of the souls can even be "treacherous" and work against the interests of the subject.[64] Thus, the souls that comprise the subject can feel alien and other. However, as the third operates to reimagine the subject as decentralized and fluid, it breaks the binary of subject-other and reconciles the subject with itself.

Jennie Skerl provides the following description of the fluid nature of the subject in Burroughs's novels: "The self is constantly changing in response to the context: the self and world are a dynamic field of forces in which there are no fixed entities, only relationships. . . . The self is defined from moment to moment by choice and action."[65] However, the self cannot be entirely defined by context, due to the fluidity and instability of contexts in the novels. If defined at all, the subject and context are defined reflexively. The Burroughsian subject is not, then, an amalgamate body composed of disparate identities or parts of identities determined by context, but a fluid self in a constant state of negotiation and renegotiation within multiple and mutable contexts under the guidance of the third.

N. Katherine Hayles designates this reconceptualization of subjectivity as the move from humanism to posthumanism. She does not, however, view the emergence of the posthuman as signaling the end of the humanist subject, but as extending subjectivity beyond the limits of the body. The posthuman is not bounded by or centered in the body but is connected to any number of environments or prostheses external to it through a feedback loop of information, "a (disembodied) entity that can flow between carbon-based organic components and silicon-based electronic components to make protein and silicon operate as a single system."[66] This loop of disembodied information operates in the same manner as Burroughs's third entity, transcending boundaries and forging connections between self and other both within the subject and in his/her technologized environment.[67]

Hayles, herself, recognizes Burroughs's anticipation of the posthuman, describing his characters as "posthuman mutations like the fish boy, whose fluidity perhaps figures a type of subjectivity attuned to the froth of noise rather than the stability of a false self."[68] The ability of the posthuman subject to extend into and integrate with its environment arises from its internal instability as its decentered status obfuscates the division between inside and outside and recasts the subject as a hybrid of both internal and external elements. Both subject and technology impact and alter one another through feedback loops of exchanged information. Like the posthuman, the Burroughsian subject gains rather than loses agency through the decentering process of self-alienation. Agency, for these subjects, arises from (re)integration of the decentered subject through and with its technological "Other Half." The soft typewriters that are Burroughs's subjects only emerge from the victimization and oppression of the "cold deck built in" by society's control structures when they embrace their technological other—"take over both halves of a body"—and use the technology into which they have integrated to actively "rewrite the message" of themselves as hybrid.[69]

Whereas postmodern theory is resigned to the dissolution of the human subject due to irredeemable self-division, the Burroughsian subject utilizes its self-division as a means to regain autonomy and agency. Through the decentering process of self-alienation, Burroughs's subjects transcend postmodern disintegration and emerge as posthuman, at once reintegrated with and dislocated from both themselves and their worlds. The Burroughsian subject, like the posthuman, is consonant with the flux of its environment, itself existing in a perpetual state of becoming. The fluidity of these subjects is made possible by feedback loops of "informational pathways connecting the organic body to its prosthetic extensions," which "can flow not only *within* the subject but also *between* the subject and the environment."[70] Fragmentation, "the froth of noise," does not disintegrate but decenters and disperses these subjects, allowing them to extend into and act upon their technologized environments.

Notes

1. Timothy S. Murphy, *Wising Up the Marks: The Amodern William Burroughs* (Berkeley and Los Angeles: University of California Press, 1997), 191.

2. For a detailed account of Hayles's posthumanism, see her *How We Became Posthuman: Virtual Bodies in Cybernetics, Literature, and Informatics* (Chicago: University of Chicago Press, 1999), esp. chap. 1, "Toward Embodied Virtuality."

3. For brief descriptions of these theories of alienation, see Richard Schacht's "Alienation Redux: From Here to Postmodernity," in *Alienation, Ethnicity, and Postmodernism*, ed. Felix Geyer, 1–16 (Westport, Conn.: Greenwood Press, 1996).

4. Jean Baudrillard, "The Ecstasy of Communication," in *The Anti Aesthetic: Essays on Postmodern Culture*, ed. Hal Foster, trans. John Johnston (Port Townsend, Wash.: Bay Press, 1983), 130.

5. John Zerzan, "The Catastrophe of Postmodernism," Primitivism.com, www.primitivism.com/postmodernism.htm, 19.

6. William S. Burroughs, *Naked Lunch* (New York: Grove Weidenfeld, 1990), 9.

7. Ibid., 9, 10.

8. Christopher Land, "Apomorphine Silence: Cutting-up Burroughs' Theory of Language and Control," *Ephemera: Theory and Politics in Organization* 5, no. 3 (2005): 461.

9. William S. Burroughs, *The Place of Dead Roads* (New York: Holt, 1983), 113.

10. Burroughs, *Naked Lunch,* 142.

11. Ibid., 195, emphasis added.

12. William S. Burroughs, *The Western Lands* (New York: Viking, 1987), 158.

13. William S. Burroughs, *Electronic Revolution* (Bonn: Expanded Media Editions, 1998), 54.

14. William S. Burroughs, *The Soft Machine, Nova Express, and The Wild Boys: Three Novels* (New York: Grove, 1980), 196.

15. Land, "Apomorphine Silence," 458.

16. Ibid., 455.

17. William S. Burroughs, *The Ticket That Exploded* (New York: Grove, 1967), 145.

18. Jacques Lacan, *The Four Fundamental Concepts of Psychoanalysis,* ed. Jacques-Alain Miller, trans. Alan Sheridan (New York: Norton, 1977), 221.

19. Interestingly, Hegel also posits alienation as a necessary stage in the process of self-realization. In her article "Alienation and Estrangement in Hegel's *Phenomenology of the Spirit*" (*Symposia: The Online Philosophy Journal*, www.journal.ilovephilosophy.com/Article/ ALIENATION-AND-ESTRANGEMENT-IN-HEGEL-S/2067), Tamela Ice notes that for Hegel, "alienation overcomes estrangement when self-consciousness

realizes that what is perceived as an independent object outside itself is in actuality a part of itself" (par. 20). And Philip J. Kain, in *Schiller, Hegel, and Marx: State, Society, and the Aesthetic Ideal of Ancient Greece* (Kingston, Ontario: McGill-Queen's University Press, 1982), writes: "Both sides here, which have become split and self-opposed, are in reality sides of one consciousness. . . . Implicit in this alienation is a movement toward universality" (43).

20. Jacque Lacan, *Ecrits: A Selection*, trans. Alan Sheridan (New York: Norton, 1977), 141.

21. Ibid., 87.

22. Burroughs, *The Soft Machine, Nova Express, and The Wild Boys*, 230.

23. Ibid., 210.

24. Burroughs, *The Ticket That Exploded*, 49.

25. Lacan, *Ecrits: A Selection*, 85.

26. Burroughs, *The Ticket That Exploded*, 159.

27. Ibid., 160.

28. Ibid., 55.

29. Burroughs, *The Soft Machine, Nova Express, and The Wild Boys*, 307–8.

30. Burroughs, *The Ticket That Exploded*, 60.

31. Lacan, *Ecrits: A Selection*, 86.

32. Burroughs, *The Soft Machine, Nova Express, and The Wild Boys*, 259.

33. Burroughs, *The Ticket That Exploded*, 202.

34. Jacques Derrida, *Writing and Difference*, trans. Alan Bass (Chicago: University of Chicago Press, 1978), 280.

35. Ibid.

36. Jacques Derrida, *Limited Inc*, ed. Gerald Graff (Evanston, Ill.: Northwestern University Press, 1988), 60.

37. Jacques Derrida, *Dissemination*, trans. Barbara Johnson (Chicago: University of Chicago Press, 1981), 4.

38. Burroughs, *The Soft Machine, Nova Express, and The Wild Boys*, 405–6.

39. Derrida, *Limited Inc*, 10.

40. Burroughs, *The Western Lands*, 158.

41. Derrida, *Limited Inc*, 9.

42. Ibid., 53.

43. Burroughs, *The Soft Machine, Nova Express, and The Wild Boys*, 37.

44. Robin Lydenberg, *Word Cultures: Radical Theory and Practice in William S. Burroughs' Fiction* (Urbana and Chicago: University of Illinois Press, 1987), 124.

45. Ibid., 124.

46. Burroughs, *The Ticket That Exploded*, 161.

47. Burroughs, *The Place of Dead Roads*, 13.

48. Burroughs, *The Western Lands*, 179.

49. Ibid., 255.

50. Ibid., 26.

51. Ibid., 27.

52. Burroughs, *The Place of Dead Roads,* 201.

53. Burroughs, *The Western Lands,* 27.

54. Ibid., 61, 39.

55. Ibid., 36, 32.

56. T. S. Eliot, "The Wasteland," in *The Wasteland and Other Poems* (New York: Harcourt, Brace, and World, 1934), 361–63.

57. Derrida, *Writing and Difference,* 300.

58. Burroughs, *The Soft Machine, Nova Express, and The Wild Boys,* 297.

59. Jacques Derrida, "Force of Law: The 'Mystical Foundation of Authority,'" in *Deconstruction and the Possibility of Justice,* ed. Drucilla Cornell, Michel Rosenfeld, and David Gray Carlson (New York: Routledge, 1920), 56.

60. Burroughs, *The Ticket That Exploded,* 129. See also William S. Burroughs, *Port of Saints* (1973; Berkeley: Blue Wind Press, 1980), 136; and Burroughs, *The Western Lands,* 57.

61. Ibid., 29.

62. Burroughs, *The Western Lands,* 4–5.

63. Ibid., 4–5.

64. Ibid., 5.

65. Jennie Skerl, *William S. Burroughs* (Boston: Twayne, 1985), 8.

66. Hayles, *How We Became Posthuman,* 2.

67. In *My Mother Was a Computer: Digital Subjects and Literary Texts* (Chicago: University of Chicago Press, 2005), Hayles applies the term "Computational Universe" to what I am here calling the "technologized environment": a space wherein the intermediation of human subjects and technologies occur.

68. Hayles, *How We Became Posthuman,* 220.

69. Burroughs, *The Ticket That Exploded,* 159–60.

70. Hayles, *How We Became Posthuman,* 2.

"I AM NOT AN I"

Performative (Self)Identity in the Poetry of Bob Kaufman

Tom Pynn

I am not an I, secret wick, I do nothing, light myself, burn.
                                        —Bob Kaufman, "Ginsberg (for Allen)"

Selfhood and Freedom: An Existential Context

When Simone de Beauvoir (1908–1986) came to the United States in the late 1940s and published her essay "An Existentialist Looks at Americans" in the *New York Times Magazine* (Beauvoir 1947), she came to many of the same conclusions that Beat writers and their consociates did about American existence. Beauvoir tasted "a flavor of death" in America. While there is an "American dynamism" that asserts "itself against the inertia of the given by dominating things, by invading them, by incorporating their structures into the world of man," she explained, most Americans are essentially "waiting for death" (13). Beauvoir characterized this "waiting" by the "indefinite flight" toward an unseen future, the lack of (inter)personal/ intersubjective accomplishment, the reduction of the compassionate plenitude of being to the calculative and quantitative achievement of making money and the self-perpetuating and self-defeating acquisitive drive to status that constitute a fatalistically morbid "flavor of death in this American existence" (13).

For the Beats, death was manifest in everyday American life as a subordination of the individual self and its freedom to the social, economic, and religious forces of conformity. Beat writers expressed unease and fear of what Allen Ginsberg in his landmark poem "Howl" (1956) called the "Moloch" mechanistic mind that both erases individual identity and mechanizes human consciousness in the service of (war) profit and the totalizing tendencies of institutional life. Like Sartre and Beauvoir, both of whom strictly insisted upon the individual's responsibility for his or her own existence, the Beats rejected any and all attempts to subordinate the individual to formalistic or essentialist construction. As Sartre famously stated, existence comes before essence. Thus, our selfhood does not precede our actions as free human beings engaged in the world. In "Forget to Not," Bob Kaufman (1925–1986) addresses Beauvoir's concern by gently redirecting the self-defeating "indefinite flight" back to the world, offering a tarrying with time rather than mindless evisceration and obliteration:

> Remember not to forget the dying colors of yesterday
> As you inhale tomorrow's hot dream, blown from frozen lips
>
> Remember you naked agent of every nothing. (1965, 55)

As an African American Beat-culture poet, Kaufman's experience of blackness took him away from an essentialist understanding of human selfhood to one of community experience. Free from the polarities of wishing to be black, or suffering from WASP privilege, Kaufman had an integrated personality that focused more on love, community, and togetherness, and not on anger. Thus, Kaufman turned to the notions of vulnerability and nakedness, to resist the totalizing tendencies of institutional life and the drive toward invincibility that subordinates all forms of embodied subjectivity to a disembodied (*sub*)jectivity of rational self-interest. Along with other Beat-culture artists, he utilized discourses about selfhood that fit his model of a performative self that could both effectively withstand the pressures of postwar America and function creatively as a counterdiscourse to mainstream American culture. Kaufman develops an aesthetics of performative personhood that emphasizes the primacy of (vocal) gesture, a nonideational and nonsubstantive somatic embodiment that traces the sources of an authentic consciousness both to vulnerability or nakedness and the fundamental intertwining of the sensory modalities of vision, touch, hearing, and sexual motility. The influence of the African American jazz traditions, especially bebop, coincides with the Beat project in general and with Kaufman's work in particular when jazz emphasizes spontaneous improvisation and integrating the subjective experience of the musician with the soundscape; thus, moving the poet from an isolated, or naïve subjectivity, toward a mature or intersubjective interplay with world and others.

In what follows I will trace these intertwining themes in order to show

how Kaufman's poetry demonstrates important Beat, existential, and Buddhist characteristics that combine in a mature, performative intersubjectivity. For the Beats, putting into question one's existence through an expressive and intersubjective performativity is key to realizing one's freedom. Kaufman underscores Beat notions of freedom with his emphasis on vulnerability and nakedness. Indeed, to be naked is to be Beat, to be naked of mind and soul, as John Clellon Holmes remarks (Holmes 1967, 110).

Expression and Intersubjectivity in Kaufman's Poetry

The uniqueness of the Beat idea of an individual was to place all human beings within an intersubjective context, a co-arising with others and the world through performance. In so doing, the expressive performative self would liberate the individual from all forms of conformity and death-in-life habits. It would release, as Kerouac wrote, "the true blue song of man" (Kerouac 1985, frontispiece). In order to attain release into the freedom of intersubjectivity, a co-arising with others and the world through performance, the urge to invincibility has to be replaced with vulnerability, a willingness to encounter and engage all forms of life on their respective terms without desiring to coerce, consume, or conquer. Thus, for Kaufman and other Beats, nakedness becomes an important leitmotif in their respective works encompassing the multivalent movement of vulnerability: rejection of totalizing consciousness and invincibility.

Rather than accept conformity and death-in-life habits, the Beats engage existential thought and are confronted and challenged by its question to bohemian aesthetics in general and Beat aesthetics in particular: "How does one realize concrete freedom?" In line with Sartre's conception of freedom, concrete freedom is realized, in the Beat project, through self-expression and responsibility for one's own self-creation. The emphasis on practice and action is in harmony with a Beat aesthetic predicated on intercorporeity; that is, embodied consciousness reversible with others. Embodied consciousness privileges expression, feeling, immediacy, and other modes of intimacy that are themselves eclipsed by rational techniques of knowing and being-with-others. Instead of empirical knowing mediating proximity, Beat writers sought freedom of self-creation and hence turned to the literary tactic of expression. Opening up the individual's subjectivity in clear, honest, and sincere ways would, they gambled, transform and liberate American literature, especially poetry, and American culture from the stultifying formalism and fundamentalism pervading postwar American life.

Existential thinkers insist that we exist as concrete human subjects coming into unique selfhood alone *and* with others through our passionate commitments that entail risk, freedom, and choice (Batchelor 1995). Our selfhood *does not* precede our actions as free human beings. Of paramount concern to existential thinkers, then, are any and all attempts to subordinate the individual to formalistic constructions of self or an essence that can be formally defined. Essentialism is the belief in a single metaphysical nature that causally determines the identity and characteristics of an individual. Instead of essentialism, existential thinkers propose that our existence makes up *who* we are as free agents performing selfhood. Selfhood cannot be reduced to any of the projects we undertake; a WHO can never be reduced to a WHAT. Since life is always changing, one can never arbitrarily stop time and declare the individual human project closed and finished. Resistance to reducing the unique human being to the same forms a core focus in both existential thinkers and Beat authors in their respective works.

Kaufman's Beat poetry expresses not only his own unspeakable visions of the individual but also acts as a counterdiscourse to what Ginsberg (1973) termed the "syndrome of shutdown" (qtd. in Tytell 1973, 309). Like his fellow Beat-culture poets, Kaufman challenges conventional patterns of selfhood and literary composition by exploring alternative philosophical, religious, and aesthetic practices in his poetry. Such an exploration leads Kaufman away from stable and rational notions of the self to a performative and para-rational conception of personhood. The pararational eschews those aspects of Enlightenment instrumental reason—technological innovation over compassionate engagement, positivism over emotion, and commercialism over expressive communication—that restrain the realization of one's humanity and interconnection with all living things.

The intertwining motifs of standing naked in one's being and *seeing* deeply into one's own self and others signifies intersubjectivity in Kaufman's work. In Kaufman's poem, "Forget To Not" the groundwork for the possibility of intersubjectivity is both remembering and nakedness. To be naked is both the (inter)active sense of remembering and the repressive prohibitive sense of not forgetting. The romantic motif of the poet's soaring transcendence is "gallivanting across the sky, / Skylarking, shouting, calling names" (Kaufman 1965, 55). At the same time, however, joyful and care*free* wandering is not care*less*. The poet advises the reader/listener would-be-poet to "Walk softly" because "Your footprint on rain clouds is visible to naked eyes" (55). In these lines, Kaufman links the work of the poet to deep ways of being that bring the heart of the poet together with the listener. Nakedness invokes not only the trope of the soul but also everything that counters the objectifying turn of postwar America. The poet's vision and the deepening connection between human beings, intersubjectivity, "fly in the face of time" (55). While the eyes of the reader/ listener are also open/ naked to the transcendental vision of the poet, the last line of this brief poem suggests that the poet must also stand in nakedness: "Remember, you naked agent of every nothing" (55).

Nakedness functioning as the condition for the possibility of intersubjectivity relies on the opening of the eyes. Whereas "Forget To Not" implies the ancient trope of the eyes as the window of/to the soul, "The Eyes Too" make this convention explicit: "My eyes too have souls that rage" (Kaufman 1965, 50). The eyes rage (in their seeing),

> At the sight of butterflies walking,
> At the crime of a ship cutting the ocean in two,
> At visions of girls who should be naked
> Sitting at lunch counters eyeballing newspapers,
> At complacent faces of staring clocks
> Objectively canceling lives
> With ticks. (50)

Raging eyes are prophetic eyes, the eyes that see into the deep present that most of us in our forgetting fail to notice. The one who sees, then, is a prophet/visionary, but to communicate such seeing is the work of the poet-prophet. As William Blake once observed, "If the doors of perception were cleansed, everything would appear to Man as it is: infinite" (Blake 1988, 14). In the above poem, "butterflies walking" are not butterflies flying, flitting in their twenty-four-hour life. In this sense, then, seeing is imaginative of flight as freedom in both the sense of *freedom to* move and *freedom from* the limitations of ratio and the senses five. Seeing reality, however, is an act of bifurcation to all eyes that do not see as deeply, the cutting of the ocean in twain by a ship. What is cut is the unity of the water signifying eternity, the Absolute, God. From a Idealist/Romantic point of view, bifurcation signifies cutting our connection with the Absolute. We are the ones who cut ourselves off from the deeper reality of our life. The "visions of girls who should be naked" have clothed their nakedness—innocence, sensuality, humanness, spirituality—in the lunch-hour rush and low-quality information typical of "newspapers" (Kaufman 1965, 50). Overseeing all is the complacency of chronological time, a mechanical ordering of temporality. Instead of direct lived experience in which one voluntarily participates in the ebb and flow of time, the mechanical ticks of the machine mind arbitrarily and coercively command and restrain what is otherwise a communal meal—the lunch counter—into "the lunch hour rush" to get back to work in the sterile, disingenuous production-consumption-waste matrix.

In "Ginsberg (for Allen)," open-naked seeing is the condition for the possibility of compassion. The Beat poet Allen Ginsberg stands in for both counterdiscourse and antidote to the institutional, mechanical, and regimented bind of religion and its "spiritual brainwashing in addition to promises of quick sainthood" (Kaufman 1965, 23). Whereas the power elite toss martyrs to the lions, Ginsberg is the liberating bard "tossing lions to martyrs" (23). Devoid of self-interest and its desire to control, consume, and possess the other, Ginsberg burns in no-self or intersubjective intentionality: "I am not an I, secret wick, I do nothing, light myself, burn" (23). The poet is one who "can cling and fall and clasp eyes with the best" (23). Kaufman imagines, sees, Ginsberg in this heroic and tragicomic light as one who is capable of transformative influence precisely because he is "stuffed with bleeding expressions of human form" (23). Unlike the success-at-all-costs, failure-is-not-an-option self-assertion of the power elite, Ginsberg leaks compassion. Hence, the poet can say, "I love him because his eyes leak" (23).

As the above poem indicates, seeing necessarily includes rather than excludes the struggle and suffering aspects of life. Nakedness is in this sense a willingness to stand open to the vicissitudes of existence, close down one's innermost or vulnerable self. In his poem "On," the poet sees with "moist prophet eyes" (Kaufman 1996, 92). Compassionate seeing into the dark corners of human history is a concern in one of Kaufman's most well-known and oft-quoted poems, "Would You Wear My Eyes?" As the poem opens, the psychophysical self has been decimated by the "loveless" transience of time: "My body is a torn mattress, / Disheveled throbbing place / For the comings and goings / Of loveless transients" (40). To what extent this is accomplished by one's self and/or the social world is fruitfully ambiguous. That he stands "Before completely objective mirrors" is a clue to the struggle between interiority, authenticity, and truth, intersubjectivity and exteriority, objectivity, distance, and alienation. His body becomes a pockmarked palimpsest of human history opposed to the "strange landscapes in my head" (40).

It is important to Kaufman's difference from other Beats that he includes in his body's remembering the map of Africans and their descendants' suffering in/from slavery. He stands naked, intimately connected to the suffering that forms a significant part of America's forgetting observed by Simone de Beauvoir: "It is true that it is in the nature of man to transcend the past toward the future without pause or stop. But to transcend is also to preserve; if uprooted, the movement toward the future becomes an indefinite flight. The aim of going faster becomes an alibi for going nowhere. The continual negation of the past in the end wounds the present and the future, also" (Beauvoir 1947, 51). The "continued negation of the past," Americans' ignorance of its own history, includes the legacy of slavery. African American thinkers-writers-artists of this period such as Richard Wright, Lorraine Hansbury, LeRoi Jones, and James Baldwin refer in their respective works to Americans' ignorance of history in general and the five hundred years of chattel slavery invented and implemented by the European colonizing powers in which America participated, from which America benefited, and which America continues to evade. Kaufman recalls the trauma of slavery inscribed on black bodies in "Would You Wear My Eyes?":

My legs are charred remains of burned cypress trees;
My feet are covered with moss from bayous, flowing across my floor. (40)

That the poem ends in the interrogative mood—"Would you wear my eyes?"—is both a provocation to remember the past wrongs visited upon people of African descent and an invitation to intersubjectivity, a communion of sorts, in which we stand in our mutual nakedness and express our shared suffering in order that we may transcend the tragic past and come into our humanity. Key to this, however, is seeing with the naked eye. The naked eye, intersubjectivity, is the way by which the alienating subject-object bifurcation of human consciousness is transcended.

Kaufman's Performative Selfhood

The Beats in general, and Kaufman in particular, stand in an American Transcendentalist tradition that redefines the place and meaning of America by a daring expression of individual creative consciousness in collective collaboration and action. John Clellon Holmes (Holmes 1967) suggests that the spiritual underpinning to the Beat quest was the vexing query, "How are we to live?," a question that spawned a plethora of feverish answers with one underlying assumption: the yearning to experience and then express a new vision of America. A vision that included rather than excluded, sought life rather than death, and, above all, propelled each participant toward a passionate life. The passionate Beat life was a life devoted to beatitude, which emerged over time from Kerouac's original conception to a complex lifestyle and aesthetic that also included religious faith. For Kaufman, the literal meaning of beatitude was spontaneity, creativity, and anonymity.

Beat privileging of intersubjective collaboration is particularly visible in the life and writings of African American Beats. In her essay "Black Beats and Black Issues," for the catalogue accompanying the Whitney Museum of Art's exhibit *Beat Culture and the New America: 1950–1965* held November 9, 1995 through February 4, 1996, Mona Lisa Saloy observes that "it was in the poetry of African-Americans that the Beat notions rang clearest" (Saloy 1995, 162). For African Americans associated with the Beat movement (e.g., Ted Joans, Ray Durem, A. B. Spellman, LeRoi Jones), this also meant that American liberalism's desire to make all things equal in order to transcend race had to be resisted in order to establish their own voices. Writers such as Kaufman and Jones sought, as Kathryn Gines has observed in a wider context of race relations and consciousness, "an authentic race consciousness that is positive, that is not merely reactional to whiteness, and that is not structured or dependent upon oppression and victimization" (Gines 2005, 15). For Kaufman, an authentic race consciousness involved "cooperation across and within traditional 'boundaries'" (Gines 2005, 16). This collaboration entailed the public support of each other at readings; in little magazines such as *Evergreen Review, Big Table, Origin,* and *Yugen*; and, in its most lasting form, the establishment of *Beatitude.* Saloy recalls Warren French's (French 1991) observation: "'*Beatitude* not only documented the Beat writing efforts,' but 'it was the only collaborative project of prominent Beats.' In 1985, the Silver Anniversary *Beatitude* issue was dedicated to Kaufman. . . . At the 1994 New York University Beat Conference, Allen Ginsberg, when asked about Bob Kaufman, insisted that it was Kaufman who had been the driving force behind *Beatitude*" (Kaufman 1996, 163).

As Sharon Mussett has cautioned, however, existential thinking challenges anyone seeking an authentic race consciousness: "How does a group avoid essentialization on the one hand (to be black *is to be* x) and vacuity on the other (there are so many experiences of blackness, all of which must be allowed in, that all sense of a unifying thread is lost)? What is the black situation and how can it be both fluid and meaningful at the same time?" (Mussett 2005, 5). It is from the ambiguous ground of expression that Kaufman conveys his racial identity as an African American poet in the wider context of Beat aesthetics.

In his first collection of poems, *Solitudes Crowded with Loneliness* (Kaufman 1965), we can read two existential elements correlative with both Beauvoir's and Beat observations of Americans and life in America: the expressive desire for an authentic America and resistance to "the flavor of death in American existence" (Beauvoir 1947, 13). At the same time that Kaufman represents the Beat attitude, he is also an African American; therefore, his poetry can be read as a tentative foray into the groundwork for a positive race consciousness, a race consciousness based not on essentialist constructions of self/group-identity, but on a performative self.

As is true of the Beat project generally, Kaufman stands in what Seymour Krim called "the American Bardic tradition" that begins with Walt Whitman (*Kerouac* 1986). Whitman's stance toward America is complex, but there are at least two important threads relevant to Kaufman's work: praise for both the progress of American inventiveness and the deep democratic project. These themes are salient to a reading of Kaufman's (1965) poem "To My Son Parker, Asleep in the Next Room." The majority of the poem is a Whitmanesque catalogue of world civilizations' identifying traits, each one differentiating itself from those past and those yet to come. One general feature of human civilization that Kaufman suggests is paradox: Neanderthals are prehuman *yet* they "mark their place in time"; Greek civilization was "bloody" *yet* perfected the art of representing human form in sculpture; Europe engaged in slavery, *but* the experience of slavery led to "chained souls [shaping] free men" (49). The poem ends with America presented as a new "shore" upon which each human being will realize concrete freedom:

> On this shore, we shall raise our monuments of stones,
>> Of wood, of mud, of color, of labor, of belief, of being,
>> Of life, of love, of self, of man expressed
>> In self-determined compliance, or willful revolt,
>> Secure in this avowed truth, that no man is our master,
>> Nor can any ever be, at any time in time to come. (49)

Unlike previous civilizations, America's monument will not be cave paintings, marble statues, or carved temples, but human freedom, "of man expressed." The explicit references to slavery in the poem make it clear that freedom is incompatible with slavery and that slavery, of any kind, is inconsistent with "self-determination," "willful revolt," and "truth" (49). It is important to notice that the cluster of idea-images indicates the promise of the Enlightenment, "a larger sense of freedom, to resist and overcome the pretensions of Authority, the audacities of government, the fanaticism of the Church, the superstitions of ignorance, the burden of poverty, the paralysis of impotence, freedom from slavery in every form" (Commager 1975, 58). Implied in both Kaufman's early poetry and the Enlightenment promise is what we might today know as freedom not only from direct violence, but also structural violence, the violence built into the fabric of social, cultural, and economic life and our conscious or subconscious consent to structural violence (hegemony). This larger sense of freedom is the basis of the democratic vision at the heart of America that Kaufman wants all Americans to realize and act upon, in spite of its violent history of the enslavement of black Africans.

Neither the Beats nor Kaufman are blindly optimistic about the prospects for an America where "all men, before, forever, eternally / free in all things" (Kaufman 1965, 49). In the poem "Benediction" Kaufman ironically, and with appropriate Beat humor, expresses the sentiment that America's promise of freedom for all has yet to be fulfilled by depicting the governor of Florida as helpless against "six hundred thousand illiterates" (Kaufman 1965, 9). Benediction, usually the utterance of a blessing and a devoted wish for the happiness, prosperity, and success of a person or enterprise, is being used ironically *and* in the sense of Christian prophetic witness for the poem is an indictment of American violence both at home:

> America, I forgive you . . . I forgive you
> Nailing black Jesus to an imported cross
> Every six weeks in Dawson, Georgia.
> America I forgive you . . . I forgive you
> Eating black children, I know your hunger. (Kaufman 1965, 9)

and abroad:

> America, I forgive you . . . I forgive you
> Burning Japanese babies defensively—
> I realize how necessary it was. (9)

As Jacques Derrida has observed in the wider context of religion, benediction "pertains to the originary regime of testimonial faith or of martyrdom," a faith arising out of lived experience testifying to what one has witnessed (Derrida 1996, 66). To forgive on Derrida's account, then, can only be forgiveness if it stems from faithful witness and is absolute. Furthermore, forgiveness is possible only if one gives up the desire for vendetta and the ethos of invincibility within which revenge arises, that is to say, *ressentiment*. Irony helps the poet make the transition from the ongoing brutality of white supremacy alluded to in the various incidents of atrocities. Therefore, a sense of humor, however ironic, is compatible with vulnerability, the ability and willingness to laugh at one's own errors as well as the errors of one's country. Furthermore, because forgiveness, in a very real sense, cannot be operationalized, Kaufman cannot be read as a moralist. He is the prophetic-poet seeing into the deep nature of reality and calling us *to see* as well.

The echo of "I forgive you" serves in the poem, among other things, to remind us of our need for forgiveness by alluding to Jesus's crucifixion and to emphasize the religious dimensions of the benediction as a prayer in the spirit of engaged hope. Kaufman was raised an African American Roman Catholic in New Orleans and knows that the priest at the end of mass sends the congregants out into the world by benediction: *stand now and prepare to receive the benediction.* The religious significance of the poem—that blood sacrifice end and that America offer up her self-interest and violence against African Americans as a holocaust—contrasts sharply with America's "generals [who] have mushrooming visions," and the Truman administration's official excuse for dropping the atomic bombs on the Japanese, that it saved thousands of *American* lives (Kaufman 1965, 9). Truman's hollow justification is indicative of the cultural ignorance, ethnocentrism, and conditional sense of obligation toward the other at the core of classical liberalism's conception of tolerance. The poem rehearses the antinomy of conditioned versus unconditioned hospitality, but whereas an antinomy calls for sustained reflection in humility, the promise of America, in reference to America's Enlightened founders, amounts to little more than "beautiful thoughts." America, "Every day your people get more and more / Cars, televisions, sickness, death dreams." America, rather than becoming free, has enslaved itself to the fictive and external absolute called the American dream.

In the poem's last two lines, Kaufman rejects Whitman's and Kerouac's optimism of mythic American progress by concluding, "You must have been great / Alive" (Kaufman 1965, 9). The ending confirms Beauvoir's insight that while America embodies dynamic innovation and freedom, it has simultaneously rejected liberation in favor of death, a withdrawal from being "Alive." "Waiting for death" is a death in life in which one has withdrawn from committing him/herself to the world and the result is that one loses one's self in the process. Such a life persists in general fear of one's self and others in which one neither "trust[s] their own individual judgments, their personal feelings," nor do they "wish to put [into] question [their judgments or their feelings], which shows how uncertain they are" (Beauvoir 1947, 51). In giving up one's freedom, one is, in any sense that makes a difference, *already dead.*

Kaufman's Buddhist Poetics and Performative Selfhood

Some of the Beats, even more so than some of the New England Transcendentalists, openly affiliated themselves with religions other than Christianity and Judaism. For many of these artists, particularly those working on the West Coast, this meant a living interest in Buddhism not only for cross-cultural poetics and aesthetics but also development of a new consciousness. Joanna McClure has commented that, "I think we were more concerned with new consciousness than with spirituality" (Charters 2001, 632). Granted, theirs was not the conventional Buddhism one might find in some Asian cultures, but it was the beginnings of what has come to be understood as the ongoing development of an American form of Buddhism. Raymond Foye recalls that "Bob always considered himself a Buddhist. He said this quite a few times. That was his religious faith" (Kaufman 1996, 16).

Of particular interest to many Beats including Kaufman is an interest in Buddhist ontology. Much like the intimate relationship between vocal and instrumental gestures and the soundscape, Buddhist ontology suggests that all phenomena are impermanent, empty of any essential or substantive self, mutually co-arising, and irreducibly karmic (Hershock 2006). Cultivating vulnerability is essential to seeing that one's deep or True Self is wisdom (about how things are) and compassion (for all sentient beings). Nakedness, on a Buddhist account, can be interpreted as *ahimsa* (nonviolence). *Ahimsa* is living life based in nonviolent responsiveness to the world one finds one's self in/with. Buddhist ontology served Kaufman and some of the Beats in their mutual quest for a performative self that would give American poetry and life a revitalizing jolt.

Even though the Beats' interest in and use of Buddhism often drew skeptical responses from some American Buddhist elites, the press, the wider public, particularly the youth culture, responded enthusiastically. In 1952, the noted Japanese scholar D. T. Suzuki gave public lectures at Columbia University for a full week to standing-room-only crowds. In 1955, *Life* magazine published not one but two feature articles on Buddhism. As noted above, Kerouac's success with *The Dharma Bums* (1957) helped sediment Buddhist thought and practice into the popular culture of Americans. Furthermore, some Beat Culture artists, especially those on the West Coast, adopted Buddhism as an antidote to the stagnancy of Western reified culture, as a way of opening American literary expression to deeper forms of poetic consciousness, and as a live option in their own respective lives.

Buddhism not only gave Kaufman a different perspective on the self but also served as a foundation for a sense of community. Allusions to Buddhist thought and practice occur both implicitly and explicitly in Kaufman's poetry. In "A Buddhist Experience," a poem he wrote at the end of his life, the poet seeks an understanding of Buddhism in his own life and in doing so reveals the wider interest in Buddhist thought in Beat culture. Buddhism is a historical phenomenon, but it is

> Also something else,
> How people emerge from the group,
> Complete, individual,
> Each responding to some higher stone
> Or order unchallenged
> In the search for meaning,
> In reaching for the pure relation,
> To interpret life and by that interpretation
> To live life more deeply in Zen. (Kaufman 1996, 161)

Kaufman expresses several of the themes dominating Beat counterdiscourse: the search for the meaningful life, the transcendence of group conformity, the urge for individual expression, and the quest "for a life that can be lived in heaven / while being lived on earth" (Kaufman 1996, 162). A life lived in heaven on earth is a life of beatitude, a concept reverently held by some Beat writers and artists that also became the title of the Beat magazine founded by Kaufman and Ginsberg. *Beatitude,* along with others such as *Yugen, Floating Bear, Evergreen Review, Big Table,* and *Origin,* all expressed in their own respective and unique ways this life the community of Beats envisioned.

In his series entitled "Jail Poems," argues Jeffrey Falla (2002, 188), Kaufman "declares a polyphonous subjectivity of 'a thousand me's.'"

> I am sitting in a cell with a view of evil parallels,
> Waiting thunder to splinter me into a thousand me's. (Kaufman 1965, 56)

From the perspective of European modernism, the "thunder" is the exigencies of modern urban life—mechanization, warfare, industrial capitalism, and philistinism—that threaten to shatter selfhood into irreconcilable fragments. Even when selfhood is conceived of as a preexisting condition that cannot be ordered by modern trends such as Freudian psychoanalysis, capitalism, Christianity, or imperialist statecraft, the "me" of the opening stanza resists "the dragging decay of Christian capitalist democracy" and its inherent alienation of the self from itself, the world and others (Mottram 1994, 7).

> It is not enough to be in one cage with one self;
> I want to sit opposite every prisoner in every hole. (Kaufman 1965, 56)

The existential "I" is autonomous in his/her uniqueness, freedom, risk, and choice not in distance from others (alienation). Far from believing that hell is other people, Kaufman expresses a desire for solidarity "for every prisoner in every hole" (56).

From the Mahayana Buddhist perspective of the interpenetration of all phenomena conditionally arising (*pratitya-samutpada*), the "thunder" can be read as the arising of wisdom that shatters all essentialist views of self and other, self and world. Furthermore, for a Buddhist it's not enough to experience selfhood in autonomy: one must also feel compassion; hence, Kaufman's desire to "sit opposite every prisoner in every hole." Kaufman's poetic "I" recognizes the interpenetration of all sentient beings in suffering when he asks rhetorically, "In a universe of cells—who is not in jail?" (Kaufman 1996, 56). Pervasiveness of suffering, the first Noble Truth of Buddhism, is particularized by Kaufman when he represents America as a wino: "Grey-speckled unplanned nakedness; stinking / Fingers grasping toilet bowl. Mr. America wants to bathe" (Kaufman 1996, 56). He echoes Beauvoir's observation of Americans' ambivalence toward life:

> Look! On the floor, lying across America's face—
> A real movie star featured in a million newsreels.

What am I doing—feeling compassion?
When he comes out of it, he will help kill me.
He probably hates living. (Kaufman 1996, 57)

The importance of nakedness as tenderness and sincerity counters the exceptionalist rhetoric of cold war, religious evangelicalism (what Cornel West has termed "Constantinian Christianity") and free-market fundamentalism. It is Kaufman's conception of nakedness, a conception he shares with Ginsberg and Kerouac, that converges with vulnerability, the condition for the possibility of *prajnaparamita,* a state of awakened perfection. The Beat aesthetic of nakedness is an approximation of Buddhist vulnerability that emancipates the self from death-in-life and freedom to live in compassion and commitment to/with others.

The emancipation of life from death is a core concern for Kaufman throughout his career and especially in his later years. This sense of liberatory freedom became acute for Kaufman when, upon hearing of President Kennedy's assassination, he took a vow of silence that lasted until 1973. Foye remembers that "he made a statement to Eileen [Kaufman] to the effect that when a president is killed things have gone too far. That the only appropriate response at that point was to take a Buddhist vow of silence" (Kaufman 1996, 16). The yogic practice of *akara-mauna* (silence) adopted by Buddhists is undertaken as a spiritual practice of liberation by deepening one's spiritual understanding (Feuerstein 1997, 185). Thus, taking a vow of silence is a voluntary aspect of a liberating practice. Given Kaufman's activism, he was a longtime union activist for the merchant marine, and from the statement quoted above that he made to his wife, one might conclude that his vow of silence was part of both his meditative practice and his activism. His vow continued until 1973. His wife, Eileen Kaufman, recalls the moment. They were attending a photography exhibit in Palo Alto, California, and "there was a little chamber group playing. I was talking to some people and all of a sudden Bob began to recite 'Murder in the Cathedral,' by [T. S.] Eliot. And that was the first thing he said when he came out of his silence" (Kaufman 1996, 17–18).

"The Trip, Dharma Trip, Sangha Trip" is Kaufman's last poem written in 1985 after a visit by fellow Beat Phillip Whalen, who by that time had become a Zen priest in San Francisco. In this poem, Kaufman suggests that Buddhism is a journey guided by teachings rooted in the truth of suffering and that the liberation from suffering (dharma) within the context of a living community (*Sangha*) "is a deliberate attempt / to rebuild a life" (Kaufman 1996, 163). Kaufman recalls the staple Buddhist notions about recollection ("something more than memory / is needed") and language ("words are not a solution, / sometimes they are a problem") (163). Buddhism, as does much of East Asian poetics, insists upon the image as the fundamental unit of poetry, a concern that the modernist imagist poets derived from their reading of East Asian poetry in translation, and that the Beats also appropriated via Ezra Pound and William Carlos Williams: *no ideas but in things.* In this poem, Kaufman's call for something more than words takes him to the symbolic mountaintop and "sky all around" of Buddha consciousness free of entangling discriminations, awareness of things as they are and compassion for all sentient beings from which there is "a view of everything spreading out / before the eyes" (163). Big-sky mind facilitates the expressive performance that burns the subjective self into an intersubjective self, ashes blowing across the Bay of Jazz, night in the city: *I am not an I.*

References

Batchelor, Stephen. 1995. *Alone with Others: An Existential Approach to Buddhism.* New York: Grove/Atlantic Press.

Beauvoir, Simone de. 1947. "An Existentialist Looks at Americans." *New York Times Magazine,* May 25, 13, 51–52.

Blake, William. 1988. *William Blake.* Edited by Michael Mason. Oxford: Oxford University Press.

Charters, Ann. 1992. *The Portable Beat Reader.* New York: Penguin.

———. 2001. *Beat Down to Your Soul: What Was the Beat Generation?* New York: Penguin.

Commager, Henry Steele. 1975. *Jefferson, Nationalism, and the Enlightenment.* New York: Braziller.

Derrida, Jacques. 1996. "Faith and Knowledge: The Two Sources of 'Religion' at the Limits of Reason Alone." In *Religion.* Edited by Jacques Derrida and Gianni Vattimo, 1–78. Stanford: Stanford University Press.

Falla, Jeffrey. 2002. "Bob Kaufman and the (Invisible) Double." Special issue on Bob Kaufman, *Callaloo* 25, no. 1: 183–89.

Feuerstein, Georg. 1997. *The Shambhala Encyclopedia of Yoga.* Boston: Shambhala.

French, Warren. 1991. *The San Francisco Poetry Renaissance: 1955–1960.* Boston: Twayne.

Gines, Katherine T. 2005. "The Debate between Sartre and Fanon: Attaining and Retaining 'Authentic' Race Consciousness." Paper presented at the Twelfth Meeting of the Georgia Continental Philosophy Circle, Kennesaw State University, February 26.

Hershock, Peter. 2006. *Buddhism in the Public Sphere: Reorienting Global Interdependence.* London: Routledge.

Holmes, John Clellon. 1967. *Nothing More to Declare.* New York: Dutton.

Jaspers, Karl. 1969. *Tragedy Is Not Enough.* Translated by Harald A. T. Reiche, Harry T. Moore, and Karl W. Deutsch. New York: Archon.

Kaufman, Bob. 1965. *Solitudes Crowded with Loneliness.* New York: New Directions.

_____. 1996. *Cranial Guitar: Selected Poems by Bob Kaufman.* Edited by Gerald Nicosia. Minneapolis: Coffee House Press.

Kerouac, Jack. 1985. *Scattered Poems.* San Francisco: City Lights.

Kerouac. 1986. Directed by John Antonelli. Mystic Fire Video.

Mottram, Eric. 1994. Introduction to *The Scripture of the Golden Eternity,* by Jack Kerouac. San Francisco: City Lights Books.

Mussett, Shannon M. 2005. "Commentary on Kathryn T. Gines' 'The Debate between Sartre and Fanon: Attaining and Retaining Authentic Race Consciousness.'" Paper presented at the Twelfth Meeting of the Georgia Continental Philosophy Circle, Kennesaw State University, February 26.

Saloy, Mona Lisa. 1995. "Black Beats and Black Issues." In *Beat Culture and the New America: 1950–1965,* edited by Lisa Phillips, 153–65. New York: Whitney Museum of American Art, in association with Flammarion.

Tytell, John. 1973. "The Beat Generation and the Continuing American Revolution." *American Scholar* 42: 308–17.

West, Cornel. 2005. *Democracy Matters.* New York: Penguin.

TONGUES UNTIED

Beat Ethnicities, Beat Multiculture

A. Robert Lee

Heavy Jewish voice heard over Kansas Radio
Varning the Jews, Take safety in Christ
> —Allen Ginsberg, *The Fall of America* (1952)

I am a Canuck, I could not speak English till I was 5 or 6, at 16 I spoke
with a halting accent.
> —Jack Kerouac, *The Subterraneans* (1958)

My parents were first-generation Americans, my grandparents Italian, and
our backyard was full of grapevines and tomato plants.
> —Diane di Prima, *Memoirs of a Beatnik* (1969)

I am the early Black Beat
I read with some of the
Best Beat minds
When the Apple was Beat Generating . . .
> —Ted Joans, "I, Too, at the Beginning," (1996)

Beat, and Beat authorship, under the auspices of multiethnicity, multicultural philosophy? The notion might at first seem a template too far, special pleading. For as a postwar American literary heritage, the terms of reference have been largely of other kinds—a circuit of poetry, fiction, life-writing, performance, and visual creativity at once countercultural, given over to the creative spirit freed and in opposition to the mainstream. This was art-and-life dissent to be seen as the very challenge to 1940s–1950s conformism at home and Cold War and U.S.–Soviet atom-bomb stasis abroad. Here was consensual Middle America defied if not stormed, a rage against Suburb, Corporation, and Pentagon. Beat into Beatnik, with Haight-Ashbury and hippiedom in their wake, could hardly not be said to have played into and through the 1960s as change era, its "alternative" banners those of drop-out, road, commune, and in the time's mantra—sex, drugs, and rock 'n' roll. Ethnic or multicultural Beat might at an opening glance seem almost incidental, peripheral fare. Yet as indeed a "tongue untied," it invites every consideration.[1]

The prime early movers, Allen Ginsberg, Jack Kerouac, William Burroughs, and Gregory Corso in New York, and Lawrence Ferlinghetti in San Francisco, and the writers around and subsequent to them were to be pitched as American authorship's quite latest tradition of the new.[2] Yet at the same time, and no doubt implicit in Beat as vanguard word and cultural politics, there was no doubting the clatter, any amount of media and institutional shock-horror. For whatever the welcome, the misgivings were equally unmistakable. To the gatekeepers of the Right, Beat amounted to antics not art, sub-zero mind, a literature, a cultural politics (if considered such) of all-too-easy shock. Norman Podhoretz spoke early and dismissively of "know-nothing barbarians."[3] Truman Capote would issue his celebrated curled-lip sneer at Kerouac's fiction—"[It] isn't writing at all—it's typing."[4] Kerouac himself, in time, came to excoriate having become "the bloody king of the beatniks," and Burroughs reflected cryptically and in amused retrospect at how "Kerouac opened a million coffee bars and sold a million pairs of Levi's to both sexes."[5]

Yet "Howl" (1956), Ginsberg's self-nominated "holy litany" and "Hebraic-bardic" chant, and *On the Road* (1957), Kerouac's Route 66 and other interstate odysseys with Neal Cassady as Dean Moriarty and under male rules of behavior and adventure, provided Beat with their great rallying insignia. Poem and novel were to be understood, indeed embraced, as iconographies for a next America. Such iconography was quick to win its following. Beat's geographies bespoke not only a changing map but a changing cultural focus, be it the New York of the postwar Village, Harlem as a redoubt of jazz and style, the lower-depths Times Square as recalled in Herbert Huncke's *Guilty of Everything* (1990), or California as variously radical or art-center Berkeley, Big Sur, and City Lights. The Mountain West, and the Denver whose streets nurtured Neal Cassady's early delinquency, were quick to beckon. Little wonder that 1974 would see Boulder's Naropa Institute (later University), founded by the Shambhala Tibetan monk Chögyam Trungpa, and then made over by Allen Ginsberg and Anne Waldman into a Buddhist meditation and creative work seminary as the Jack Kerouac School of Disembodied Poetics.

Mexico City holds its own Beat signification, famously as south-of-the-border road destination in Kerouac's *On the Road* and, in 1955, for the stay where he wrote and found titling for the verse-jazz improvisations of *Mexico City Blues* (1959). It also gathers a dark shadow as the site of Burroughs's William Tell accident-or-not shooting of his common-law wife, Joan Vollmer Adams, in 1951. Other Mexico, for Ginsberg, would involve Chiapas and Yucatán in 1953–54 exploring the Mayan ruins, and for Neal Cassady, the Guanajuato of his death-place—where more indicatively than by a railway track? In 1963, Ginsberg would add Cuba to his travels, only to be expelled on grounds of "decadence" by the Castro regime. For Bonnie Bremser, in *Troia: Mexican Memoirs* (1969), Mexico represents the landscape of her flight from the United States after a robbery by her poet-husband Ray Bremser and where she becomes the seller of her own flesh to keep them solvent. If her text functions as Abelard and Eloise journey narrative, it also limns "Mexcity," Vera Cruz, and the coastal towns. Even the Amazon enters Beat cartography in the form of Burroughs's researches into psychotropic drugs like ayahuasca, which in turn gave rise to *The Yage Letters* as edited by Allen Ginsberg in the 1963 City Lights collection and the various tropical-gothic episodes in *Naked Lunch* (1959, 1962).

Further itineraries look to the French capital, for Corso in his poem "Paris" the "Childcity," the "April city," the city of "beautiful Baudelaire, / Artaud, Rimbaud, Apollinaire."[6] In "Apollinaire's Grave," Ginsberg writes in fondness, "Here in Paris I am your guest."[7] Paris famously also means 9 Git-le-Coeur "Beat Hotel," each shabby room a studio, a scriptorium, which at different times and among others housed Burroughs, Ginsberg, Orlovsky, Corso, Harold Norse, and Bryon Gysin.[8] Paris equally drew Ted Joans, most of all to André Breton's apartment at 42 Rue Fontaine, epicenter for the surrealism first evident in his *Beat Poems* (1957) and threaded into a writing and performance career whose span is reflected in *Teducation: Selected Poems 1949–1999* (1999). Amsterdam held sway for its liberal drugs policy, cheap housing, and Van Goghs and other paintings at the Rijksmuseum, the latter a special draw to both Ginsberg and Corso. In the North Africa of Tangiers, with Paul and Jane Bowles as expatriate literary doyens, Burroughs and entourage would establish their own edge-of-Sahara drugs-and-boys outpost. Beat Asia yields Benares as Vedic and sadhu locale (not least in a Ginsberg poem like "Describe: The Rain on Dasaswamedth Ghat" in his *Planet News: 1961–1967* [1968]), and Kyoto for its Zen temples, Gary Snyder–Joanne Kyger residency, and the more than three decades of the keystone poetry journal *Origin* under the editorship of the Ukrainian-descended and Boston-raised Cid Corman.

Creative lineages were to be recognized and honored, Whitman as bardic first presence; the Melville of *Moby-Dick* as literary ocean epicist; William Carlos Williams for his "no ideas but in things" and innovations of "variable foot"; and Charles Olson for his open-breath prosody. Cognizance of Beat's spiritual affiliations has become mandatory, Zen to Veda, Torah to mystic St. John of the Cross Christianity, and whether refracted in a Kerouac Sierra Mountain sojourn like *The Dharma Bums* (1958), or Ginsberg's lyrically memorial *Kaddish* (1959), or a lifetime of Gary Snyder's contemplative verse spanning *Riprap & Cold Mountain Poems* (1959) to, say, *Mountains and Rivers without End* (1996). Jazz and blues, with Charlie Parker and John Coltrane as patron martyr-saints, have met with necessary recognition. Gender, or at least sexuality, hugely came to weigh, the lifelong same-sex love of Ginsberg and Orlovsky, the bisexual turns of Burroughs, or the seeming early absence of women writers and yet the abundant feminine call to the literary muse and nuanced varieties of feminism in Diane di Prima, Joanne Kyger, Janine Pommy Vega, Joanna McClure, and Anne Waldman.[9]

Within, and alongside, these patterns of Beat reception, one dimension oddly continues to go underaddressed, that of race, ethnicity, and in respect of both main players and outriders. In an era of multicultural debate, politics, ideology—philosophy if you will, and to be sure literature and art, and of which a cross-disciplinary collection (sociology, life-writing, popular culture, family, and economics) like *Mapping Multiculturalism* (1996) is symptomatic, and for all the importance of Beat's other expressive points of compass, that has to look discrepant, the risk of a negligent eye.[10] For virtually every Beat name, and its writings, carries the one or another ethnic-cultural footfall. If no one overarching ethnographic accord or grand aesthetic holds—how in truth could it?—that is not to say that Beat imagination has been other than route-marked or philosophically overlapping in ethnic presence.[11] Indeed, I want to suggest that we look at the Beat body of literature as foreshadowing the debates and terms that will come to make up the field of multicultural studies.

Beat's Jewish provenance runs not only through Ginsberg but Carl Solo-

mon as the illustrious dedicatee of "Howl" and himself author of the Dadaist chapbook *Mishaps Perhaps* (1966); Hettie Jones (née Cohen), whose
How I Became Hettie Jones (1988) with its unrecriminatory Village portrait
of interracial marriage; Barbara Probst Solomon in her portrait of postwar
alienation and Manhattan Jewish-Gentile young coupledom in *The Beat
of Life* (1960); Jack Micheline (né Harold Martin Silver), poet-painter who
bowed in with *Rivers of Red Wine* (1959) with an introduction by Jack Kerouac; Elise Cowen, with her early blighted love for Ginsberg and brilliant
few poems; Joyce Johnson (née Glass), whose Jewish family roots and subsequent affair with Kerouac are given in distinctive style in *Minor Characters: A Beat Memoir* (1983); Irving Rosenthal in his dedicatedly reflexive and
homoerotic *vita sexualis* in *Sheeper* (1968); and Ira Cohen, founder-editor
and poet of the vanguard literary magazine *Gnaoua*. From the related arts
came the Beat-connected composer David Amram and the photojournalist
Robert Frank, for whose iconic album *The Americans* (1958) Kerouac wrote
a preface and who codirected the Beat film whimsy *Pull My Daisy* (1959).

Within his New England upbringing, Kerouac draws upon the *jual* of
his French Canadian family (English he would not begin using until early
boyhood) and recognition of his family's cross-blood Algonquin line. Black
Beat, Afro-Beat, has its leading avatars, and community and jazz affinity,
not only in Ted Joans but LeRoi Jones/Imamu Amiri Baraka, Bob Kaufman,
and a verse-writing horn man like Archie Shepp. Italian America yields its
diversity of trace in Lawrence Ferlinghetti and from *Pictures of the Gone
World* (1955) as the inaugural volume of City Light's Pocket Poets series,
in Gregory Corso despite his early orphaning and New York street education, and in a necessary contributing Beat name like the Brooklyn-raised
Diane di Prima. Albert Saijo reminds of Japanese American heritage from
the Beat-inflected writing of *Trip Trap: Haiku on the Road* (1973), cowrit-
ten with Jack Kerouac and Lew Welch, to *Outspeaks: A Rhapsody* (1997).
Maxine Hong Kingston's *Trickmaster Monkey: His Fake Book* (1989) offers
Wittman Ah Sing, "Chinese beatnik," at once derived from Whitman, Frank
Chin as Cantonese American trickster novelist and dramatist, and her own
Beat and alternative Berkeley 1960s.

WASP voice, or at least culturally "white" voice, inevitably enters the
reckoning. One such is to be met within the Massachusetts-raised John
Clellon Holmes, be it his early Beat novel *Go* (1952) or his signature essay
"This Is the Beat Generation" published in the *New York Times Magazine* in
November 1952 and providing one of the movement's earliest literary atlases.

Another kind of benchmark has to be Michael McClure's *The Beard* (1965), which not only remains Beat's best-known play but became the center of court proceedings on grounds of obscenity after its first staging at the San Francisco Actor's Workshop. In its pairing of Billy the Kid and Jean Harlow as American myths—their arguments, trade of insults, but eventual sexual coupling—McClure explores as though in a dream afterlife both the violence and beauty of American history, along with Hollywood and other media constructions of whiteness. It also satirizes the dubious yet lavish cult of "celebrity" at a time of the all-too-actual Vietnam War.

But few have more weighed than William Burroughs himself, born to wealth as a St. Louis, Missouri, and Harvard-educated scion of the Burroughs Adding Machine family, and whose laconic assaults on WASP political and social writ in the multinovel mythographies that follow *Naked Lunch* might best be thought cultural insider-trader dissent, as it were. Burroughs so envisions the world as *l'univers concentrationnaire,* to be given further early narrative expression in *The Soft Machine* (1961), *The Ticket That Exploded* (1962), *Dead Fingers Talk* (1963), and *Nova Express* (1964), and control and addition under a mainly white-Anglo power structure.[12]

None of this is to seek overemphasis of ethnic traits, a literary or philosophical agenda in which the one or another lineage is smuggled in under cover of Beat. But nor is it to allow ethnicity to pass invisibly from due recognition of the legacies in play. It does not take account, either, of a whole Beat line of affinity beyond America, from Michael Horovitz in England to Nanao Sakaki in Japan or from Simon Vinkenoog in the Netherlands to Alik Olisevich in the Ukraine. Yet at every turn ethnicity leaves a calling card within Beat, its own discernible filter or seam. Nor is it to suggest that multiculturalism as a politics, a philosophy, does not look to a long discursive American hinterland—be it Crèvecoeur's "What then is an American, this new man?" in *Letters from an American Farmer* (1782), Tocqueville on America's racial makeup and discordances in *Democracy in America* (1835), or in a long prevalent metaphor of the process of immigrant Americanization in Isaac Zangwill's play *The Melting Pot* (1908). Few voices, however, more cannily anticipate the plies and contra-flows of current debate than Randolph Bourne in his "Trans-National America" (1916): "America is already a world-federation in miniature . . . not a nationality but a trans-nationality . . . [a] cosmopolitan vision."[13] Latterly an encompassing fuller account has been available in Ronald T. Takaki's *A Different Mirror: A History of Multi-*

cultural America (1993), the mapping of the nation's ethnic-cultural longi-
tudes and latitudes given due update.

How, then, best to frame Beat writing, verse and fiction, autobiography
and discursive work, as inveterately caught up in a multicultural ethos or
philosophy? Debate about multiculturalism in life and art, and in literary
terms across both theory and eyes-on-the-page critique, has been fractious,
often fiercely so, a call both to offense and defense. The terms have circled
one around the other: mainstream-minority, postcolonial (and internal
colonial), hegemony, orientalism, subalternism, alterity, whiteness studies,
Toni Morrison's distinction in her Massey lectures of 1990 between "racial"
and "racist" writing, and even postethnicity.[14] Whether they qualify as philosophers as such, many of the lead discursive players have exhibited their
own philosophical turn, at least if the ever-burgeoning scholarly allusion
and footnotings are to be believed.

Edward Said's *Orientalism* (1978) has become almost foundational, an
attempt with due allusion to both Enlightenment and colonial thought to
decenter Western taxonomies of the Islamic world. Gayatri Spivak's "Can
the Subaltern Speak? (1988), in line with her other Derridean analysis,
emerges as virtual poster child for an end to essentialist or totalizing versions of non-Western (and especially South Asian) culture. Colonialism,
and its counterdialectic of postcolonialism, finds its further (and for some
coagulated) deconstruction in Homi Bhabha's vintage essay collection *Nation
and Narration* (1990) and the monograph *The Location of Culture* (1994)—
both with their acknowledgments of Said along with Foucault, Lacan, and
Baudrillard. In Epifanio San Juan's *Racism and Cultural Studies: Critiques of
Multiculturalist Ideology and the Politics of Difference* (2002), multiculturalism came under Marxist critique to invite rebuke as tokenism, mere bou-
tique politics in the face of ongoing globalized capital and cheap-labor flows
with the Philippines as prime case study.[15] From another angle came Arthur
Schlesinger's *The Disuniting of America: Reflections on a Multicultural Society*
(1992), a long-serving historian's fears that multiculturalism had led to ethnic encampment, the fracture of any agreed American "political contract."

A professional philosopher like Anthony Appiah, Ghanaian by birth,
British-educated, one of Princeton's professorial luminaries, and arguing
from a "cosmopolitan-intellectual" stance, has much turned his attention to
ethnicity as interstitial, an inescapable historical lattice, not least in his 1996
Tanner Lectures on liberty and the multicultural under the rubric "Race, Cul-

ture, Identity: Misunderstood Connections."[16] At a yet further reach, Charles Taylor, who brings a Canadian as well as political-philosopher perspective to American and other Western multicultural discourse, has sometimes been invoked, especially his arguments as to rights, dialogics, and "the politics of recognition" for each cultural identity-formation within a liberal society.[17]

Each may or not provide an exact fit with Beat writing, but they offer a suggestive contour, a reminder that Beat grew prominent as the whole issue of majority-minority relationship in the United States took on new impetus. Its span encompasses civil and voter rights and the marches they engendered (as figured and literally embodied in Martin Luther King and Fanny Lou Hamer) from the 1950s onward, Betty Friedan's first-wave feminism, the Black Power of Malcolm X and the Panthers, La Raza and related Hispanic activism, tribal and AIM Native politics, Asian American self-assertion, and the gay politics whose symbol was to be found in the 1969 Greenwich Village stand-off centered on the Stonewall Club. America, in other words, could not but become increasingly aware of an un-othering, a national culture at once indeed historically ethnic and, in Bourne's still wholly pertinent term, transnational. The ethnicities that have severally gone into the formation of Beat authorship, and Beat philosophy, in this respect deserve their recognition. A panel of the writings, however selective, makes for both close tracking and overall linkage.

It would be hard not to start with Allen Ginsberg, Beat luminary as always yet also Jewish-born Bad Boy. Was it not he who famously wrote "Fuck the Jews" on his Columbia dorm window when the room went neglected by cleaners? "Howl," of necessity, enters the lists, not least in the introduction by William Carlos Williams with its allusions to the poem as redemptive of Ginsberg's Golgotha, his inescapable awareness of "the Jews in the past war." The successive witness-paragraphs to an America of "best minds," "hipsters," sex-and-drug road-journeyers, Buddhists and other religionists pledged to countermand the sterility of Moloch as fire-god of dollar and war have long become familiar—"Howl" could not more remain the classic Beat anthem. Its Jewish seams are several. An Old Testament scale or measure runs alongside, and into, the Whitman verse chants. Behind the Greek of Ginsberg's cited "eli eli lamma lamma sabacthani" lies its Hebrew etymology, not to mention Jewish sacrifice. Ironic allusions to the "Hebrew socialist revolution," the Manhattan "whose skyscrapers stand in the long streets like Jehovahs!," or even the wry recollection of pogrom and shtetl in the line, "America I still haven't told you what you did to Uncle / Max after he came over from Russia," all play into the poem's constituent texture.

No Ginsberg poem, however, more draws from a Jewish schema than "Kaddish" (1957–59), prayer-for-the-dead memorial fugue or psalm, at once mourning and scar tissue, in the name of his mother, Naomi. It is also rightly argued to rank among Ginsberg's best poetry, rich in the detail of New Jersey family lore and setback, bravely confessional, and nothing if not poignant in its contemplation of human frailty. From the start, and throughout, the poem eschews easy-on-the-wrist filopiety ("Strange to think of you now, gone without corsets & eyes while I walk on / the sunny pavement of Greenwich Village"). Rather this is grief, accusation, memory, love as pain.

The contours of Naomi's life, from Lower East Side immigrant Russian Jewish girl to marriage with the poet and teacher Louis Ginsberg in Paterson, New Jersey, and from Trotskyist communism to nervous breakdown, all bespeak a Jewish history. Invoked are due Yiddish, YPSL membership, her sister Elanor, and the unhinging haunt of "Hitlerian invisible gas," "mysterious capitalisms," and a psychotic diet of "sticks," "wires," and "spies." Each hospitalization, Naomi's creviced and lobotomized body, her self-fissure (to include a Catskills conversation in which she offers to cook for God), and her vision of redemption in sunlight ("I have the key"), is given as though almost anatomical riposte. Her face, young-woman beauty, the crazed euphoria, the demeaning undress of body and genitals, play against a Jewish poet-son's love ("wrote hymns to the mad—works of the merciful Lord of Poetry") and homocentrism ("Orlovsky in my room"). The poem finally likens Naomi to the biblical Ruth, Ginsberg himself to Svrul Avrum (Israel Abraham), and the presiding God-reference to the Elohim of Torah and Bible. As told by Ginsberg, "Kaddish" makes for a brilliant lyric of embattlement and redemption, an America of particularized Jewish mother-son family yet inextricably plied into a wholly wider multicultural national kinship.

In Jack Kerouac, Beat authorship again has a figure of wholly particular lineage—the Kerouac baptized Jean-Louis Lebris de Kerouac, raised in Lowell, Massachusetts, to immigrant French Canadian parents and known in childhood as Ti Jean (Petit Jean), and whose best-known novel first took form in French as *Sur le chemin*.[18] Upbringing and text no doubt presaged the variety of multicultural types and landscapes to be found across his writing. That embraces the San Francisco interracial love between Leo Percepied ("I am a Canuck," he says early [3]) and the African American Mardou Fox in *The Subterraneans* (1958), the tantric Buddhism personified in the

Gary Snyder figure of Japhy Ryder in *The Dharma Bums* (1958), the cross-ethnic relationship in Lowell as 1950s milltown blue-collar New England of Kerouac's French Canadian persona, Jean Duluoz, and the Irish American Maggie in *Maggie Cassidy* (1959), and the Italian American and other ethnicity in play (especially in the Ferlinghetti figure of Lorenzo Monsanto) throughout the harrowing fame-and-alcoholic descent of Kerouac's Duluoz figure in *Big Sur* (1963).[19]

This multicultural vista, however, and as evidently as anywhere, holds in *On the Road*, first in the novel's very geography—from Bear Mountain in New York, through "the great hugeness" (32) of the prairie Midwest and Plains, to California ("My ah-dream of San Francisco" [157]), and into a Mexico that Sal Paradise as narrator calls "these vast and Biblical areas of the world" (274). Afro-jazz Chicago and New Orleans; farmland Nebraska; Central City, Colorado; and the yet farther Far West (albeit, Sal comes to understand, vulnerable to cowboy chic) each add to the panorama. As Sal accompanies, and monitors, Dean Moriarty along "the 'holyboy road, madman road, rainbow road'" (229), the novel in fact offers whole networks of ethnicity. In Denver he speaks of "wishing I were a Negro" (163) and of swapping his soi-disant dull cultural whiteness in favor of becoming "Denver Mexican, even a poor overworked Jap" (164). The dramatis personae looks to Beat's usual suspects—Ginsberg, for instance, as Jewish-surreal Carlo Marx—but also to Sal's *campesina* lover Terry, the Cajuns near Bull Lee's Louisiana drug farm, fellow drinkers in black Detroit, the Scandinavian Minnesota farm-boy truckers, the Québecois Remi Boncoeur, and the Mexicans among whom Sal finds both the heat of Latin sexuality and wrack of his fever. *On the Road*, Beat's co-classic with "Howl," in all of these aspects gives its own more than passing grounds and reference to be situated in the multicultural literary column.

Italianità as life and literary heritage makes any number of literary entrances into Beat, and not least as refracted in the video *Little Italy* (1995), in which Lawrence Ferlinghetti and Diane di Prima both feature. Corso, parentless in his childhood, nonetheless among interests in the jazz of Charlie Parker, Miles Davis, and bebop, Shelley and *les symbolistes,* always held to an awareness of his Italian heritage. His poem "Uccello," in *Gasoline* (1956), early gives evidence. The Florentine painter's three San Romano canvases of peace and war, sight and sound, bespeak both Corso's ancestral affinity and a refraction of his own best-known poetry like "Bomb" and "Columbia U. Poesy reading—1975." Diane di Prima as historic woman Beat writer but also self-aware Italian Brooklynite can be said to be mirrored in two texts from the abundance that has been her career. In "No Problem Party Poem," from her *Selected Poems 1956–1975* (1975), she works the "no problem" paradigm into a pattern-poem similar in genre to Anne Waldman's "Fast Speaking Woman" and in which Beat is given parsing from Corso and Ginsberg to Berkeley and Naropa. In "Backyard," from her City Lights collection *Pieces of a Song* (1990), di Prima invokes a Brooklyn of Caruso, Gobbi, Gigli, and Lanza, Italy's music carried on pulse and memory into America. The two offer a Beat and ethnicity cultural overlap infinitely to the point.

Beat poet, or simply publisher of Beats as he has often insisted, Lawrence Ferlinghetti has from the start exhibited a multicultural range and flair. How, almost, not to do so given his mixed Italian, French, and Sephardic heritage, his New York, New England, and, since 1953, San Francisco years, his lifelong affinity and practice of painting and sketch work? Dante and Sarolla, at the outset, make their appearances in *Pictures of the Gone World,* just as Cellini, the love-call *"Dove star amore,"* and Sarolla again, do in *A Coney Island of the Mind* (1958). But few of Ferlinghetti's always painterly poems more affectingly summon Italy-in-America than "The Old Italians Dying," with its fond yet tough envisaging of Little Italy and other citizenry—churchgoers to pigeon feeders, Garibaldi-ists to Mussolini-ists—"in faded felt hats . . . sunning themselves and dying." The poem enumerates "the Piedmontesi the Genovese the Siciliani smelling of garlic and pepperoni," each joined in "telling the unfinished *Paradiso* story." Vintage Beat homily or memoir, vintage Beat poetics or otherwise, it is equally a tribute full of its own ethnic-cultural affiliation.

Other Beat, or Beat-influenced, domains help extend and aggregate this multicultural dimension, neither still sufficiently given its due. In her "The Beats and Beyond," a 1999 memoir contributed to Anne Waldman's edited collection *Beats at Naropa* (2009), Lorna Dee Cervantes recalls how her Chicano and California indigenous Chumash origins have also braided into Beat influence. Her Mission District birth and San Jose upbringing, early publication in *Revista-Riqueña* and elsewhere, and her own small-press publication of poets like Gary Soto, Sandra Cisneros, Jimmy Santiago Baca, and Ray Gonzalez, coexist with her sense of debt to the Beats (she nicely terms Ginsberg "the first American pachuco," perceptively judges Bob Kaufman "a very underrated poet," and avers that "I know that my roots come out of the Beat movement").[20] Both ethnicity and a "spoken word" Beat measure fuse across her two signature collections, whether in a poem like "Refugee Ship" in *Emplumada* (1981), with its "I feel I am a captive / aboard the refugee ship," or like "Pleiades from the Cables of Genocide" in *From the Cables of Genocide* (1991), with its eulogy to her grandmother as guide to the Seven Sisters' Beat-Transcendent "strange stories of epiphanies of light."

Oscar Zeta Acosta, tenant lawyer, autobiographer, rowdy, and the rambunctious "gonzo" co-spirit remembered in Hunter Thompson's New Journalist *Fear and Loathing in Las Vegas: A Savage Journey to the Heart of the American Dream* (1971), calls up his own species of Beat *chicanismo,* not to say in mirror fashion, *chicano* Beat.[21] His two fiction-of-fact autobiographies, *The Autobiography of a Brown Buffalo* (1972) and *The Revolt of the Cockroach People* (1973), give any number of grounds for thinking them a Beat-connected vita. A whole chain of Beat patois and allusion presses, even, and indeed not least, when he takes shies at "Ginsberg and those coffee houses" or beatniks "shouting Love and Peace and Pot."[22] Much as he positions himself as "a fat, dark Mexican—a Brown Buffalo" or "last of the Aztecs," he also assumes his place as "a faded beatnik, a flower vato," "a singer of songs."[23] The effect is to suggest a dual Chicano-Beat passport, joined and at the same time bifurcated in cultural identity and philosophy.

Frank Chin, ideological godfather to the Asian American renaissance, battler-royale against each and every China and other Asian stereotype—notoriously to include his charges against Maxine Hong Kingston, Amy Tan, and David Hwang of transforming China into at once fortune-cookie exotica and misogynist dungeon, might almost be thought to have been also the reflexive begetter of a Beat credential.[24] Oakland-Berkeley, drugs and radicalism 1960s, the debut of *The Chicken-Coop Chinaman* (1972) and *The Year of the Dragon* (1974) as first-ever Asian American plays, and his groundbreaking multicultural *Aiiieeeee* anthologies (1974, 1991) all call up both ethnic counterculture and Beat-radical voice. *Gunga Din Highway* (1994), Chin's most commodious novel, gives both impulses a quite canniest memorial and philosophical overlap, the China–United States dynasty of Longman Kwan as a mural of Charlie Chan movies, San Francisco Chinatown, and the Hawai'i of beach and pot, with the 1960s in the role of presiding Beat-centered interlude.

Beat's black ligatures, the wells of life encoded in Harlem's jazz or Chicago's South Side, along with the Dixie they memorialize, and then carried over into Beat authorship, have been unmistakable and provide a wholly appropriate place to conclude. Ginsberg's "negro streets at dawn," Corso's "Bird" in its eulogy to Miles Davis and Charlie Parker, or Norman Mailer's *The White Negro* (1957) as would-be hipster philosophic manifesto bring to bear the one Beat array of voice. In Jones/Baraka, Joans, and Kaufman, Afro-America, however, offers its own Beat multicultural stylings, each a poet of hugely individual register and of necessity implicated in all the daunting skeins of American race history.

In *The Autobiography of LeRoi Jones/Amiri Baraka* (1984), Jones/Baraka makes emphatic his own early Beat affiliations. As recollection of his pre–Black Nationalist and Marxist phases, he is decidedly the young writer in search of a true voice ("I'd come to the Village *looking*, trying to 'check', being open to all flags. Allen Ginsberg's *Howl* was the first thing to open my nose" [156]).[25] A 1980s interview, in turn, sets this within historical context ("Beat came out of the whole dead Eisenhower period, the whole of the McCarthy Era, the Eisenhower blandness, the whole reactionary period of the 50s").[26] In *Preface to Twenty Volume Suicide Note* (1961), the collection most associated with his Beat phase, Jones/Baraka offers a variety of open-prosody registers—"Way Out West" dedicated to Gary Snyder with its Zen perception of space-time; "One Night Stand," for Ginsberg, with its teasing send-up of Beat's claim to creating the New Bohemia ("We entered the city at noon! The radio on . . ."), or "Look for You Yesterday, Here You Come Today," with its allusive interplay of blues, Lorca, and Baudelaire. "In Memory of Radio" delivers an ode to the lost innocence of listening to old radio heroes, the execution of Caryl Chessman, and violence toward black Americans, and, notably, "Hymn for Lanie Poo" (his sister's nickname) takes its slaps at black imitations of a white middle class ("the huge & loveless / white anglo-sun / of benevolent step mother America") and his sense of moving on from Beat self-absorption into black militancy.

Given more than thirty volumes of verse beginning with *Beat Poems* (1957) and culminating in *Teducation: Selected Poems 1949–1999* (1999), and his different incarnations as troubadour, painter, trumpeter, European and African traveler, jazz aficionado, and surrealist, Ted Joans gives reason to be thought more than only a Beat figure. His best-known banners, after all, became "Jazz is my religion" and "Surrealism is my point of view." Yet from his Mississippi River birth to his Village years (and not least his enlistment in Fred McDarrah's performance-art Rent-a-beatnik circuit), Beat, Black Beat, clearly played a decisive role in his improvisational riffs and versifying. In "The Sermon," he lays down for white would-be hipster women a veritable menu of desiderata: jazz, blues, Jelly Roll, "Howl," Kerouac, *The White Negro,* Dada, and surrealism. No poem, however, more figures Beat into jazz, white hipsterism into black "cool" than "The Wild Spirit of Kicks," written in Harlem in 1969 in memory of his friendship and jazz with Jack Kerouac just as other poetry had eulogized similarly important friendships with his one-time roommate Charlie Parker and Langston Hughes:

> JACK IN RED AND BLACK MAC
> RUSHING THROUGH DERELICT STREWN
>   STREETS OF NORTH AMERICA . . .
>   RUNNING ACROSS THE COUNTRY LIKE A
>   RAZOR BLADE GONE MAD . . .
> OLE ANGEL MIDNIGHT SINGING MEXICO
>   CITY BLUES
> IN THE MIDST OF BLACK HIPSTERS AND
>   MUSICIANS
> FOLLOWED BY A WHITE LEGION OF COOL
>   KICK SEEKERS
> POETRY LIVERS AND POETRY GIVERS
> PALE FACED CHIEFTAIN TEARING PAST
>
> THE FUEL OF A GENERATION
>
> AT REST   AT LAST
>
> JK SAYS HELLO TO JC
> JOHN COLTRANE THAT IS[27]

The capitalizations add height, and weight, a philosophy in majuscule, it might be said, to a historic cross-ethnic Beat kinship.

From his New Orleans birth, through merchant marine service and labor activism in New York, to San Francisco's North Beach, where he became a larger-than-life Bohemian feature, Bob Kaufman lays every claim to Beat status. The often destructive heat and noise of his drugs-and-poetry life, several jail terms, together with his Buddhist vow of silence from 1963 to 1973 after the John Kennedy assassination, do not diminish his creative track, the jazz and imagism of an African American cultural heritage. Besides his three major collections, *Solitudes Crowded with Loneliness* (1959, *Golden Sardine* (1960), and *The Ancient Rain: Poems 1956–1978* (1981), these elements play into the Dadaist "rejectionary philosophy," as he called it in his *Abomunist* manifestos.

An early poem like "Afterwards They Shall Dance" pays dues to both Billie Holiday and Dylan Thomas, Poe and Baudelaire, but also to Beat ethos in its line, "drinking cool beatitudes." In "Ginsberg (for Allen)," he adopts a suitably playful voice ("I love him because his eyes leak"). "West Coast Sounds—1956" invokes California's Beat world, whether "Allen on Chesnutt Street," Corso with his "God eyes," Rexroth and Ferlinghetti "swinging," or Kerouac "writing Neil / on high typewriter." "A Remembered Beat" offers homage to Charlie Parker. But no poem more captures Beat's multicultural-philosophical inscription than "Like Father, Like Sun." Invoking a panorama from New Orleans and the Mississippi to the "Apache, Kiowa and Sioux ranges" and "Africa's black handkerchief," he looks to an America of compassion not loss or conflict, an America of healing Beat blues:

> America is a promised land, a garden torn from naked stone,
> A place where the losers in earth's conflicts can enjoy their triumph.
> All losers, brown, red, black and white: the colors from the
> Master Palette.

If Beat ethnicity, Beat multiculture, can look to a tongue untied, and with links of philosophy, as of word, back to "Howl" and *On the Road,* it surely lies in Kaufman's lines.

Notes

Ginsberg epigraph: Allen Ginsberg, "Dr. Michaelson and the Hebrew-Christian Hour—P.O.B 707 Los Angeles 53–," in "Hiway Poesy LA–Albuquerque–Texas–Wichita," in *The Fall of America: Poems of These States 1965–1971,* Pocket Poet series no. 30 (San Francisco: City Lights, 1972), 25.

Kerouac epigraph: Jack Kerouac, *The Subterraneans* (New York: Grove, 1958), 3.

Di Prima epigraph: Diane di Prima, *Memoirs of a Beatnik* (New York: Olympia, 1968; repr., New York and London: Penguin, 1998), 48.

Joans epigraph: Ted Joans, "I, Too, at the Beginning," in "Je Me Vois (I See Myself)," in *Contemporary Authors Autobiography Series,* vol. 25, ed. Shelley Andrews (Detroit: Gale, 1996), 242.

1. The term has its own multicultural life in Marlon Riggs's stirring and greatly pioneering movie of the lives of gay black men's lives, *Tongues Untied* (1980).

2. I borrow the phrase from Harold Rosenberg, *The Tradition of the New* (New York: Horizon, 1958), a landmark analysis of modern American visual art.

3. Norman Podhoretz, "The Know-Nothing Bohemians," *Partisan Review* 25, no. 2 (Spring 1958): 301–11, 313–16, reprinted in *Doings and Undoings: The Fifties and after in American Writing* (New York: Farrar, Straus, 1964).

4. Truman Capote's jibe was made in 1959 on David Susskind's TV show, *Open End*.

5. Kerouac's observation is quoted in Joyce Johnson, *Door Wide Open: A Beat Love Affair in Letters, 1957–1958* (New York: Viking, 2000), xxii. The Burroughs observation is to be found in "Remembering Jack Kerouac," 1985, 1986, reprinted in William Burroughs, *Word Virus: The William S. Burroughs Reader* (New York: Grove, 2000).

6. Gregory Corso, "Paris," in *Gasoline/The Vestal Lady on Brattle* (San Francisco: City Lights, 1969), 54.

7. Allen Ginsberg, *Reality Sandwiches: 1953–1960* (San Francisco: City Lights, 1963).

8. The fullest account remains Barry Miles, *The Beat Hotel: Ginsberg, Burroughs and Corso in Paris, 1957–1963* (New York: Grove, 2000).

9. The rebalancing of Beat as also woman-centered is reflected in anthologies and interview collections like the following: Nancy M. Grace and Ronna C. Johnson, eds., *Breaking the Rule of Cool: Interviewing and Reading Beat Women Writers* (Jackson: University Press of Mississippi, 2004); Ronna C. Johnson and Nancy M. Grace, eds., *Girls Who Wore Black: Women Writing the Beat Generation* (New Brunswick, N.J.: Rutgers University Press, 2002); Richard Peacock, ed., *A Different Beat: Women of the Beat Generation* (New York: Serpent's Tail, 1997); and Brenda Knight, ed., *Women of the Beat Generation: The Writers, Artists, and Muses at the Heart of the Beat Generation* (Berkeley: Conari, 1996).

10. Avery F. Gordon and Christopher Newfield, eds., *Mapping Multiculturalism* (Minneapolis: University of Minnesota Press, 1996).

11. I have been at some pains over the recent years to map the ethnic and cultural diversity within Beat authorship. See *Modern American Counter Writing: Beats, Outriders, Ethnics* (New York: Routledge, 2010), chaps. 1–4; "Pocket Poets to Global Beat: Andrei Voznesensky, Kazuo Shiraishi, Michael Horovitz," *Orbis Literarum* 59, no. 3 (June 2001): 218–37; and "Black Beats: The Signifying Poetry of LeRoi Jones/Amiri Baraka, Ted Joans and Bob Kaufman," in *The Beat Generation Writers*, ed. A. Robert Lee (London: Pluto, 1996), 158–77.

12. In one of his celebrated signed postcards, Burroughs speaks of *The Naked Lunch* as "shitting out my educated Middlewest background once and for all. It's a matter of catharsis" (Web: William Burroughs, Postcards for Sale).

13. Randolph S. Bourne, "Trans-National America," *Atlantic Monthly*, July 1916, reprinted in *War and the Intellectuals: Collected Essays, 1917–1919* (New York: Harper and Row, 1964).

14. Toni Morrison, *Playing in the Dark: Whiteness and the Literary Imagination* (Cambridge: Harvard University Press, 1992), xii–xiii. The postethnic notion is best argued in David A. Hollinger, *Postethnic America: Beyond Multiculturalism*, rev. ed. (New York: Basic, 1996).

15. Specific ethnicities have found their theorists in studies like Henry Louis Gates Jr., *The Signifying Monkey: A Theory of Afro-American Monkey* (1988); Ramón Saldívar, *Chicano Narrative: The Dialectics of Difference* (1990); Gerald Vizenor, *Fugitive Poses: Native American Indian Scenes of Absence and Presence* (1998); Sau-ling Wong, *Reading Asian American Literature: From Necessity to Extravagance* (1993); Karen Brodkin, *How Jews Became White Folks and What That Says about Race in America* (1999); Fred Gadar-phé, *Italian Signs, American Streets: The Evolution of Italian American Literature* (1996); Valerie Babbs, *Whiteness Visible: The Meaning of Whiteness in American Literature and Culture* (1998); Noel Ignatiev, *How The Irish Became White* (1995); and Matthew Frye Jacobson, *Whiteness of a Different Color: European Immigrants and the Alchemy of Race* (1999). Ishmael Reed's collection, *Multi-America: Essays on Cultural Wars and Cultural Peace* (New York: Viking-Penguin, 1997) bears every witness to how the different arenas of multicultural cultural and literary debate has evolved. I also map these developments in *Multicultural American Literature: Comparative Black, Native, Latino/a and Asian American Fictions* (Edinburgh University Press; University Press of Mississippi, 2003), 1–19.

16. Anthony Appiah, "Race, Culture, Identity: Misunderstood Connections," in *The Tanner Lectures on Human Values* (Salt Lake City: University of Utah Press, 1996), 51–136. Another helpful analysis in this connection is his "But Would That Still Be Me? Notes on Gender, 'Race,' Ethnicity as Sources of Identity," *Journal of Philosophy* 87, no. 10 (October 1990): 493–99.

17. Charles Taylor, *Multiculturalism and "The Politics of Recognition"* (Princeton, N.J.: Princeton University Press, 1994).

18. In *"Beatific: The Origins of the Beat Generation,"* Kerouac speaks also of his own origins as "Breton, Wiking, Irishman, Indian, madboy . . ." (reprinted in Ann Charters, ed. *The Portable Kerouac* [New York: Viking-Penguin, 1995], 567).

19. There can also be added Jack Duluoz's outburst in *Desolation Angels*—"I know they cant understand a word of my speech with its French-Canadian and New York and Boston and Okie accents a mixed up and even Español and even Finnegan's Wake" (*Desolation Angels* [New York: Coward-McCann, 1965; repr., New York: Riverhead Books, 1995], 97).

20. Lorna Dee Cervantes, "The Beats and Beyond," in *Beats at Naropa*, ed. Anne Waldman and Laura Wright (Minneapolis: Coffee House Press, 2009), 113–16.

21. I offer a full account of Acosta as putative Beat in *"Chicanismo's Beat Outrider? The Texts and Contexts of Oscar Zeta Acosta,"* in "Teaching Beat Literature," special issue, *College Literature* 27, no. 1 (Winter 2000): 58–76.

22. Oscar Zena Acosta, *The Autobiography of a Brown Buffalo* (San Francisco: Straight Arrow, 1972), 18.

23. Ibid., 86, 140; Oscar Zena Acosta, *The Revolt of the Cockroach People* (San Francisco: Straight Arrow, 1973), 53, 207.

24. Chin's work I have addressed in "Bad Boy, Godfather, Storyteller: The China Fictions of Frank Chin," in *China Fictions/English Language: Literary Essays in Diaspora, Memory, Story,* ed. A. Robert Lee (Amsterdam and New York: Rodopi, 2008), 79–100.

25. Imamu Amiri Baraka, *The Autobiography of LeRoi Jones/Amiri Baraka* (New York: Freundlich, 1984).

26. "LeRoi Jones in the East Village," interview by Debra L. Edwards, in *Beat Vision: A Primary Sourcebook,* ed. Arthur Knight and Kit Knight (New York: Paragon, 1986), 123–38.

27. Published in *The Beat Vision: A Primary Sourcebook,* ed. Arthur Knight and Kit Knight (New York: Paragon, 1986), 269.

JOANNE KYGER "DESCARTES AND THE SPLENDOR OF"

Bridging Dualisms through Collaboration and
Experimentation

Jane Falk

In the late 1990s, two seminal anthologies, Brenda Knight's *Women of the Beat Generation* and Richard Peabody's *A Different Beat,* focused on women writers of the Beat Generation who had not previously been considered part of the male-dominated Beat canon. The West Coast poet Joanne Kyger was one of these. Coming to San Francisco from Santa Barbara in the spring of 1957, Kyger was first drawn to the San Francisco Renaissance poets Robert Duncan and Jack Spicer, joining their circle. However, through her acquaintance with and subsequent marriage to Gary Snyder, and her friendships with Philip Whalen and Lew Welch, Kyger also became associated with the Beat movement.[1]

A characteristic Kyger shared with other Beat writers in the late 1950s and 1960s was the search for an alternative to Western culture, seemingly bankrupt after World War II. Kyger's prose poem "Descartes and the Splendor Of," her rewrite of the seventeenth-century Enlightenment philosopher Rene Descartes's *Discourse on Method* and script for her video *Descartes,* exemplifies this move away from the Eurocentric as well as a rejection of Descartes's privileging of the rational.[2]

Background in Philosophy

Kyger's interest in Descartes and what she considered the problematic nature of his "mind-body dualism" had originated in her college years at the University of California, Santa Barbara, where she studied philosophy in a tutorial program. One of her more influential teachers at Santa Barbara was Paul Wienpahl, and she took a required course in the history of Western philosophy as well as two semesters of contemporary philosophy with him.[3] Kyger notes that "Descartes' mind-body dualism was discussed as having made a 'problem' in philosophic thinking that needed to be surmounted."[4] Wienpahl makes his own position clear in regard to Descartes in the first chapter of *Zen Diary*.[5] For Wienpahl, Descartes's "fatal flaw" is the way he "separates the subjective from the objective. . . . But in doing so not only makes man an alien in this world, but alienates him from his fellows and ultimately from himself."[6] The project of modern philosophy, according to Wienpahl, was to move away from Cartesian dualism.

A Beat interest in Buddhism was another aspect of this counter to a dualistic Western point of view, which Kyger, as well as Wienpahl, shared. "When I arrived in San Francisco Spring 1957, 'Zen' was in the air, like a buzz word," she notes.[7] Beat connections are also evident in the summer 1958 issue of the *Chicago Review,* known as the Zen issue, which contained work by Snyder, Kerouac, and Whalen, among others, as well as Wienpahl's essay "Zen and the Work of Wittgenstein." Here Wienpahl points out correspondences between the two, claiming that Wittgenstein had "attained a state of mind resembling that which the Zen master calls *satori,*[8] the Buddhist term for enlightenment or liberation and a goal of Buddhist practice. When Kyger saw this article, she realized Wienpahl had "made the bridge, from the 'west' to the 'east.'"[9]

In a 1995 interview about Zen master Shunryu Suzuki, Kyger corroborates the idea that Zen became of greater interest for her than Western philosophy: "My own interest in Zen came about because I had been studying Wittgenstein and Heidegger in Santa Barbara. Their philosophy just comes to an end saying you just have to practice the study of nothing. Then I got DT Suzuki's book on Japanese Zen and I thought oh! This is where you go with this mind." She adds that "the way of Western philosophy had come to a real dead end . . . and it was a very natural kind of progression into what was available about Zen Buddhist teachings. Like no mind."[10] However, it is not through reading and the study of abstract concepts that Kyger undertakes to counter dualism and to reject Eurocentric academic culture, but through performance art, specifically her video *Descartes,* created for the National Center for Experiments in Television (NCET) in 1968.

The NCET Project: Collaboration and Experimentation

The NCET project, under the direction of Brice Howard and funded by the Rockefeller Foundation and the NEA, can best be described as experimental or avant-garde television. The purpose of this collaborative and cross-disciplinary project was for guest artists to challenge conventional notions of television through the use of experimental video techniques to present their art forms. This was especially true of its first year, that of Kyger's internship, which was officially titled "The Experimental Project." Various artists were invited to participate: Kyger, the representative poet, along with William Allen, painter-sculptor; William Brown, novelist; Richard Felciano, musician; and Loren Sears, filmmaker. Of the artists involved, Kyger's principal collaborators would be Felciano and Sears.

According to Howard, these artists were to be "free to move and think and create in the television environment in a unique way. They need not produce anything."[11] Experimentation or process was privileged over program production, so as to expand the medium, often resulting in images that, per Howard, the technical crew of KQED might consider "aberrations and distortions" involving such effects as feedback, tape loops, and tape delay. The artists would be working with and in what Howard called "videospace."

The influence of the psychedelic movement, a dynamic aspect of the San Francisco Bay Area art scene in the 1960s, is also evident to a contemporary eye in this experimental work, something on which Kyger comments: "In 1967 fall, the Summer of Love and the Hippy thing in the Haight Ashbury had come to an end. . . . But psychedelics were still in the air. Along with the visual stimulus of LSD-inspired rock posters, psychedelic colors and designs. The world was looking different."[12] The critic Catherine Elwes characterizes such video experimentation as a scrambling of image with LSD visual simulation.[13] The artists took advantage of what Howard called "multiple evolution,"[14] involving video's ability to use simultaneity and superimposition in the production of kaleidoscopic and strobe-like effects with layered, ghostly, metamorphic, and swirling images.[15]

Kyger's Subversion of Descartes

In the NCET project, each artist was required to create one representative work by residency's end, and Kyger's *Descartes* is what she had considered a "complete and finished composition."[16] She describes the video as an

"11-minute translation of Descartes' six part *Discourse on Method* into video, using various techniques to visualize thoughts."[17] For Kyger, video seemed like a medium in which body, speech, and mind could come together, hence one suited to the resolution of Cartesian dualism, and one reason to turn to this text for her video project. As she put it, Descartes's "body mind problem could be resolved in videospace."[18]

Discourse on Method is a record of Descartes's quest to discover a way of thinking whereby he could determine the nature of reality, his conclusion being that the mind is ultimately privileged over the body. This idea is epitomized by his famous statement, "I think, therefore I am,"[19] in Latin, *cogito ergo sum*, often known simply as the cogito.[20] His purpose is to demonstrate that reality and the existence of God can be validated rationally and logically through the mind, not the senses, thereby setting up a mind-body duality. The text presents a narrative of Descartes's quest to truly understand man's relation to both God and the world and his method for doing so, based on his rejection of tradition and his reliance solely on his own powers of reasoning.

In part 1, Descartes describes his educational background and his decision to give up his studies. Although he had been to "one of the most celebrated Schools in Europe where I thought that there must be men of learning," at the end of his course of study he found himself "embarrassed with so many doubts and errors."[21] He relates that he had read "good books," knew "languages and . . . the reading of the literature of the ancients,"[22] but was still not satisfied with a traditional education. He determines to abandon book learning: "And resolving to seek no other science than that which could be found in myself, or at least in the great book of the world, I employed the rest of my youth in travel . . . in proving myself in the various predicaments in which I was placed by fortune."[23] However, this preliminary solution proves unsatisfactory, and ultimately Descartes decides "to believe nothing too certainly of which I had only been convinced by example and custom," resolving to make himself "an object of study."[24]

Describing his return to France from Germany in part 2, Descartes notes that he isolated himself so as to use his own reason rather than "custom" or the ideas of others to develop his method of determining Truth. This is comprised of four laws, the first of which is "to accept nothing as true which I did not clearly recognize to be so: . . . to avoid precipitation and prejudice in judgments, and to accept in them nothing more than what was presented to my mind so clearly . . . that I could have no occasion to doubt it."[25] In the third part, he describes traveling again for nine years and continuing to be skeptical about what he encounters, stating that he "I rooted out of my mind all the errors which might have formerly crept in."[26]

In part 4, Descartes uses his method of rejecting everything of which he cannot be absolutely certain to arrive at his first principle, the cogito. In reasoning his way to "Truth," he finds it necessary to "reject as absolutely false everything as to which I could imagine the least ground of doubt, in order to see if afterwards there remained anything in my belief that was entirely certain."[27] Here Descartes draws on dreaming as a way to strip the senses of all authority by asking, "How do we know that the thoughts that come in dreams are more false than those that we have when we are awake, seeing that often enough the former are not less lively and vivid than the latter?"[28] He concludes that senses deceive, and his only certainty lies in his mind: "I noticed that whilst I thus wished to think all things false, it was absolutely essential that the 'I' who thought this should be."[29] Hence the cogito. Refining his ideas about mind, body, and soul in part 5, in the process differentiating humans and animals, he further applies these principles to natural phenomena in part 6. In concluding his discourse, Descartes debates publication, considering the controversial nature of his ideas, but ultimately decides to publish in French, not Latin, so as to be accessible to all.

Kyger's highly condensed six-part poem script "Descartes and the Splendor Of" follows the basic outline of *Discourse on Method,* with close paraphrasing and key points of Descartes's text indicated by capitalization.[30] Kyger's purpose here then is to subvert and critique Descartes, though seeming to espouse his position, a parody, according to Alicia Ostriker's 1972 review of *Places To Go.* In her paraphrases, for example, Kyger sometimes uses slang and colloquialisms to deflate serious philosophical language, a technique she shares with other Beat writers.[31] For example, in part 1 of "Descartes and the Splendor Of," the speaker compares her natural mind to Yosemite National Park, an ignorant state, and decides to travel, listing all the friends she has met by first name. She ends somewhat flatly and succinctly: "So I traveled a great deal." At this point in the video, newsreel-like images of contemporary life, such as American flags, are superimposed over the speaker's face, a subtle allusion to the Vietnam War then in progress as well as to Descartes's participation in European wars. She then adds the suggestive phrase, "This being some trip," with its 1960s slang allusion to *trip* as in drug trip or tripping out.[32] In part 4, Kyger paraphrases Descartes's famous statement, "I think therefore I Am," as "I THINK hence I AM," followed by the aside, "You get the picture." In the next paragraph she adds that "to doubt is a drag,"[33] in both cases effectively mixing levels of language using sarcasm and slang.

Kyger also decontextualizes Descartes, substituting Buddhist, Taoist, and Confucian terminology for his seventeenth-century phraseology as another way to subvert his meaning. In the third part of his discourse, for example, Descartes refers to the need to act with moderation, stating that of "many opinions all equally received, I chose only the most moderate, both because these are always most suited for putting into practice, and probably the best (for all excess has a tendency to be bad), and also because I should have in a less degree turned aside from the right path, supposing that I was wrong."[34] Kyger here substitutes the phrase, "choosing the Middle Way for convenience"[35] in her corresponding part 3, recalling the historical Buddha's avoidance of extremes in his path to Enlightenment.

Kyger also decontextualizes Descartes in his part 4, where he comments on the delusional nature of thoughts which come in dreams: "And since all the same thoughts and conceptions which we have while awake may also come to us in sleep, without any of them being at that time true, I resolved to assume that everything that ever entered into my mind was no more true than the illusions of my dreams."[36] Kyger paraphrases here by alluding to the Taoist parable of Chuang Tzu questioning whether he is dreaming he is a butterfly or a butterfly dreaming he is Chuang Tzu: "AM I A BUTTERFLY DREAMING I AM ME or ME DREAMING I AM A BUTTERFLY or am I MOTHER *GOD* in Glory and Splendor?"[37]

A third example of decontextualization appears in the sixth part, where Descartes discusses his lack of resolution in publishing the *Discourse* due to its controversial nature. He notes that he had decided not to publish three years previously, but subsequently changed his mind. Kyger restates this with the phrase, "The *I* that is the Pivot, must not wobble,"[38] an allusion to the modernist poet Ezra Pound's translation of a Confucian classic, *The Unwobbling Pivot.*

Kyger's most radical move is to feminize Descartes, shown dramatically in her video production. She provides the voice-over, simultaneously narrating and acting out her poem, as she takes on the role of both the contemporary woman/Descartes and Mother God/God. Her powerful and hieratic female voice is an important and effective part of her parody. Inflections and shifts in tone provide additional commentary and critique moving between the formality of her straight paraphrase of seventeenth-century prose and her own casual, slangy, sarcastic, and often humorous female voice.

Her impersonation of Descartes, male seeker after truth, is central to her deconstruction and subversion of the masculine. Kyger subtly undermines male privilege as she replaces Descartes with a female persona in a domestic space. In impersonating Descartes, recontextualizing him as it were, the preeminent male philosopher becomes female, in the process feminizing this most masculine of professions.[39] The feminist critic Judith Butler, in *Gender Trouble,* her study of gender identity and feminism, comments on the "resignification and recontextualization" involved in gender parody.[40] She claims that parodic practices can "disrupt the categories of the body, sex, gender, and sexuality."[41] Here, Kyger's acting out of Descartes's figurative language rooted in the domestic (his sweeping away of conventions, for example) is a clever way of literalizing his metaphors while commenting on and subverting his message of male authority.

Butler also connects Cartesian dualism with mind/body and male/female distinctions: "In the philosophical tradition that begins with Plato and continues through Descartes . . . the ontological distinction between soul (consciousness, mind) and body invariably supports relations of political and psychic subordination and hierarchy." She goes on to claim that "any uncritical reproduction of the mind/body distinction ought to be rethought for the implicit gender hierarchy that the distinction has conventionally produced, maintained, and rationalized."[42] Describing the body seen as a "passive medium that is signified by an inscription from a cultural source figured as 'external' to that body," she claims "Christian and Cartesian precedents to such views."[43] Cartesian dualism is thus implicit with a devalued body associated with the female.

In reference to Christianity, Kyger also feminizes Descartes by referring to his masculine God as Mother God. In doing so, she conflates Descartes's references to a female Nature with those to God, recalling Mother Nature and commenting on Descartes's opposition of God and nature. For Descartes, God is masculine, always referred to in the *Discourse on Method* as "He." Nature, on which God acts, is feminine. In part 5, for example, Descartes notes that he has "observed certain laws which God has so established in Nature . . . we cannot doubt their being accurately observed in all that exists or is done in the world."[44] He goes on to refer to Nature specifically as female and dominated by God, as He (God) lends "His concurrence to Nature in the usual way, leaving her to act in accordance with the laws which He had established."[45] Here Descartes uses the uppercase *He* in reference to active God and the lowercase *her* in reference to passive Nature. This opposition is also paralleled by Descartes's opposition of mind/soul and body and the senses which deceive, clearly stating that "the soul by which I am what I am, is entirely distinct from body."[46] He maintains that "neither our imagination nor our senses can ever assure us of anything, if our understanding does not intervene."[47]

A closer examination of *Descartes* further reinforces these claims about the feminization of *Discourse on Method.* In part 1, Kyger's voice is high-pitched and squeaky and her facial image jumpy, adding a comic touch to announce the beginning of what seems to be Descartes's more serious quest: "We are now on an adventure of RIGHTLY APPLYING our VIGOROUS MINDS TO THE STRAIGHT ROAD." In part 2, Kyger/Descartes inhabits a domestic scene. Here she is shown sweeping, literal accompaniment to Descartes's decision "to sweep away everything in my mind and start over again; not adding one little iota until I was absolutely sure of it."[48] Her cleaning actions speed up; then she begins mending. The section ends with Kyger relaxing and smoking to the words, "I THEREBY EXERCISE MY REASON WITH THE GREATEST ABSOLUTE PERFECTION (ATTAINABLE BY ME)."[49]

Part 3 continues the domestic scene as she places objects on a tray and takes them outside to a camper to these words: "So my reason may have a place to reside, I thus build myself temporarily a small house of commonly felt rules . . . until I arrive at the grand castle of my PURELY EXECUTED REASON." Part 3 ends with her smile of satisfaction and the words: "And having furnished my cottage, I begin the establishment of the castle."[50] The house is an important extended metaphor for Descartes.[51] He knocks down the old house of mind to rebuild a new one on the foundation of rationality in *Discourse on Method,* noting that in tearing down the old, we use the "debris to serve in building up another so in destroying all those opinions which I considered to be ill-founded, I made various observations and acquired many experiences, which have since been of use to me in establishing those which are more certain."[52] In the video, the new house is a camper, "a hippie version of a cottage," according to Kyger, and another deconstructive touch, one that literally belittles Descartes's ideas.[53]

In Part 4, Kyger's tone turns authoritarian, like a teacher instructing a pupil, as she presents Descartes's breakthrough moment. The section begins with abstract images multiplied and swirling, which give way to Kyger's head, so huge it takes up the whole screen, signifying mental power. The talking head announces her arrival at the first fundamental truth in stentorian tones: "I THINK hence I AM," concluding that perfection has come from Mother God, a realization accompanied by a musical fanfare. This section ends sarcastically, as she states that "reason must be wielded at all times to guard against ERROR, error of IMAGINATION and error of the SENSES."[54] Here sarcasm turns Descartes's words back on themselves, suggesting that reason, itself, is in error, not the senses.

The most significant electronic distortion of sound and image occurs in part 5, emphasizing the powerful, otherworldly nature of Mother God. According to Kyger: "Loren Sears was really responsible for encouraging many of the special effects that were used in *Descartes,* and they were discovered at the time we were doing the piece in the studio, like the great mother god Byzantine feedbacks, when I raised my arms. I'm watching the studio monitor, to notice the effects."[55] Mother God appears with voice and tone distorted by an echo chamber and figure elongated by video image manipulation to emphasize her hieratic and larger-than-life qualities. As Kyger moves her arms up and down, feedback loops create a halo effect.

Part 6, the conclusion, shifts back to the contemporary scene with shots of the studio set with lights, cameras, and booms visible. Kyger notes that this last part "shows the unadorned studio (signifying the difficulty of trusting and using your own mind)."[56] The camera moves from a close-up of the ceiling boom to Kyger/Descartes seated in lower right speaking softly. She then stands and takes center stage, concluding, "ONE CANNOT SO WELL LEARN A THING WHEN IT HAS BEEN LEARNED FROM ANOTHER, AS WHEN ONE HAS DISCOVERED IT FOR HIMSELF." The video ends with her curtsy and the words, "Mother God in the Castle, of Heaven."[57]

Interestingly, Kyger has downplayed the feminist nature of this work. In response to the entry on *Descartes* in the NCET exhibition catalogue of 2000 by the Videospace curator, Steve Seid, in which he remarked on the video's "feminist spin," she states that she "didn't have a clue as to what feminism was in those days."[58] She has likewise downplayed or denied a feminist position in her work at other times. For example, in a 2002 interview, Kyger offered this response to a question about whether her poetry is woman-centered: "It's always a danger to set a male/female dichotomy or duality; the self is more than the sum of its parts."[59] Her comment here is reminiscent of her put-down of dualism in Descartes.[60]

Is Kyger then a subconscious feminist, a prefeminist, or an unwilling feminist? Certainly in much of her work there is simultaneously a valorization of typical female roles side by side with a defiance and critique of being kept in that domestic role and a refusal to play second fiddle to men (for example, her rejection of the domestic role with then-husband Gary Snyder in Japan as evidenced in her *Japan and India Journals,* dating from 1960 to 1964.[61] This move is combined with a denial of a feminist agenda. Such an ambiguous attitude toward the feminist position seems to be a constant in Kyger's early work and may be connected with a need to play down the feminist aspect for acceptance by her early mentors, Duncan and Spicer, or perhaps a refusal to dichotomize.[62] In this case, Kyger's ambiguous stance may be an aspect of the postmodern impetus to disrupt the binary.

The Impact of *Descartes* and "Descartes and the Splendor Of" on Kyger's Later Work

Despite the fact that *Descartes* was the only video from her NCET internship that Kyger considered a finished work, the video project as a whole had a significant effect on her subsequent development. The heightened importance of voice for Kyger is one result of her year in videospace. In much of her video work, Kyger does voice-overs with tone of voice varying from hieratic and imperious or distorted and squeaky in *Descartes* to chatty in *I, Nevertheless,* and hypnotic and incantatory in *Slip Back Into the Shining Sea.* Video thus enabled Kyger to hear how tone and voice could change in relation to the poem's written words, facilitated by video's ability to incorporate feedback and to amplify and distort. Voice and tone are key elements in Kyger's poetics, creating interest, excitement, and nuance.[63]

The emphasis on voice also relates to Kyger's interest in the poetic line as discussed in a roundtable discussion of 1974 published in *Credences,* "Three versions of the Poetic Line." In comparison with poems in *The Tapestry and The Web,* where the line was determined more by its relation with other lines on the page, after *Descartes* she claims an interest in a line where the "poem gets to be more like a score for the voice."[64] Such an interest may also derive from video's aural echo chamber–like effects and reverberation possibilities.

In addition, the space of videospace might be considered an open field wherein the oral and visual aspects of *Descartes* intersect for the viewer as well as the poet. This is similar to Charles Olson's ideas about the field of the poem in his essay "Projective Verse," expressed as the "large area of the whole poem . . . where all the syllables and all the lines must be managed in their relations to each other."[65] The idea of a field in which varying oral and visual aspects interact and intersect may also relate to Kyger's subsequent interest in phenomenology, the world, itself, being one huge space, and the poet the recorder through the viewfinder of her eye.[66]

Kyger, the Beats, and *Descartes*

This examination of Kyger's video *Descartes* and its subsequent impact on her work makes its experimental nature clear. As well, its relationship with the Beat avant-garde scene with its collaborative practices and emphasis on poetry as performative and spontaneous is also apparent. Perhaps the most famous Beat collaborative moment can be considered the typing and assembling of William S. Burroughs's *Naked Lunch* manuscript by Jack Kerouac, Allen Ginsberg, and Alan Ansen in Tangier. The Beats also strove to break down barriers between mind and body, for example Ginsberg's glorification of the body and its sexuality in his revolutionary poem "Howl." They were also generally interested in poetry as performance, which could be considered a way to resolve the mind-body split. The Six Gallery reading, for example, where Ginsberg read "Howl" in the company of East and West Coast Beats, is one of the most famous examples of Beat poetry as performance rather than silent text on the page, while Kerouac's spontaneous prose method is a hallmark of Beat compositional practice.

However, Kyger's interest in visual experimentation as evident in *Descartes's* camera work, aural effects, and voice reverberations, allying her with a West Coast aesthetic, indicates a divergence from such Beat productions as *Pull My Daisy*, a collaboration between the filmmaker Robert Frank and the Beat writer Jack Kerouac, adapted from Kerouac's play *Beat Generation*. Kyger had seen this work in 1959 before she went to Japan.[67] Kyger's video is seemingly more experimental and avant-garde than Kerouac's film, especially in its nonlinear approach with juxtaposition of images and oral and visual distortion. In comparison, *Pull My Daisy*, a narrative of a day in the life of a band of bohemians, seems more conventional, maintaining visual continuity using fade-outs and panoramic shots. Kyger seems to have more in common with *Towers Open Fire* (1963) and *The Cut-Ups* (1967), by William S. Burroughs collaborating with Antony Balch, in her emphasis on nonlinearity and intentional distortion of sound and image, as well as superimposition of imagery and kaleidoscopic and strobe-like effects. In retrospect, Kyger not only contributes to, but furthers Beat multimedia aesthetics.

More significantly, in undermining Descartes's privileging of the masculine, Kyger subtly demonstrates her affinity with other women writers associated with the Beat Generation, in contrast to the male-centered aspect of much Beat writing. The gender parody evident in *Descartes* performs an important function in the subversion of the masculine and the supplanting of male domination. Butler states that "parody by itself is not subversive, and there must be a way to understand what makes certain kinds of parodic repetitions effectively disruptive . . . in a way that destabilizes the naturalized categories of identity and desire."[68] She concludes in the affirmative that "there is a subversive laughter in the pastiche-effect of parodic practices."[69] Kyger's parody effectively exposes what might be considered "the natural" to scrutiny, especially true in the Mother God sequence with its powerful voice-over and visuals. Ultimately, the body seen as passive by Descartes becomes actor and active participant in Kyger's video, changing attitudes toward masculine and feminine roles, especially the masculine God and the male philosopher, epitomizing Western bourgeois culture of the 1950s and 1960s.

Kyger's unique perspective is also evident, especially in the way she references and includes philosophical texts, in the process implicitly contrasting West and East. Her video interlude, though taking her in new directions, reflects this reliance on her educational background, expertise in philosophy and knowledge of its history. Her subsequent interest in the phenomenological and more recent poems collected in *About Now: Collected Poems* (2007) demonstrate that philosophy's thread continues to run through Kyger's work.

Notes

1. Kyger, however, has commented on problematic aspects of being labeled a Beat in a panel discussion at Naropa in 2000 (see Hettie Jones et al., "Women and the Beats," in *Beats at Naropa,* ed. Anne Waldman and Laura Wright [Minneapolis: Coffee House Press, 2009], 45–60).

2. Similar to Kyger's other prose poems of the period, "Descartes and the Splendor Of" blends autobiography, dream, and activities of daily life. Included as the penultimate work in *Places To Go,* her second poetry collection, its serial aspect was influenced by Duncan and Spicer, Kyger's early mentors, according to a May 18, 2009, letter from Kyger to the author.

3. Joanne Kyger to author, May 18, 2009.

4. Joanne Kyger to author, January 10, 2006.

5. Though written in 1969 and published in 1970, *Zen Diary* records Wienpahl's experiences in Japan in the early 1960s studying with Zen master Zuigan Goto Roshi, while his interest in Zen stems from the 1950s.

6. Paul Wienpahl, *Zen Diary* (New York: Harper and Row, 1970), 4–5.

7. Joanne Kyger to author, May 18, 2009.

8. Paul Wienpahl, "Zen and the Work of Wittgenstein," *Chicago Review* (Spring 1957): 69.

9. Joanne Kyger to author, May 18, 2009.

10. Joanne Kyger, interview by David Chadwick September 29, 1995, www.cuke.com/Cucumber%20Project/interview/Kyger.html, 19.

11. Brice Howard, "Experimental Project," *KQED Focus* (1968): 6.

12. Joanne Kyger to author, January 10, 2006.

13. Catherine Elwes, *Video Art: A Guided Tour* (London: Taurus, 2005), 28.

14. Howard, "Experimental Project," 6.

15. For Sears, per a February 6, 2006, e-mail to author, video experimentation was also furthered by its "ability to mix images in real time."

16. Joanne Kyger, e-mail to author, January 21, 2006. In addition to *Descartes*, she collaborated on several other videos, all daringly avant-garde visually and aurally: *Slip Back into the Shining Sea* with Sears, and *I, Nevertheless* with Robert Zagone, a member of the technical crew. In these videos, Kyger contributes text, voice-overs, visual effects, and acting.

17. Joanne Kyger, "Joanne Kyger," in *Contemporary Authors Autobiography Series,* ed. Joyce Nakamura, vol. 16 (Detroit: Gale Research, 1992), 200. This use of Descartes as source text is similar to Kyger's use of Homer's *Odyssey* as what she calls in a 2002 interview "structure or reference" for poems in her first published volume, *The Tapestry and the Web*. According to Kyger, in an interview by Nancy Grace and Ronna Johnson in their edited volume *"Places To Go: Joanne Kyger": Breaking the Rule of Cool* (Jackson: University Press of Mississippi, 2004), his strategy enabled her to use an "old narrative that could go through [your] life that was common to all humans" as well as to avoid the "dangers of confessional writing" (144).

18. Joanne Kyger to author, January 10, 2006.

19. Rene Descartes, *The Philosophical Works of Descartes,* trans. Elizabeth S. Haldane and G. R. T. Ross, vol. 1 (New York: Dover, 1955), 101. Unless otherwise noted, all citations to "Descartes" refer to this volume.

20. Descartes and his ideas have had a major influence on Western intellectual history and continue to do so, according to David Weissman, editor of a critical edition of *Discourse on the Method and Meditations on First Philosophy* (trans. Elizabeth S. Haldane and G. R. T. Haldane [New Haven: Yale University Press, 1996]); in his introduction to this edition, Weissman specifies a "variety of lineages" and a "range of effects" produced by Descartes (119–20). This could be countered by Wienpahl's claim that one move of twentieth-century intellectual history has been a rejection of Descartes. Thanks also to Eric Sotnak for an enlightening discussion of this key philosopher.

21. Descartes, 83.

22. Ibid., 84.

23. Ibid., 86.

24. Ibid., 87.

25. Ibid., 92.

26. Ibid., 99. Descartes discusses the benefits of doubting at greater length in the first of his *Meditations on First Philosophy,* first published in 1641.

27. Ibid., 101.

28. Ibid., 105.

29. Ibid., 101.

30. In the video, the text's capitalized passages will often be given additional emphasis by Kyger.

31. Note the effective use of slang in Ginsberg's "Howl" or Whalen's "Slop Barrel" to move poetry from its more academic and high cultural status on the page to a more antibourgeois, radical, or colloquial oral voice. However, Bertrand Russell comments on Descartes's "unpedantic style" in his history of Western philosophy, one of Kyger's texts from the 1950s.

32. Joanne Kyger, *Places To Go* (Los Angeles: Black Sparrow, 1970), 89. Note that page numbers for quotes from both the poem and the video with poem as script refer to the text of "Descartes and the Splendor Of" from *Places To Go,* Kyger's second poetry collection.

33. Ibid., 91.

34. Descartes, 95.

35. Kyger, *Places To Go,* 90.

36. Descartes, 101.

37. Kyger, *Places To Go,* 91. Interestingly, Kwang-Sae Lee, in his book *East and West: Fusion of Horizons* (Parnassus, N.J.: Homa and Schey, 2006), also provides Chuang-Tzu's butterfly dream as an "interesting counterpoise to the Cartesian legacy" (45).

38. Kyger, *Places To Go,* 92.

39. Even in the twenty-first century only a few women are considered to be philosophers. *The Oxford Dictionary of Philosophy* lists Mary Wollstonecraft and Simone de Beauvoir. Suzanne Langer, Hannah Arendt, and others could also be added to this list.

40. Judith Butler, *Gender Trouble* (New York: Routledge, 1990), 138.

41. Ibid., x.

42. Ibid., 12.

43. Ibid., 129.

44. Descartes, 106.

45. Ibid., 107.

46. Ibid., 101.

47. Ibid., 104.

48. Kyger, *Places To Go,* 89.

49. Ibid., 90.

50. Ibid.

51. Descartes uses building metaphors at least five times in the *Discourse.*

52. Descartes, 99.

53. Joanne Kyger to author, January 10, 2006.

54. Kyger, *Places To Go,* 91.

55. Joanne Kyger to author, January 10, 2006.

56. Ibid.

57. Kyger, *Places To Go,* 92.

58. Joanne Kyger, letter to author, January 10, 2006.

59. Kyger, *"Places To Go: Joanne Kyger,"* 148.

60. In her essay on Kyger and the San Francisco Renaissance, Linda Russo has described Kyger as "proto-feminist." The feminist overtones in *Descartes,* however, are similar to those in the Penelope poems in *The Tapestry and the Web.*

61. In 1960, Kyger left for Japan to marry Snyder, who had been associated with the First Zen Institute of Japan in Kyoto since 1956. She lived in Kyoto for four years, immersing herself in Japanese culture, but left Japan in 1964; Snyder and Kyger subsequently divorced.

62. Kyger's position is never truly clear-cut, however, and in her poetry, her feminist stance is strong. For more on her relationship with Duncan and Spicer, see her interview by David Meltzer in *San Francisco Beat,* ed. Meltzer (San Francisco: City Lights, 2001). Note that Butler implies a similarly conflicted or ambivalent position for Simone de Beauvoir in *Gender Trouble,* perhaps part of a mid-twentieth-century feminist cultural sensibility.

63. The poet Alice Notley begins her essay "Joanne Kyger's Poetry," in her *Coming After* (Ann Arbor: University of Michigan Press, 2005), by remembering the first time she heard Kyger read, noting "that her poetry is vocally sculpted is its most overwhelming characteristic" (15).

64. Joanne Kyger, "Three Versions of the Poetic Line," *Credences* 2, no. 1 (March 1977): 64.

65. Charles Olson, "Projective Verse," in *Selective Writings of Charles Olson,* ed. Robert Creeley (New York: New Directions, 1966), 20. Kyger comments on the importance of Olson's "Projective Verse" essay in a 1997 interview with Dale Smith ("Energy on the Page: Joanne Kyger in Conversation with Dale Smith," *Jacket Magazine* 11 [2000], www.jacketmagazine.com/11/Kyger-iv-date-smith.html).

66. Kyger today is associated with the philosophical movement of phenomenology, although she claims to interpret it in her own way. This interest may have grown out of her involvement in the poet Charles Olson's project, "A Plan for a Curriculum of the Soul," and her work written for this project, *Phenomenological* (Canton, N.Y.: Glover, 1989), a journal of her trip to the Yucatán in 1984. Olson, himself, became interested in phenomenology through reading Maurice Merleau-Ponty's *Phenomenology of Perception.* Merleau-Ponty's chapter on the phenomenal field in this work would be relevant here, as would his statement that "both universality and the world lie at the core of individuality

and the subject, and this will never be understood as long as the world is made into an object. It is understood immediately if the world is the *field* of our experience" (406). Thanks to Thomas Kasulis for an enlightening discussion of phenomenology and Zen; Kasulis also makes connections between the two in his study, *Zen Action, Zen Person* (Honolulu: University of Hawaii Press, 1981).

67. Kyger had seen other experimental film productions by Stan Brakage in the Bay Area and by Andy Warhol in New York. She was even a stand-in for a film Jack Smith was shooting during her New York stay, per Kyger's letter to the author of January, 18, 2006. Here she notes that viewers need to remember that film and video are different media.

68. Butler, *Gender Trouble*, 139.

69. Ibid., 146. Although Butler is specifically addressing gender identities parodied in "drag, cross-dressing, and the sexual stylization of butch/femme identities," here, I believe these ideas can also be applied to Kyger's parody.

III

Beat Avant-Garde

Spontaneity and Immediacy

JOHN CLELLON HOLMES AND EXISTENTIALISM

Ann Charters

"Yes, hell must be like that," Camus has said, "streets filled with shop signs and no way of explaining yourself." Full of choice Existentialist texts, I walked along 57th Street one icy morning, the solemnly radical veteran, certain he understood the anxiety and bewilderment of the middle class while studying the sparkling Impressionist paintings in the sparkling Christmas windows: so many menacing shadows had swarmed up out of those dappled hues. I threw up my first real belly-full of martinis, right over the side of the bed, after a party arguing about the "reactionary rot" in Koestler.... A passion for order was my reigning passion then: that the world would *be* coherent, after all.

—John Clellon Holmes, *Passionate Opinions*

When Holmes wrote this statement he was remembering back to the Christmas of 1947, when he was a twenty-one-year-old unpublished, aspiring novelist living in Manhattan at Fifty-Sixth Street and Lexington Avenue, soon to meet another young aspiring novelist, Jack Kerouac. In the autumn of 1948, shortly after they had met and become friends, they were deep into a long conversation in Holmes's apartment when John—always temperamentally a writer in search of order and coherence—asked Jack to come up with a term describing the "questing" quality of their group in the fervent years after the end of World War II. As Holmes recalled: "Everyone I knew felt it in one way or another—the bottled eagerness for talk, for joy, for excitement, for sensation, for new truths. Whatever the reason, everyone of my age had a look of impatience, unreleased ecstasy, and the presence of buried worlds within."[1]

Inspired by Holmes's question, Kerouac replied: "It's a kind of furtiveness. Like we were a generation of furtives . . . a kind of beatness . . . a weariness with all the forms, all the conventions of the world. . . . So I guess you might say we're a *beat* generation," and he "laughed a conspiratorial, the Shadow knows kind of laugh at his own words and at the look on my face."[2]

At the moment they were talking, existentialism was so fashionable among intellectuals in New York City that had Kerouac shared Holmes's passion for philosophy, he might have said "we're an *existentialist* generation," and the word "beat" might not have come up at all. Just as well. No doubt the multisyllable word "existentialist" quickly would have been abbreviated to "X," and who would have remembered for very long the writers associated with the bland name "the X Generation"? Let alone the term "X-nik" instead of Beatnik, a word coined a decade later by a hostile San Francisco columnist who might have been implying that the Beats were a "Russian secret weapon" during the Cold War.[3] Unhelpful as the word "beat" is, at least it's better than "X." And of course it's in the spirit of a true American literary rebellion to reject all previous labels—especially European—and come up with one of your own. Yet for what would become the loosely associated group of postwar American writers known as the Beats, the existentialist quest to redefine the meaning of existence would be at the heart of their poetry and fiction.

Existentialism is the name used for several different revolts against tradition in philosophy carried on for more than a century by European philosophers such as Kierkegaard, Nietzsche, Heidegger, and Jaspers, though Gabriel Marcel was the first philosopher to call himself an existentialist.[4] The vagueness of the label "existentialist" is similar to the inexactitude of the label "Beat," which loosely describes the condition of the group of American writers in the 1940s and 1950s associated with Kerouac and his friends Holmes, Ginsberg, and Burroughs, in revolt against tradition in literature, social conformity, and, as Kerouac later said, "something but not everything."[5] The word "existentialist" as a philosophical term preceded the word "beat" by only a few years, emerging into the consciousness of a large public in 1945, when Sartre lectured on existentialism in Brussels and Paris in the immediate aftermath of World War II and presented his philosophy as a doctrine for the postwar age.[6] A year later, in *Existentialism and Human Emotions,* Sartre clarified that existentialism actually began at the point when the Russian writer Dostoevsky wrote, "If God didn't exist, everything would be possible."[7] The assertion that God does not exist and the consequences that each human consciousness must accept the absurdity of existence and have the courage to create meaning in a meaningless world implied a frightening moral vacuum for many of the early critics of existentialism. As the writer Hayden Carruth understood in his introduction to Sartre's novel *Nausea*:

> Existentialism entered the American consciousness like an elephant entering a dark room: there was a good deal of breakage and the people inside naturally mistook the nature of the intrusion. What would it be? An engine of destruction perhaps, a tank left over from the war? After a while the lights were turned on and it was seen to be "only" an elephant; everyone laughed and said that a circus must be passing through town. But no, soon they found the elephant was here to stay; and then, looking closer, they saw that, although he was indeed a newcomer, an odd-looking one at that, he was not a stranger: they had known him all along. This was in 1946 and 1947. And in no time at all Existentialism became a common term. No question of what it meant; it meant the life re-emerging after the war in the cafes of the Left Bank—disreputable young men in paint-smeared jeans, and their companions, those black stockinged, makeupless girls who smoked too many cigarettes and engaged in who knows what follies besides.[8]

In *Existentialism and Human Emotions,* Sartre wrote that "man is nothing else but what he makes of himself."[9] He defined the basis of his philosophy as his insight that "existence precedes essence," by which he said he meant that "subjectivity must be the starting point."[10] Sartre didn't use the word "subjectivity" in the way that it is commonly understood to mean an individual's interior life or thoughts. Sartre didn't believe that an individual had a separate subjective interior life, since he argued that everything is external to the basic fact of human consciousness. As the critic Arthur C. Danto explained: "Existence precedes essence has a fairly clear meaning in the case of human beings: they are not determined to be what they are through a fixed human nature in which they participate."[11] Instead, "their lives are spent in a quest of self-definition."[12] Once liberated to live their own lives, they can choose to live authentically, taking responsibility for their own freedom to make decisions, "which is solely theirs and cannot be shrugged off onto politics or sexuality or whatever."[13]

In the immediate postwar years, existentialism had a powerful effect on artistic and literary developments in Europe and the United States. Initially Holmes was attracted to it for two reasons. First, because existentialism redefined what it meant to think and act rationally after the catastrophic disasters of World War II, specifically Hitler's rise to power in western Europe, the "ethnic cleansing" of the Jews in concentration camps, and the American use of atomic bombs to end the war in the Pacific. In the late 1940s, Holmes, like many others, believed that existentialism "stood for the hope that a new age would at last break free of the illusions of the past."[14] Second, Holmes recognized that Sartre was a brilliant writer, as much a creator of fiction, essays, and drama as he was a philosopher. Danto notes, and Holmes would agree, that in his philosophical writing Sartre "energized terms like dread and anguish, engagement and nothingness, nausea and shame; terms whose central meaning is quite sober when introduced through the contexts of argument and system which Sartre the philosopher develops, spill beyond these into affective and emotional spaces which Sartre as a literary person exploits."[15]

Although Holmes was not initially aware of it, Sartre's existentialism was to be only a stage in his radicalization, which had begun in 1944, when John was still in the navy. Holmes never endorsed Sartre's defense of the actions of the Communist Party after the outbreak of the Korean War because John had only a brief flirtation with communism. As a nineteen-year-old hospital orderly at St. Albans Naval Hospital on Long Island, he had been introduced to Marxism through his friendship with James Brady Macguire, an editor of the hospital newspaper. Holmes spent hours talking to Macguire, a 1938 graduate from Brown University who had earned a doctorate in history from Trinity College in Dublin. Later John's sister Elizabeth, who also met Macguire, remembered him as a "sharp, acerbic little man—thick glasses, small jolly eyes and quick little stabs of insight and prejudices."[16] After several months working at the hospital, Holmes was waiting to be mustered out of the navy with a medical discharge because he had begun to suffer excruciating migraine headaches while caring as an orderly for mutilated servicemen shipped back to the United States after they had been severely wounded in Europe. Just before his headaches began, Holmes had discovered he had lost his faith in God when he tried to pray at the St. Albans chapels.

On April 29, 1945, Holmes wrote in his journal that he was "more than willing to listen" to Macguire. "So I trailed him about the halls, ate chow with him, talked to him in the library."[17] Macguire was the first intellectual whom young Holmes had ever met, and Holmes admired his belief that ideas were essential in order for people to feel themselves fully alive. To his friend, "there was something stimulating about people who thought." Passionate about Marxist theory, Macguire had tried to convince Holmes that a new world order would arise after the war when communism would ultimately triumph, bringing with it economic and political freedom for everyone on earth.

In the long run, Holmes's searing experiences as a medic in the hospital wards changed him even more deeply than the new political consciousness he absorbed from Macguire and the existentialism he later encountered reading Sartre. His months in the navy caused a shift in the values he had absorbed as an adolescent from his family, and for the rest of his life he remained a pacifist. It was only years later that he was able to clarify what had happened: "Anti-fascist though I had been since twelve, the experience [of the Second World War] ended war for me. . . . War-memories encourage romanticization, and my paltry-few would be demeaned by that approach, being mostly visceral, having to do with the simple frailty of the body, and the hard fact of the scarred future. It grew to seem a grotesque madness to me. Though ours was perhaps the last 'just' war, a war in which my youth and ignorance 'believed,' I came into the conviction that though there are things worth dying for, there is nothing worth killing for."[18]

After Marxism what was waiting for Holmes, as for many other intellectual veterans at the end of the war, was existentialism. On January 3, 1946, just having taken a graduate course at Columbia University from Suzanne Langer on the philosophy of art, Holmes wrote his friend Howard Friedman, another navy buddy studying on the GI Bill, that he distrusted politics but believed in art: "Artists are eager to remake the world into something new and beautiful and effective. We have only seen the beginnings of what these men have started. . . . It is the beginning of a new life for all of us."[19] By September 1946, Holmes was gravely disillusioned with the Communist Party, writing in his journal, "I waited for the high ethical speeches to strike me."[20] A year later, he wrote a letter to the editor of *PM*, a leftist journal opposing the United States' policy in Germany, noting, "I'm not a Communist but economics speak very loud these days."[21] At Christmas parties in 1947, he argued about the writing of Arthur Koestler,[22] the Communist who had become disenchanted with Stalinism after "the show" Moscow trials in the late 1930s. By the end of 1948, after the failed presidential campaign of

Henry Wallace, Holmes had given up on both the Communist Party and mainstream American politics.

In the spring of 1948, Holmes was reading Sartre's essays in translation in radical magazines such as *Partisan Review* and *Politics,* and writing pages of notes in his journal about Sartre's play *The Unburied Dead.* By May 1948, he noted that Camus's novel *The Plague* had sold over one hundred thousand copies in English translation. That month Holmes began to publish his poetry in *Partisan Review* in an issue that featured a chapter of Sartre's long essay "For Whom Does One Write?," which considered "what happens to literature when the writer is led to reject the ideology of the ruling classes."[23] That issue also contained a review of Marjorie Grene's *Dreadful Freedom: A Critique of Existentialism* published by the University of Chicago Press, and the young poet Delmore Schwartz's humorous article "Does Existentialism Still Exist?," spoofing the philosophical movement that everyone at the New York parties was talking about.[24]

At the end of the 1940s, existentialist writers such as Camus and Sartre argued that since all individuals lived within a world of infinite possibilities, it was the ability to choose—in absolute freedom—that was the vital determinant in human activity.[25] A few years later, Sartre's extension of this basic existential concept was that activism was justified against anything that restricted a human being's freedom to choose. He also claimed that existentialism had the power to rescue Marxism and Maoism from false assumptions about society,[26] a stance that Ginsberg took to heart in his political activism during the Vietnam War and throughout his later life.

The initial influence of existentialism on Holmes, however, was nonpolitical. Sartre's influential novel *Nausea* was not published in English until 1949, but works of Camus and Kierkegaard had been available in English for many years, Kierkegaard's *Fear and Trembling* appeared in 1939 and *Either/Or* in 1944. Camus's *The Stranger* was published in 1946 followed by *The Fall* and *The Plague* in 1948. The 1956 edition of *The Rebel* included Camus's influential philosophical "Essay on Man in Revolt," which argued for the necessity of each individual to take moral action after the so-called "logical crime" by which 70 million human beings were killed or enslaved during the appallingly cruel wars of the first half of the twentieth century.[27] In *The Rebel,* Camus makes his case for a spiritual dimension to human experience that had nothing to do with political theory or orthodox religions of any kind. Reading Camus taught Holmes that all acts of rebellion indicated the presence of a moral choice. This idea became his religion and his politics after his disenchantment with Sartre in the early 1950s.

Initially attracted to the fiction of Dostoevsky before he began reading Sartre and Camus, Holmes had completed his first novel, *The Transgressors*, after his navy discharge. Attempting, as he told his friend Mira Kent on April 13, 1949, "to isolate the social, psychological, and moral implications of rebellion on the basic level," he used a quotation from Sartre as the book's epigraph.[28] After this manuscript failed to find a publisher, Holmes told Kent in the letter that he had begun to plan another novel about what he described as the "transcendental rebellion" he had observed in his new friends Jack Kerouac and Allen Ginsberg. This was to become his novel *Go*, the first book to describe the Beats. In *Go*, John wrote a roman à clef that would become the primary inspiration for Kerouac's scroll version of *On the Road* in the spring of 1951, three weeks after Jack read John's newly completed manuscript. Considering that Holmes was steeped in existential texts at the time he started *Go*, the question legitimately arises, Is *Go* an existential novel?

The answer is yes. The first readers of *Go* were dismayed by the book, since it appeared to them to be a depressing novel without a moral center describing the aimless search for "kicks" in New York City by Holmes's crowd of young writers and their friends. *Go* included a portrayal of John as his protagonist Paul Hobbes (the pseudonym referred to Holmes's eighteenth-century English philosophical predecessor, the rationalist Thomas Hobbes) along with the characters Gene Pasternak (Jack Kerouac), David Stofsky (Allen Ginsberg), Hart Kennedy (Neal Cassady), and Albert Ancke (Herbert Huncke). In their rebellion against the "anxiety and bewilderment" of square life, Holmes considered these characters beat.[29] They may or may not have argued about Sartre's books at their drunken parties, but they were existentialists.

Go can be interpreted in terms of the definition of the Beat Generation that Holmes gave during a lecture at Yale University in April 1959, where he systematically defined the "Beat attitude" and the existentialism behind it. The Beat attitude consisted of three distinguishing characteristics: (1) Disassociation from the conventions of society; (2) a belief that the source of truth, as well as joy, lies in the intuitive faculties; and (3) a longing for spiritual values. Holmes then went on to say that underlying this attitude is an existential "conception of the nature of man," the belief that "man is free and he is capable of transcending himself."[30] In *Go*, the only nihilist character in Paul Hobbes's wild crowd was Bill Agatson (William Cannastra), who was not free because he was self-destructive. He was crushed to death after he attempted the crazy stunt of climbing through the window of a subway car as it pulled out of the Sheridan Square station. In his Yale lecture, Holmes cleared up the misconception of many of *Go*'s readers that to be Beat is to be "nihilistic and negative." The nihilist attitude wants to introduce chaos, anarchy, and disorder for their own sake. It seeks to destroy, whereas Holmes believed that "the Beat attitude merely says 'no' in order that it may say 'yes.' As Albert Camus has said in *The Rebel,* in our time it seems that you can't be positive without first being negative."[31]

Agatson's suicidal action momentarily put a stop to the revels. His death was the event that caused Hobbes to question their lifestyle, though his wife, Kathryn, like all the women in the novel, had questioned it many times before. Emotionally dependent on their male partners, the women portrayed in *Go* were not existentialists. In denying his female characters independent minds, Holmes accepted the sexism of his time and disregarded the example of Simone de Beauvoir, Sartre's brilliant lifelong companion, who emerged from Sartre's shadow with a book that was destined to become a feminist classic, *The Second Sex,* first published in English translation in 1953.

In *Go*, Hobbes regarded his Beat friends as "children of the night: everywhere wild, everywhere lost, everywhere loveless, faithless, homeless."[32] But except for Agatson, all of them are survivors and possess the potential of saying "yes." Hobbes is the first to do so. After the impromptu wake held at a Hoboken bar to commemorate Agatson's death, Hobbes asks himself: "But why did I dignify their madness? And why does everything else seem spiritually impoverished?"[33] He transcends his negative thoughts when he understands that his vision of "unending lovelessness" will corrupt his soul, since it will suffer "the most unbearable of all losses: the death of hope. And when hope dies there is only irony, a vicious senseless irony that turns to the consuming desire to jeer, spit, curse, smash, destroy."[34]

In the last poignant scene of the novel, Hobbes and his wife stand on the Hoboken ferry en route to Manhattan as if crossing back over the River Styx, and he senses the unstated possibility of rebirth into a different, more authentic life. As the sad couple look at the lights of Manhattan ahead in the darkness, Holmes ends his book with a question given to his brooding alter ego Hobbes, an aspiring novelist, which remains unanswered in *Go*: "'Where is our home?' he said to himself gravely, for he could not see it yet."[35] The anguish, violence, and claustrophobic atmosphere of Holmes's novel characterize it as an example of existential art. Also its theme is existential. The book dramatizes the quest for meaning exemplified in the chaotic lives of aspiring New York writers searching for new forms of expression, intuitively enacting "the Existential predicament of man."[36]

Shortly after the publication of *Go,* Holmes included a reference to Sartre in the essay "This Is the Beat Generation," which Holmes wrote in 1952 for the *New York Times* at the request of the reviewer Gilbert Milstein, who later quoted Holmes's essay as evidence of the importance of Kerouac's *On the Road* when Milstein reviewed it in 1957. In an eloquent paragraph in "This Is the Beat Generation," Holmes described how in the course of their rebellion the traumatized members of his generation were inexorably led to Sartre before they became Beat, having first endured "the collective bad circumstances of a dreary depression" and "the collective uprooting of a global war":

The fancies of their childhood inhabited the half-light of Munich, the Nazi-Soviet pact, and the eventual blackout. Their adolescence was spent in a topsy-turvy world of war bonds, swing shifts, and troop movements. They grew to independent mind on beachheads, in gin mills and USOs, in past-midnight arrivals and pre-dawn departures. Their brothers, husbands, fathers, or boy friends turned up dead one day at the other end of a telegram. At the four trembling corners of the world, or in the home town invaded by factories or lonely servicemen, they had intimate experience with the nadir and the zenith of human conduct, and little time for much that came between. The peace they inherited was only as secure as the next headline. It was a cold peace. Their own lust for freedom, and the ability to live at a pace that kills (to which the war had adjusted them), led to black markets, bebop, narcotics, sexual promiscuity, hucksterism, and Jean-Paul Sartre. The beatness set in later.[37]

Six years later, in "The Philosophy of the Beat Generation," an article Holmes wrote for *Esquire* in 1958 after *On the Road* and *Howl and Other Poems* had officially launched the Beat Generation, he connected the dots between existentialism and the Beats for his readers—and revealed his shift away from Sartre's brand of existentialism—when he declared, "To be beat is to be at the bottom of your personality looking up; to be existential in the Kierkegaard, rather than the Jean-Paul Sartre, sense."[38]

In 1959, when Holmes published his only essay on existentialism, "Existentialism and the Novel: Notes and Questions" in the *Chicago Review,* he opened it by comparing *Crime and Punishment* with *An American Tragedy,* asking "Which is the existentialist novel?"[39] His answer isn't hard to find after he tells us, "Dreiser thought of Clyde as a misguided citizen; Dostoevsky thought of Raskolnikov as a misguided soul." Years before he had discovered existentialism, both Holmes and his friend Kerouac had taken the Russian writer Fyodor Dostoevsky as a hero. As the critics Maria Bloshetyn and Jesse Menefee have noted, both of these early Beat writers claimed Dostoevsky—the original existentialist—as a major influence on their work. Kerouac even credited Dostoevsky's short novel *Notes from Underground* as the model he took in 1953 for his novel *The Subterraneans.*[40]

For the most part in "Existentialism and the Novel" Holmes cited Dostoevsky, Dreiser, and a few other American novelists—among them Nelson Algren, John Steinbeck, Ernest Hemingway, F. Scott Fitzgerald—rather than Camus and Sartre. In fact, valuing only "the evidence of soul in a work," Holmes concluded that "Sartre's novels often seem brittle and contrived."[41] In the second paragraph of the essay, Holmes defined the core issue of existentialism as he understood it. At its center for him was the question "religious or atheist?": "In Dostoevsky's sense of the word, existentialism is the most *realistic* philosophical attitude precisely because of its remorseless subjectivity. The deepest realism is what makes sense, not alone to the mind or eye, but to the deep, intuitive logic in a man who knows the fullness of life. We are not omniscient philosophers, at best, we are living men, philosophizing. But the key existentialist question today is: what sort of existentialism? Religious or atheist? Kierkegaard or Sartre?"[42] Holmes believed that Sartre, the atheist existentialist—by 1957, Sartre had split with Camus and moved on to embrace his own kind of Marxism after denouncing communism as a political system—had ceased "to be a living man, philosophizing," and had become "a philosopher, studying life as if he, himself, was not embroiled in it." Holmes then asked: "But does this knowledge of freedom make the despair of uncertainty bearable? Doesn't the atheist engagement palliate the power of reality no less than the wishful immortality it was intended to replace?"[43] In other words, does Sartre feel "compelled to become God to alleviate his own despair? Doesn't he value his atheism more than his existentialism?"[44] Holmes's answer was: "To value the evidences of soul in a work; this is all that interests me now. Not craft, not style, not 'truth.' I've read all the books. I say to a man whose book I open: Give me something peculiar to yourself, and thus news to me."[45]

Holmes never clarified how he understood the idea of being existential in the sense of Kierkegaard rather than Sartre, nor did he ever explain how he read Kierkegaard. At the end of "Existentialism and the Novel," instead of discussing his own novel *Go* as an existentialist text, Holmes analyzed Kerouac's novels. He maintained that the characters in Kerouac's books

> escape into sheer existentialist experience itself. They are great ac-
> cumulators of sensations, they are great celebrators of life. But like
> Dmitri Karamazov, the deeper they go into undifferentiated reality
> (which is actually the American version of Camus' concept of the
> absurd), the more they discover that man cannot live in meaning-
> lessness... [in] the valueless abyss of modern life. Kerouac assumes
> it, and his characters are introduced to us in flight from despair, "the
> square life," "the drag." But unlike Hemingway or Sartre or even Al-
> gren, who stop short, or short-circuit the last connection, Kerouac
> remains subjective (and consistent) to the end: the realization that
> only spiritual convictions will sustain a living man, and illuminate
> the darkness of his life.[46]

Holmes concluded "Existentialism and the Novel" with his insight that "all non-existentialist philosophies are really only imaginary birdcages"[47] because "it is the bird's nature to fly. All he has to do is realize it."[48] He rejected Sartre's claim that humans were self-sufficient and accepted Kierkegaard's belief that there is something beyond individual human consciousness that resists proof. Holmes believed in a relationship with God based on faith, an objective uncertainty that nevertheless involved a total commitment of the self, unlike Sartre's belief that we always have alternatives from which to choose. Agreeing with Kierkegaard's intuition that silence *is* God's presence, Holmes had moved on from Sartre's atheistic existentialism, and he remained a Kierkegaardian existentialist for the rest of his life. Later he discovered that this philosophical stance was also sympathetic to his brief study of Buddhism, since Buddha's insight at the start of the Dhammapada was "nothing less than the quintessence of Sartre's thought: 'All that we are is the result of what we have thought.'"[49]

For Holmes's friend Kerouac, who was born, raised, and died a Roman Catholic despite his intense immersion in Buddhist studies for several years of his life, existentialism as a philosophy held little attraction. In drunken rants he belligerently derided Sartre and his atheism. Kerouac also dismissed Camus's books, believing that the French writer "would have had us turn literature into mere propaganda, with his 'commitment' talk."[50] In *The Sub-terraneans,* Kerouac dismissively labeled the self-absorbed behavior of the junkies in his crowd as "Existentialism" after his lover Mardou described their philosophy as "you take care of yourself, I'll take care of me."[51]

In 1965, on a visit to John and Shirley Holmes's home in Old Saybrook, Connecticut, Kerouac jokingly confided to them that he'd never understood "Existentialism" and asked John and Shirley to explain it to him. Nor did Jack concern himself very much with the concept of "existentialism" as it diminished to a small "e" in Webster's dictionary along with its common usage as the freedom of a self-determining agent. After two decades, the postwar intellectual framework of alienation and rebellion had frayed into egocentrism, when a new generation began to attempt a new art in communion with others and their environment.[52]

Does it matter whether or not Kerouac believed that he wrote as an existentialist? Steeped in existentialism, Holmes understood near the end of his life that as young writers he and his friends were attracted to it because it was "the only philosophic insight that seemed to smack exclusively of our times."[53] In this statement he echoed Camus's words from nearly a half century earlier, "that only one thing has ever been asked of our generation—that it should be able to cope with despair."[54]

Notes

1. John Clellon Holmes, *Passionate Opinions* (Fayetteville: University of Arkansas Press, 1988), 54.

2. Ibid., 54.

3. John Clellon Holmes, Yale lecture on the Beat Generation, 1959.

4. Ted Honderich, ed., *The Oxford Companion to Philosophy.* (Oxford: Oxford University Press, 1995), 259.

5. Bill Morgan, *I Celebrate Myself: The Somewhat Private Life of Allen Ginsberg* (New York: Viking, 2006), 258.

6. George Myerson, *Sartre* (London: Hodder and Stoughton, 2001), 60–61.

7. Jean-Paul Sartre, *Existentialism and Human Emotions,* trans. Bernard Frechtman (New York: Philosophical Library, 1957), 22.

8. Hayden Carruth, introduction to *Nausea* by Jean-Paul Sartre (New York: New Directions, 1959), v.

9. Sartre, *Emotions,* 15.

10. Ibid., 13.

11. Arthur C. Danto, *Jean-Paul Sartre* (New York: Viking, 1975), 25.

12. Ibid.

13. Ibid., 27.

14. Myerson, *Sartre,* 8.

15. Danto, *Sartre,* 12.

16. Elizabeth Von Vogt, e-mail to Ann Charters, 2009.

17. Unpublished manuscript in the John Clellon Holmes Archive in the Howard Gotlieb Archival Research Center in the Mugar Library, Boston University. See also Ann Charters and Samuel Charters, *Brother-Souls: John Clellon Holmes, Jack Kerouac, and the Beat Generation* (Jackson: University Press of Mississippi, 2010).

18. John Clellon Holmes, *Interior Geographies* (Warren, Ohio: Falls Printing, 1981), 3.

19. Unpublished manuscript in the Holmes Archive, Gotlieb Archival Research Center at Mugar Library, Boston University.

20. Ibid.

21. Ibid.

22. Ibid.

23. Ibid.

24. Ibid.

25. Ibid.

26. Myerson, *Sartre,* 73.

27. Albert Camus, *The Rebel,* trans. Anthony Bower (New York: Knopf, 1956), 3.

28. Jaap Van der Bent, "On the Road to Go—John Clellon Holmes' First Novel *The Transgressor,*" *Beat Scene* 63 (2010): 32.

29. Holmes, *Opinions,* 15.

30. Holmes 1959 Yale lecture.

31. Ibid.

32. John Clellon Holmes, *Go* (1952; New York: Thunder's Mouth, 1997), 310.

33. Ibid.

34. Ibid.

35. Ibid., 311.

36. Amy Dempsey, *Styles, Schools and Movements* (London: Thames and Hudson, 2002), 176.

37. Holmes, *Opinions,* 59.

38. Ibid., 66.

39. John Clellon Holmes, "Existentialism and the Novel: Notes and Questions," *Chicago Review* 13, no. 2 (1959): 144.

40. Ann Charters, *A Bibliography of Works by Jack Kerouac* (New York: Phoenix, 1967), 9.

41. Holmes, "Existentialism and the Novel," 145.

42. Ibid., 144.

43. Ibid., 145.

44. Ibid.

45. Ibid.

46. Ibid., 149.

47. Holmes, "Existentialism and the Novel," 151.

48. Ibid.

49. Walter Kaufmann, introduction to *Existentialism from Dostoevsky to Sartre* (New York: New American Library, 1975), 46.

50. Jack Kerouac, "Letter from Jack Kerouac on Celine," *Paris Review* 31 (1964): 136.

51. Jack Kerouac, *Road Novels 1957–1960* (New York: Library of America, 2007), 489.

52. Dempsey, *Styles,* 178.

53. Holmes, *Opinions,* 52.

54. Dempsey, *Styles,* 176.

WHOLLY COMMUNION

Poetry, Philosophy, and Spontaneous Bop Cinema

David Sterritt

One rarely turns to the movies for insights into Beat poetics. Apart from avant-garde shorts by Bruce Conner, Ron Rice, Robert Frank, and Alfred Leslie, and a few others, not many films offer more than dim reflections of the Beat sensibility.[1] Given this scarcity, it's unfortunate that Peter Whitehead's unique *Wholly Communion* has been almost entirely overlooked since its completion in 1965. Filmed at a massively attended poetry event that included readings by Allen Ginsberg, Gregory Corso, and Lawrence Ferlinghetti, among others, the movie stands with the most vigorous expressions of Beat consciousness in any medium. In this essay, I use it as a vehicle for exploring the rhizomatic flux and nomadic, polyphonic flows that I see as quintessential attributes of Beat poetry and poetics. To this end, I focus on the portions of *Wholly Communion* that best reflect and embody these properties: Allen Ginsberg's partial reading of his 1963 poem "The Change: Kyoto-Tokyo Express" and (secondarily) performances by the sound poet Ernst Jandl and the antiwar poet Adrian Mitchell, considering them through the aesthetics of Mikhail Bakhtin and the schizoanalysis of Gilles Deleuze and Félix Guattari.

The phrase "wholly communion" is a recurring motif in Whitehead's film and fiction, punning on the holy communion of Christianity and on at least two forms of communion that Whitehead aimed to achieve in his cinema of the 1960s. One is the communion that breaks down borders between artist and theme, figure and ground, subjective and objective, document and reality; the other is that which blurs boundaries among people who simultaneously share an aesthetic experience that is authentic and powerful enough to propel consciousness beyond the temporal and material limits that habitually hem it in.

These phenomena are vividly present in *Wholly Communion,* a sponta-neously filmed account of the International Poetry Incarnation, an evening of literary performances involving members and fellow travelers of the Beat Generation that took place at London's venerable Royal Albert Hall on June 11, 1965. The improvisational nature of *Wholly Communion,* conjoined with the heterogeneous content of the Incarnation itself, place the film under the rubrics that Bakhtin calls the dialogic and the carnivalesque. Although dialogism is a polyvalent term in Bakhtin's vocabulary, it takes one of its most important meanings from his concept of "many equally privileged and fully valid consciousnesses" dynamically posed "on the *boundary* between one's own and someone else's consciousness," revealing that the "very being of man (both external and internal) is the *deepest communion.*" This is an excellent précis of the spirit that is heard, seen, and felt in Whitehead's film, which portrays each consciousness involved in the Incarnation as a singu-larity that is "turned outward, intensely addressing itself, another, a third person," seeking the state of "eternal co-rejoicing, co-admiration, con-cord" that constitutes the "world symposium" in its ideal form, which is to say, the "dialogic fabric of human life."[2] In capturing Beat performances at the moment of their unfolding, *Wholly Communion* enacts the Beat values of collaboration, intuitiveness, and all-embracing creative energy.

At the center of all this, Whitehead may be seen as a psychic interme-diary linking the singular Incarnation with the mythic meanings it started acquiring while it was happening and has kept accruing ever since. *Wholly Communion* is less a *record* of the event, therefore, than an *extension, amplifi-cation,* and *intensification* of it—a point that becomes clear if we think of the film not as an object for beholding but as a component of a dispersed, mul-titudinous system constituting what Deleuze and Guattari term a "machinic assemblage," a set of intertwined networks that perform, regulate, effectuate, and guide converging and diverging flows of desire, expression, content, and becoming. Considered within this framework, Whitehead's movie resembles a music recording as theorized in Deleuzian terms by Drew Hemment, who observes that when a recording is played and listened to, "the final statement is deterritorialized and set adrift in multiple, uncertain circumstances that can never be fully prescribed in advance," presenting "only a snap shot of . . . materials and codes circulating in technological networks."[3] Considered this way, the matter at hand in *Wholly Communion* is understood not as that which was seen, spoken, and heard while Whitehead's camera and sound recorder rolled but rather as a set of multiple, mobile strata that territorialize and deterritorialize afresh every time the film is viewed. Whitehead has described *Wholly Communion* as the movie that "also 'happened' that night" alongside the performances it depicts,[4] and it "happens" again every time it is watched, heard, or thought about, under an infinity of circumstances by an infinity of minds.

In addition to their dialogic qualities, the Incarnation's flows of meaning are steeped in what Bakhtin terms the carnivalesque, the cultural domain populated with "popular-festive images" of the unruly, excessive, inverted, reverted, and perverted, which, like François Rabelais's boisterous prose, embody currents of "change and renewal [and] growth and abundance," expressing "the general [happy] funeral of a dying era, of the old power and old truth."[5] Such was the ethos of the 1960s, which began its full, imperfect flowering in the storied year of 1965. Such also was the ethos of White-head's tumultuous aesthetic during that fruitful time; of the Beat Genera-tion as personified by Ginsberg, a lord of misrule down to his bones; and of the Incarnation, which was less an intellectual conclave than a gathering of adventurous minds eager to see gladiators of creativity "rage and battle with one another, and their audience"[6] in the mandala-shaped space at the center of Royal Albert Hall.

Minor Cinema

Wholly Communion had an almost accidental origin. After participating in the London phase of Bob Dylan's tour of England in 1965, which included a sold-out engagement at Royal Albert Hall, Ginsberg floated the idea that he and other well-known Beats could draw an equally enthusiastic crowd to a reading of their work. Ginsberg was traveling at the time with Barbara Rubin, an underground filmmaker, and she promptly booked the capacious hall for an evening with Ginsberg and friends. The program was soon "hijacked by a posse of native poets," as a London film historian later wrote,[7] but the final lineup still included Ginsberg along with Corso, who read intently and introspectively from *The Mutation of the Spirit: A Shuffle Poem*, published by Death Press the previous year, and Ferlinghetti, who proffered a rollicking version of "To Fuck Is to Love Again." A tape recording brought William S. Burroughs's voice into the mix, too.[8]

Rubin's plan to film the occasion was hijacked as well; organizers told her to desist because "her experimental double-exposure technique was deemed unlikely to preserve the poems as read."[9] It's unclear why Rubin didn't proceed anyway: Who would or could have stopped her, given the anarchic atmosphere that prevailed? In any case, the joke was on the hijackers, since her replacement was Whitehead, who showed up at the four-hour event with forty-five minutes' worth of film stock, hardly enough to preserve the poems as read even if preserving had been as high on his agenda as communing. The finished movie came in at about thirty-three minutes after Whitehead eliminated material that was, in his words, "out of focus, or falling over, or looking for something, or trying to find where the poet had gone to, because Allen Ginsberg pushed me over at one point for getting in his way. I suddenly thought, 'What's happen[ing]?,' he was yanking me down saying, 'Get out of the fucking way. Bloody photographers!' or something similar."[10]

Wholly Communion neither preserves (most of) the poems as read nor provides a legible record of the evening's trajectory; yet its attunement to the unique wavelength of the occasion feels thrillingly right. And it was quite an occasion. By most accounts some seven thousand people were in the hall, and two thousand more were reportedly turned away. Over the course of the evening, an eyewitness wrote, "flowers were distributed; weird papier-mâché creatures strolled about the aisles . . . the dry eerie voice of Burroughs crackled from a tape-recorder . . . poets and hecklers interrupted each other; and a girl in a white dress danced under the pall of potsmoke with distant gestures of dream."[11] Given this material and Whitehead's proclivity for artistic risk, it isn't surprising that *Wholly Communion* evokes the politics of counterculture so dynamically.

The film also amounts to an illustration and defense of Beat poetry as a *minor* literature in the sense devised by Deleuze and Guattari, since virtually all of the readings partake of the three basic characteristics that the philosophers attribute to such texts: "the deterritorialization of language, the connection of the individual to a political immediacy, and the collective assemblage of enunciation" whereby "what each author says individually already constitutes a common action."[12] Marked by these traits as well, *Wholly Communion* is an instance of minor cinema, enriched by the anarchic circumstances under which Whitehead shot it and the fortuitous rifts and fissures these imposed upon the finished work. The limited film supply, dodgy equipment, constant interruptions and misunderstandings, heterodox cast of characters, and so forth serendipitously fractured what Deleuze calls the "general system of commensurability" that habitually orders perception and action in space, time, and cinema. Only in the presence of such a rupture can film perform its liberating function of bringing thought "face to face with its own impossibility" and animating the "higher power of birth" that this encounter can catalyze. "The sensory-motor break," Deleuze declares, "makes man a seer who finds himself... confronted by something unthinkable in thought."[13]

Seeking to do exactly this—to find the unthinkable in thought—Whitehead works the assemblages of cinematography and montage into volatile folds that reveal, refract, and reflect upon their own becomings-flows.[14] In the process he creates a film equivalent of what Ginsberg praised Kerouac for originating: "spontaneous bop prosody," based on the conviction that if poetic lines are lived, breathed, and felt with the skill and sensitivity of an improvising musician, then words can "approach pure prosody," as the culture scholar Daniel Belgrad correctly notes, functioning as "musical elements with physical origins and effects" and achieving what Kerouac described as "the raciness and freedom and humor of jazz."[15] *Wholly Communion* is spontaneous bop cinema.

Into the Chaosmos

Wholly Communion starts with a montage of voices on the sound track—those of Ginsberg, Corso, and Ferlinghetti, the best-known Beats on the program—that offers an impressionistic preview of coming attractions. This is a sophisticated Bakhtinian gambit, since it is often hard to tell where one voice leaves off and another begins (the word "sun" is uttered by all three), and the resulting slippage of identity inscribes the inseparability of individual and collective consciousnesses as a fundamental theme of both the evening and the movie. The most striking contribution is recognizably Ginsberg's, though, as he recites the last lines of "The Change":

And the Sun the Sun the
Sun my visible father
Making my body visible
Thru my [own] eyes![16]

It is hard to overstate the aptness of this poem, which is read at greater length near the end of the film. Ginsberg wrote it during a train ride from Kyoto to Tokyo, at the very moment of a life-changing realization that self-acceptance, the imperative "to be and be alive now," was infinitely more important than the so-called moral obligations—to seek God through drugs and visions, to seek truth and beauty by elevating mind over body—that had long dominated his life. At this moment, he explained a year later, he suddenly understood that "there is only one universe where we can all be together, and *that* universe is the universe where we do exist *here* in our bodies and accept each other's bodies in tenderness. Because that's the only common place where everybody can meet—where everybody is invited to the festival."[17] The festival was literal as well as figurative at Albert Hall, and Whitehead did well to open and close *Wholly Communion* with a poem that crystallizes those ideas.

To those familiar with Deleuze's thought, the "only one universe" that Ginsberg discovered during his fateful trip is surely the plane of immanence. This is the infinitely faceted field of forces and processes of which all beings and bodies are expressions, manifestations, or modes that exist not as essences but as networks and assemblages of intersecting linkages, relationships, and flows that can be diverted into states of static *being* or liberated into streams of boundless *becoming*. Like all of the core Beat writers, Ginsberg celebrated the powers of idiosyncrasy, excess, and paradox, using them to create destabilized and destabilizing texts that might purge the era's psychopolitical consciousness of ingrained dogmas, credos, habits, and beliefs. Anticipating developments in Deleuzian philosophy with uncanny accuracy, he closes "The Change" with an ecstatic vision of becoming, presenting himself as

> [. . .] a universe of skin and breath
> & changing thought and
> burning hand & softened
> heart in the old bed of
> my skin From this single
> birth reborn that I am
> to be so—
>
> My own Identity now nameless
> neither man nor dragon or
> God
>
> But the dreaming Me full
> of physical rays' tender
> red moons in my belly &
> Stars in my eyes circling

Ginsberg here enters the *chaosmos*. This is a portmanteau word that Deleuze and others have borrowed from James Joyce's novel *Finnegans Wake*, refer- ring to the intersecting properties of *cosmos* and *chaos,* order and disorder; the philosopher Keith Robinson calls the chaosmos "a self-organizing sys- tem that creatively advances through the immanent construction of its own generative principles."[18] This describes the becomings-flows of Ginsberg's poem as well as those of the Incarnation and Whitehead's film.

Ginsberg's full-bore deconstruction of his physical self also places him in the stimulating company of the body without organs (BwO), whom Deleuze and Guattari themselves discovered in a poetic work: Antonin Artaud's extraordinary 1947 radio play *To Have Done with the Judgment of God,* which maintains that "there is nothing more useless than an organ" and that when the "badly constructed" human animal has been given a body without them, "then you will have delivered him from all his automatic reactions/ and restored him to his true freedom," teaching him "again to dance wrong side out . . . and this wrong side out will be his real place."[19] In schizoanalytic theory, the organ-ized body is "a phenomenon of accumulation, coagulation, and sedimentation" that always already territorializes the BwO with "forms, functions, bonds, dominant and hierarchized organizations, organized tran- scendences."[20] The body without organs is the antithesis of this theological entity, a surface freely traversed by machinic flows, fluxes, intensities, sin- gularities, and becomings of autotelic desiring-production. As such it is a chaosmic being—the "body without an image," on which "the proportions of attraction and repulsion . . . produce, starting from zero, a series of states in the celibate machine; and the subject is born of each state in the series, is continually reborn of the following state . . . consuming-consummating all these states that cause him to be born and reborn."[21] Making himself a BwO as he writes, Ginsberg begins "The Change" with a vision of his own rebirth, which takes him through "the portals of the festival" into "what Is" and thence to the immediate fall that happens when

> The schemes begin, roulette,
> brainwaves, bony dice
> Stroboscopic motorcycles
> Stereoscopic Scaly
> > Serpents winding thru
> > cloud spaces of
> > > what is not—

The poem that serves as the unofficial anthem of *Wholly Communion* thus evokes the state of organ-ized body from which the poet now seeks a line of schizo-flight via intensities of revolutionary language.

Ginsberg's intensities reside in his delivery as well as in his words, moreover, and his oral performance ideally supplements the radical unruliness of his text. This is most evident when he returns near the end of *Wholly Communion* to read from "The Change" and another poem, "Who Be Kind To." By this time, the program had been going on for two and a half hours, and Ginsberg was now "completely drunk," Whitehead recalled later. "For the audience it was great but for Ginsberg who was waiting to read . . . I suppose he was just sitting there drinking, thinking, 'When the hell am I going to get up and do it?'" Far from criticizing Ginsberg for his intoxication, Whitehead recognized it as an energizing state for the poet: "Ginsberg was trapped in this drunken mess and then he went out (because he is very inward-looking a lot of the time), then suddenly he gets out and does this amazing extroverted thing, really projecting it out."[22] Even as Ginsberg's poems do purposeful violence to the frozen forms of ordinary language, his drunken delivery does determined violence to the reified formalities of official art and culture, producing a dis-organized flow of deterritorializing thought that partakes of what Deleuze calls the encounter. "Something in the world," he writes in *Difference and Repetition,* "forces us to think. This something is an object not of recognition but of a fundamental *encounter.* . . . It may be grasped in a range of affective tones: wonder, love, hatred, suffering. In whichever tone, its primary characteristic is that it can only be sensed."[23]

In an interesting gloss of this concept, the literary scholar Jon Clay observes that insofar as the Deleuzian encounter brushes against otherness, it necessarily touches on "that which is other than a subject and potentially other than human." This takes on special interest in the sphere of poetics, since a poem is itself "both human and other," made of sensations that "exist independently and virtually in the unperformed poem" yet can be actualized "through a performative conjunction with a reader." By proffering "counter-words" that defy the "order-words" of society's dominant discursive orders, the innovative poem mobilizes percepts and affects to transform the reader-poem assemblage immediately and corporeally, in contrast with the incorporeal effects of order-words, which operate in abstract rather than physical ways; and counter-words are made all the more forceful by the poem's own "intractable materiality." The counter-word is therefore "an act of freedom (or more precisely, perhaps, a line of flight) rendered as a material inscription in the body of a reader as poetic sensation." Such inscription takes place even when a poem is read silently to oneself, since the "virtual speech apparatus" in the reader's mind generates affects analogous to those produced by actual speech.[24]

I agree that all poetry, properly approached, is oral poetry. But the act of inscribing acquires particular force, I think, when a poem is recited by the poet, whether for a live audience or via technological mediation—and perhaps especially in the latter case, when the assemblage poet-text-audience is expanded to include networks of technology and varying conditions of reception, as discussed earlier. The against-the-grain flows of Ginsberg's dissident counter-words, inflected by the nonhuman-becomings of his intoxicated voice in communion with movie viewers via cinema technology, thus open an exceptionally galvanic space in the matrices of Whitehead's counter-film.

Sensation

Wholly Communion breaks into a different kind of poetic ruckus when the spotlight turns to Ernst Jandl, an Austrian sound poet and translator of Robert Creeley and John Cage, among others. Here is his poem "schmerz durch reibung" (pain through friction):

frau

frfrauau

frfrfrauauau

frfrfrfrauauauau

frfrfrfrfrauauauauau

frfrfrfrfrfrauauauauauau

frfrfrfrfrfrfrauauauauauauau

frfrfrfrfrfrfrfrauauauauauauauau[25]

The work is entirely logical, rational, and reasonable, from its pyramidal shape to its eight-line structure, corresponding to the octave of the diatonic scale. Its impact as it leaps from Jandl's growling, spluttering mouth is another matter, however, drawing (like Michael McClure's animal poetry) on all that is illogical, irrational, and unreasonable in the anarchic world of unfettered oral expression. This is as invigorating in the movie as it is inexpressible in the book from which I quote. The audience responds in kind to this and further Jandl poems, morphing by turns into "football crowd,

Boy Scout rally, and wolfpack," as eyewitness Alexander Lykiard described the scene.[26] Here we have poetic performance as pure *sensation,* freed from even the hallucinatory traces of semiotic representation found in Ginsberg's recitations. "The violence of sensation is opposed to the violence of the represented (the sensational, the cliché)," Deleuze writes in *Francis Bacon: The Logic of Sensation.* "The former is inseparable from its direct action on the nervous system, the levels through which it passes, the domains it traverses."[27] Precisely.

The Loophole Left Open

I said at the outset that *Wholly Communion* substantiates its title by breaking down aesthetic borders, blurring boundaries among people, and propelling consciousness beyond the norms that ordinarily define and bind it. These are carnivalesque actions par excellence, but it is crucial to remember that the interplay of consciousnesses, discourses, and worldviews loses its fecundity if it becomes a form of fusion in the literal sense—the many united into "an innate one-and-only"—rather than a "dialogic *concordance* of unmerged twos or multiples."[28] Dialogism is not a matter of mere dialogue between communicating people or competing ideas; construed in its full sense, it comprises an open-ended heteroglossia of links and processes of consciousness, geared to the awareness that relativity, mutability, and instability are bedrock qualities of human interaction, just as difference, contradiction, and undecidability are inherent aspects of the human condition itself. Monologic discourse is antithetical to this knowledge, allowing no "play with its borders," affording no "spontaneously creative stylizing variants," and entering consciousness "as a compact and indivisible mass."[29]

Interestingly, one of the Incarnation's most vocal admirers and participants felt a monologic one-and-only coming perilously close to the surface at one point during the event, to wit, the recital of sound poetry by Jandl and associates. "As his sound-poems rose to a crescendo, a rhythmic furore aided and abetted by the claps and cries of the crowd," Lykiard wrote later,

> so, suddenly, the destruction of words and their conversion to a shouted, half-hysterical series of sounds seemed sinister—took on a Hitlerian aspect: the hall became almost a Babel. It was perhaps the most extraordinary event of the evening: parody and warning, cacophony with its own logic, rational collapse of reason, and despair

of communication communicating itself. Artaud, who understood the sanity of madness, would have relished it.[30]

As his artfully clashing descriptive terms attest, Lykiard appears to have felt pleasure and alarm simultaneously and in equal measure. And in the end, his ambivalent response is an effective antidote to the dark side of the furor, by virtue of its very ambivalence: being of two minds is a good way to fight the monologic one-and-only, opening possibilities for dialogic "playing with distances, with fusion and dissolution, with approach and retreat."[31]

One hardly needs reminding that those processes and forces are all dynamically alive in Whitehead's film, a teeming multiverse of shifting positions, mutating contexts, fusing and dissolving discourses, and other manifestations of the polyphonic instability that distinguished the Beat spirit at its mutinous, ungraspable best. Here we have the interplay of minds and bodies as an unstable and participatory phenomenon that subverts authority and propriety in positive and productive ways. Madness certainly plays a role, but it is a madness that liberates propulsive energies, not one that fades into the deracinated mob.

Difference in Repetition

Linking contemporary language poets with Deleuze and Guattari, the critic James Pate observes that they are no longer "content to simply examine the world, or to stay within the fairly safe (by now) discourse of the semiotic," but instead use a "renewed interest in the materiality of the body" to explore an aesthetic that is "politically subversive" and also "highly grotesque/excessive," employing "the extreme logic of the grotesque" such that it "relates fundamentally to the logic of radical politics."[32] While this point is unarguable, neither language poets nor sound poets have a monopoly on subversive politics, and the semiotic is by no means obsolete as a vehicle for radical expression. A case in point is Adrian Mitchell's poem of protest against the Vietnam War, "To Whom It May Concern," which provides *Wholly Communion* with some of its most powerful moments through a regularly repeated, incrementally expanding list of incantatory metaphors for entrapment, deception, violence, and death, ending thus:

You put your bombers in, you put your conscience out
You take the human being, and you twist it all about

So scrub my skin with women
So chain my tongue with whisky
Stuff my nose with garlic
Coat my eyes with butter
Fill my ears with silver
Stick my legs in plaster
Tell me lies about Viet Nam[33]

The poem's intellectual and emotional sharpness arises in part from Mitchell's ingenuity in decrying the eternal recurrence of war in a poem that invokes the eternal recurrence in Friedrich Nietzsche's sense of a crushing psychospiritual weight that only one with an authentic *amor fati* can endure without fear and trembling *ad aeternitatem*.[34]

Explicating the ethics of this concept, Deleuze asserts in *Difference and Repetition* that the eternal return "seems to make repetition itself the only form of a law beyond morality" by casting repetition in "the brutal form of the immediate, that of the universal and the singular reunited, which dethrones every general law, dissolves the mediations and annihilates the particulars subject to the law."[35] Interpreting this idea in another context, the critic Marco Abel suggests that in Patricia Highsmith's fiction, "repetition of violence operates by the logic of [iterating] intensification where what is repeated is only that which ultimately can return differently," creating repetition that is "not based on the generality of law but on the specificity of actions."[36] At once transparent/polemical and grotesque/excessive, "To Whom It May Concern" performs a similar operation. Offered as an intensive howl of rage against a sociopolitical evil that law has proven utterly unable to ameliorate, Mitchell's poem enacts that which it advocates by conjuring up the difference within repetition, deploying iterative poesis as a materialist line of flight that pierces, traverses, destratifies, and deterritorializes the world of order-words in the name of counter-words, encounters, and becomings-other that animate higher powers of birth and life by pushing thought beyond space, time, and itself.

Rhizomatic Film

Whitehead was profoundly in sync with what he witnessed at the Incarnation, despite—or thanks to—his concurrent immersion in the mechanics and poetics of the shoot. "I chose to call it *Wholly Communion*," he later underscored. "That was my title, not the name of the event. It was inside the womb, the church, it was this sort of religious experience."[37] As a filmmaker, he also emphasized, he was never quite the same: "Any pretensions I had as a cameraman about the objectivity of film have, since making this movie, also been abandoned."[38] From a Deleuzian perspective, we can understand the assemblage constituted by the polyvalent voices of the Incarnation and Whitehead's spontaneously created film in terms similar to those of music improvisation whereby, in the words of the theorist Jeremy Gilbert, the "lines between composers, producers, performers and audiences are all deliberately blurred, and the relationship between authorial intention and sonic [or audiovisual] product is radically destabilized." In such circumstances, "a continuous experience of trans-personal intensity—a body without organs—is generated by the deliberate subversion of any simple process of composition, expression and interpretation."[39] This sounds to me like something strange, familiar, and marvelous: spontaneous bop creativity, BwO style.

According to Deleuze and Guattari, the supreme act of philosophy is "not so much to think *THE* plane of immanence as to show that it is there, unthought in every plane, and to think it in this way as the outside and inside of thought, as . . . that which cannot be thought and yet must be thought."[40] This self-contradictory play of schizo-thought can be sensed and felt when Ginsberg and the others read, chant, personify, and *become* their subversive texts in Whitehead's film, magnified and expanded by the techno-assemblages of cinema. Deleuze has credited Jean-Luc Godard with forging a new kind of film: a rhizomatic cinema of *between* and *and* that "does away with all the cinema of Being = is" and renders "the indiscernible" visible.[41] Whitehead has a similar agenda, seeking in cinema what the best Beat poets seek in language. They usher us into the chaosmos where thought folds around and upon itself to manifest liberating new becomings-modes of speech, action, and imagination.

Notes

A substantially different version of this essay appeared as "*Wholly Communion:* Scenario, Film, Novelization," in *Framework* 52, no. 1–2 (2011), published by Wayne State University Press.

1. After many false starts, Francis Ford Coppola's adaptation of *On the Road*, directed by Walter Salles from a screenplay by Jose Rivera, is scheduled for completion in 2011.

2. Mikhail Bakhtin, *Problems of Dostoevsky's Poetics,* trans. Caryl Emerson (Min-

neapolis: University of Minnesota Press, 1984), 287, 251–52, 293, emphases in the original.

3. Drew Hemment, "Affect and Individuation in Popular Electronic Music," in *Deleuze and Music,* ed. Ian Buchanan and Marcel Swiboda, 76–94 (Edinburgh: Edinburgh University Press, 2004), 78.

4. Peter Whitehead, "Notes on the Filming," in *Wholly Communion: International Poetry Reading at the Royal Albert Hall, London, June 11, 1965* (New York: Grove Press, 1965), 9.

5. Mikhail Bakhtin, *Rabelais and His World,* trans. Hélène Iswolsky (Bloomington: Indiana University Press, 1984), 99.

6. Peter Whitehead, *Tonite Let's All Make Love in London* (Pytchley, U.K.: Hathor, 1999), 110. The quasi-coherent story of this novel, named after a line from Ginsberg's poem "Who Be Kind To," relates in part to the Incarnation. Ginsberg wrote the poem in his journal for 4–6 A.M. on June 8, 1965, three days before the Incarnation, and *Wholly Communion* shows him reading it at the event. It appeared later in Allen Ginsberg, *Planet News: 1961–1967* (San Francisco: City Lights, 1968), 95–99.

7. Henry K. Miller, "Notes from Underground," *Film Comment* (July/August 2006), www. filmlinc.com/fcm/ja06/peterwhitehead.htm.

8. Other readers included Anselm Hollo, Alexander Trocchi, Michael Horovitz, Pablo Fernandez, Christopher Logue, Pete Brown, Harry Fainlight, John Esam, Paolo Lionni, Simon Vinkenoog, Dan Richter, and George Macbeth.

9. Miller, "Notes from Underground."

10. Jack Sargeant, *Naked Lens: Beat Cinema* (Berkeley: Soft Skull, 2008), 136, brackets in original.

11. Alexis Lykiard, introduction to *Wholly Communion: International Poetry Reading at the Royal Albert Hall, London, June 11, 1965* (New York: Grove, 1965), 3–4.

12. Gilles Deleuze and Félix Guattari, *Kafka: Toward a Minor Literature,* trans. Dana Polan (Minneapolis: University of Minnesota Press, 1986), 16–17.

13. Gilles Deleuze, *Cinema 2: The Time-Image,* trans. Hugh Tomlinson and Robert Galeta (Minneapolis: University of Minnesota Press, 1989), 169, 277, 168, 169.

14. For discussion of these points in relation to Jean-Luc Godard, an important artist for Deleuze and a culture hero for Whitehead, see David Sterritt, "Schizoanalyzing Souls: Godard, Deleuze, and the Mystical Line of Flight," *Journal of French and Francophone Philosophy* 15, no. 1 (Fall 2010).

15. Daniel Belgrad, *The Culture of Spontaneity: Improvisation and the Arts in Postwar America* (Chicago: University of Chicago Press, 1998), 203–4. See also Allen Ginsberg, "Dedication," in Howl *and Other Poems,* by Ginsberg (San Francisco: City Lights, 1956), 3.

16. Allen Ginsberg, "The Change: Kyoto-Tokyo Express," in Ginsberg, *Planet News,* 55–63.

17. Michael Schumacher, *Dharma Lion: A Critical Biography of Allen Ginsberg* (New York: St. Martin's, 1992), 394, 395, emphases in original.

18. Keith Robinson, "Introduction: Deleuze, Whitehead, Bergson—Rhizomatic Connections," in *Deleuze, Whitehead, Bergson: Rhizomatic Connections,* ed. Keith Robinson (New York: Palgrave Macmillan, 2009), 23.

19. Antonin Artaud, *To Have Done with the Judgment of God,* trans. Helen Weaver, in *Antonin Artaud: Selected Writings,* ed. Susan Sontag (Berkeley and Los Angeles: University of California Press, 1976), 571.

20. Gilles Deleuze and Félix Guattari, *A Thousand Plateaus: Capitalism and Schizophrenia,* trans. Brian Massumi (Minneapolis: University of Minnesota Press, 1987), 159.

21. Gilles Deleuze and Félix Guattari, *Anti-Oedipus: Capitalism and Schizophrenia,* trans. Robert Hurley, Mark Seem, and Helen R. Lane (Minneapolis: University of Minnesota Press, 1987), 8, 20.

22. Sargeant, *Naked Lens,* 134, 138.

23. Gilles Deleuze, *Difference and Repetition,* trans. Paul Patton (London: Columbia University Press, 1993), 139, emphasis in original.

24. Jon Clay, *Sensation, Contemporary Poetry and Deleuze: Transformative Intensities* (London: Continuum, 2010), 93, 99, 103.

25. Ernst Jandl, "schmerz durch reibung" (pain through friction), in *Wholly Communion,* 60.

26. Lykiard, introduction, 4.

27. Gilles Deleuze, *Francis Bacon: The Logic of Sensation,* trans. Daniel W. Smith (Minneapolis: University of Minnesota Press, 2004), 34–35.

28. Bakhtin, *Problems of Dostoevsky's Poetics,* 289.

29. M. M. Bakhtin, *The Dialogic Imagination: Four Essays,* trans. Caryl Emerson and Michael Holquist (Austin: University of Texas Press, 1981), 344.

30. Lykiard, introduction, 4.

31. Bakhtin, *Dialogic Imagination,* 344.

32. James Pate, "Wittgenstein, Deleuze, and the Political Grotesque," *ActionYes* 1, no. 12 (Winter 2010), www.actionyes.org/issue6/pate/pate1.html. Pate chiefly discusses works by Arlana Reines, Lara Glenum, and Daniel Borzutzky.

33. Adrian Mitchell, "To Whom It May Concern (Tell Me Lies About Viet Nam)," in *Heart on the Left: Poems 1953–1984,* by Mitchell (Newcastle Upon Tyne: Bloodaxe, 1997), 292–93.

34. See, for example, *The Gay Science: With a Prelude in Rhymes and an Appendix of Songs,* trans. Walter Kaufmann (New York: Vintage, 1974), 341.

35. Deleuze, *Difference and Repetition,* 7.

36. Marco Abel, *Violent Affect: Literature, Cinema, and Critique after Representation* (Lincoln: University of Nebraska Press, 2007), 126, 127.

37. Sargeant, *Naked Lens,* 137.

38. Whitehead, "Notes on the Filming," 9.

39. Jeremy Gilbert, "Becoming-Music: The Rhizomatic Moment of Improvisation,"

in *Deleuze and Music,* ed. Ian Buchanan and Marcel Swiboda, 118–39 (Edinburgh: Edinburgh University Press, 2004), 120–21.

40. Gilles Deleuze and Félix Guattari, *What Is Philosophy?,* trans. Hugh Tomlinson and Graham Burchell (New York: Columbia University Press, 1994), 59–60, emphasis in original.

41. Deleuze, *Cinema 2,* 180.

HIGH OFF THE PAGE

**Representing the Drug Experience in the Work of
Jack Kerouac and Allen Ginsberg**

Erik Mortenson

Just what is the body's knowledge? A scar traces the history of a laceration; a pain in the back indicates bad posture; a runny nose predicts a cold. The body is ours to read like a text, provided something occurs. Otherwise, it becomes all too often a mere given, an instrument used to grasp, to move, to live. Only through the prism of a rent do we witness the body itself in all its fullness and possibility. For those of us who desire such a glimpse, alteration becomes a necessity. But how should we attempt such a mutation without damaging our precious vessel? Drug use is one answer. Perhaps no other term creates such a wealth of connotations—addiction, transgression, criminality, overdose. With all the dangers attached to them, drugs seem an unlikely candidate for such experimentation.[1] Yet there are advantages. Drugs provide a temporary alteration with fairly predictable results. A user can ingest a substance, experience the embodied consciousness of the drugged state, and return with their tale. What is needed, then, are such accounts of drugs that can provide the user and nonuser alike with insights into how drug use intersects with subjectivity.

Fortunately, such an account already exists in the work of Jack Kerouac and Allen Ginsberg. These writers were involved in a postwar project that saw drug use as an invaluable means of expanding their range of experience beyond accepted channels. Written during the period of intoxication, Kerouac's and Ginsberg's works provide not just an abstract comment but a concrete record of the effects of drug use on embodied consciousness. The gains these writers experienced while mapping this terrain are twofold. On the one hand, the drug-inspired works of Kerouac and Ginsberg reveal an emphasis on the temporality of the drug experience in each author's individual life. Their works become studies in speed, concerned with the increases, decreases, and stoppages in the perception of time that drug use enacts. Not only do their drug writings relate their own personal experiences, but they likewise seek to explore the interstice between the drugged state and the other who stands outside that experience. We become privy to the changes drug use inaugurates both within the single body and between multiple ones. Kerouac's and Ginsberg's willingness to experiment on themselves and bring back the results in the form of literature provides us with accounts of drug consumption's effects on subjectivity and, ultimately, sheds light on what it means to alter the body and to portray this alteration to another.

Before exploring the specific results of the drug state, one must first understand the literary process by which information concerning this state is conveyed from writer to reader. For these two authors, communication between the reader and the drugged other can take place only when writing attains the status of original speech. In his work *Phenomenology of Perception*, the philosopher Maurice Merleau-Ponty differentiates between two types of language: original and secondary, writing: "I may say that 'I have been waiting for a long time,' or that someone 'is dead,' and I think I know what I am saying. Yet if I question myself on time or the experience of death . . . there is nothing clear in my mind. This is because I have tried to speak about speech, to re-enact the act of expression" (391). Original, "authentic" expression is already full, since in the act of saying something we attain an "immediately apprehended clarity" (391). Problems arise only when we attempt to speak about speech. The sentence turns into a reified object that loses its immediacy and thus its immanent meaning. This is precisely the reason writers like Kerouac and Ginsberg are so adamant that writing should emanate from elsewhere than the "ego." Thus in his "Essentials of Spontaneous Prose," Kerouac advises, "If possible write 'without consciousness in semi-trance' (as Yeats' later 'trance writing'), allowing subconscious to admit in own uninhibited interesting necessary and so 'modern' language what conscious art would censor" (70). What Kerouac is advocating is writing from what phenomenology terms the "intentional consciousness." Instead of writing about objects and ideas, the writer is advised to transcribe the workings of their "subconscious" as objects and ideas are grasped intentionally.[2] In "Notes Written on Finally Recording 'Howl,'" Allen Ginsberg explains it thus: "Mind is shapely, Art is shapely. Meaning Mind practiced in spontaneity invents forms in its own image—gets to Last Thoughts" (81). The ego is an impediment. Forcing the world through the filter of the "I" reduces externality into easily manageable representations.

Original speech, however, is tied closely to the body. This can be seen in Merleau-Ponty's conception of linguistic communication, which is built on the gesture. In discussing a threatening gesture, Merleau-Ponty explains that "the gesture does not make me think of anger, it is anger itself" (184). One need not search his or her experience of gestures or reason by analogy in order to understand the meaning of a raised fist since this gesture contains the significance of "anger" within it. For Merleau-Ponty, the spoken word is also a gesture, and thus "the meaning of words must be finally induced by the words themselves . . . their conceptual meaning must be formed by a kind of deduction from a gestural meaning, which is immanent in speech" (179). Original speech is not concerned with simply communicating a set of facts to the listener, but aims at conveying a style of being from one body to another. Thus Kerouac has recourse to the simile of gesture in explaining his technique. In his "Essentials of Spontaneous Prose," Kerouac compares the line to "a fist coming down on a table with complete utterance, bang!" (69). This "bang!" denotes the "telepathic shock and meaning-excitement" (69) that the reader receives from such expression. Language is not first a matter of communication, but of alteration. Merleau-Ponty claims that "I begin to understand a philosophy by feeling my way into its existential manner, by reproducing the tone and accent of the philosopher" (179). Before content comes to form, a certain style of being gets communicated from the speaker to the listener, causing not a "process of thinking on my part, but a synchronizing change of my own existence" (183–84). Original speech can bridge the gap between self and other since, as Kerouac maintains, the listener has the "same laws operating in his own human mind" (69).

The importance placed on corporeality should come as no surprise, since the body figures prominently in all of Kerouac's and Ginsberg's manifestoes. Jack Kerouac claims that his work relies on "the vigorous space dash separating rhetorical breathing (as jazz musician drawing breath between outblown phrases)" ("Essentials" 69). Here the body becomes a privileged site for poetics. Breath is tied to the body, and by breathing life into the poem, the poet breathes a part of himself into the poem as well. Allen Ginsberg deepens this connection between breath, body, and writing in his essay "Improvised Poetics." He declares that "physiologically in the body . . . is . . . the key to suddenly wakening up . . . a whole Reichian chain of muscular reactions . . . it's like having the basic patterns of physiological reactions built into the language, into the alphabet" (36, ellipses in original). Writing that takes its cue from the body imbues language with a physical presence. As Daniel Belgrad observes in his book *The Culture of Spontaneity,* such a poetic act is possible "only because of the very physicality of the poet's body-mind, which situated him or her as an object in place and time" (130). The Beat poet Michael McClure uses a different metaphor but to the same effect. In *Scratching the Beat Surface,* McClure speaks of a "systemless system" which "alters itself in the waves with a living anarchism" (54). The poet allows energy to flow through the body in order to create a "systemless system" that is the poem. McClure writes that poems become "extensions of myself as much as my hand or arm are extensions of me" (89). Again, physicality is infused directly into the work in order to embody the poem. But if the body is the basis for poetics, then an alteration of that body through the use of drugs is going to alter the writing as well.[3] Composing through the drug-altered body allows the effects of the drug to be transferred onto the written page, providing the reader with a novel account of the drug experience unavailable through mere descriptions of the event.

But how exactly does a reader experience the written drug account? Here again the work of Merleau-Ponty is instructive. Merleau-Ponty's conception of the body grounds the individual in the world. But it also provides a means for intersubjective communication. Merleau-Ponty claims that "as the parts of my body together comprise a system, so my body and the other person's are one whole, two sides of one and the same phenomenon" (354). It is only through encountering the other's body that communication can be established, that this "system" can be comprised. Writing done "through the body" allows for intersubjectivity to be established between bodies via the medium of the text. McClure explains it thus: "Blake is as present today as if he were biologically alive. His works are extensions of himself. . . . Blake's works, like all artifacts of all high artists, are his body. Gestures come so directly from his physical being that their presence is real and physical" (137–38). Blake's works are traces of his body, and from them we are able to connect with a man dead for over a century. Discussing the use of mantra in his poetry, Ginsberg explains in "Improvised Poetics," "the . . . rhythmic . . . units . . . that I'd written down . . . were basically . . . breathing exercise forms . . . which if anybody else repeated . . . would catalyze in them the same pranic breathing . . . physiological spasm . . . that I was going through . . . and so would presumably catalyze in them the same affects or emotions" (33–36, ellipses in original). When the text is infused with a bodily presence, the reader is able to connect with the work on a visceral level. Merleau-Ponty claims that "aesthetic expression confers on what it expresses an existence in itself" (183). While it is the writing itself that we phenomenologically confront, this "existence" that is the text retains bodily properties that allow the reader to experience it physically as well as mentally.[4]

Yet Merleau-Ponty's paradigm of bodily intersubjectivity is only one side of the coin. If drugged writing is working through an altered body to record new experience for the reader, how do we theorize this reorientation toward the world? In contrast to Merleau-Ponty's reliance on the body as a means to ground experience, the philosophers Gilles Deleuze and Félix Guattari call for an experimental body in constant flux and change. In *A Thousand Plateaus,* Deleuze and Guattari describe a "set of practices" which create a limit known as the "Body Without Organs" (150).[5] The "Body Without Organs" is championed as a way of breaking down this reified body in order to find a new means of experiencing phenomena by opening the body up to sensations and "intensities" that were previously imperceptible. Rather than relying on a rigid, fixed conception of the body as a means of experience, these philosophers are calling for a reorganized body where "experimentation has replaced all interpretation" (162). Although Deleuze and Guattari warn of the dangers involved in creating a drugged body, it is clear that in crafting a "Body Without Organs" the drug user is attempting to open herself up to new experience and phenomenological data by altering the very foundation of knowledge itself: the body.

But if the bodily consumption of drugs is a means of altering perception, the question becomes: What novel perceptions are drugs inaugurating? According to Deleuze and Guattari, the fundamental issue here is one of speed: "The problem is well formulated if we say that drugs eliminate forms and persons, if we bring into play the mad speeds of drugs and the extraordinary posthigh slownesses . . . if we confer upon perception the molecular power to grasp microperceptions, microoperations, and upon the perceived to emit accelerated or decelerated particles in a floating time that is no longer our time" (283). The body as "ground" gives way to the "Body Without Organs." These alterations created through drug use, these "accelerations" and "decelerations," provide the drug user with a means to perceive what was before imperceptible. This new sense of time opens up new vistas of the "molecular" for the drug user and allows for what Deleuze and Guattari call a "hecceity." Subjectivity is replaced by a becoming that involves both speed and affect: "You are longitude and latitude, a set of speeds and slownesses between unformed particles" (262). If speed is what you are, altering your speed will change your very being, allowing the world (and yourself) to be perceived in new ways. Writings about the drug experience often address this notion of an altered temporality, but they do so on the level of content. How might an investigation of the formal nature of literary work shed light on Deleuze and Guattari's emphasis on speed? These thinkers downplay the individuality of the drug substance, preferring to organize their thinking under the rubric of speed. Yet a closer inspection of writing under the influence reveals that each drug creates a specific "hecceity" that should not be overlooked. Deleuze and Guattari may be concerned with the overall effect of drugs, but it is important to flesh out some of the distinctions in speed between various drugs if we are to fully understand both their effects on temporal perception and their possible literary representations.

The fundamental problem in discussing the speeds associated with drug use is that there is no objective yardstick with which to measure deviations from a norm. Philosophy has attempted to solve this problem by positing the notion of a "real" present that elides perceptual difference. As Richard Gale notes in *The Philosophy of Time,* this solution has the result of making any perceptual present "specious" with regard to a "*real* or *true* present, which is supposed to be punctual" (294). Experience dictates, however, that the present always remains relational—a second for one person is never a second for another. What do "acceleration" and "deceleration" mean in such a situation? An answer can be found in an appeal to the notion of attention. In his work *Patterning of Time,* Leonard W. Doob presents the results of a study that discovered "subjects under the influence of the depressant tapped and drew a mirror image more slowly than when affected by the antidepressant" (313). Let's call the time it takes to draw the "mirror image" the present. Under the influence of a depressant like marijuana, the subject expends more attention to the process than he would under the influence of an antidepressant such as amphetamines. The person high on marijuana thus experiences an expansion of the present that concomitantly leads to the feeling that objectified clock time has slowed. As Peter Hartocollis claims in *Time and Timelessness,* under the influence of marijuana there is a "concentration on the present" (133). The amphetamine user, by contrast, attends to her task more quickly, leading to a contraction of the present, which means the next present will be encountered more rapidly. Here objective clock time seems to speed up.

This expansion of the present that occurs under marijuana use is literally "captured" in Kerouac's texts. Writing under the influence of marijuana, Kerouac's work is able to represent the distinct attentional effects of the experience to the reader. Take a passage from *Visions of Cody*, where Kerouac explains a "gray afternoon" to the reader: "that kind of day, that'll only know a rosy cloud at sundown when the sun will find its tortured way through masses and battles of fevered darkening matter—raw, dank, the wind going like a gong through your coat and also through your body—the wild woolly clouds hurrying no faster in the heavens above than the steam from the railyards hurrying over the fence and up the street into town— fantastic, noisy" (85). According to Kerouac's friend and fellow Beat writer John Clellon Holmes, such passages in *Visions of Cody* were written while under the influence of marijuana: "He'd blast, get high, and then he'd write all night. And the reason why those sentences are so long and exfoliating and so incredible is because of pot" (Gifford and Lee 77). Sentence length expands correspondingly as Kerouac's perceptions "exfoliate" into additional clauses that nuance the overall description while slowing down the reading process. By the time the reader comes to the end of the line, the idea of a "gray afternoon," registered momentarily by a sober observer, has been explored in the extreme depth that marijuana use allows. Kerouac's passage not only presents his thinking process while under the influence of marijuana, but conveys the speed of the experience as well.

For Kerouac, this expansion of the present that marijuana produces allows for what is known as "digging." Consider a letter Kerouac wrote to his friend Neal Cassady:

> First let me say that I have been digging the World Series and the tones of the various announcers. This morning I did the World Series the honor of getting up early and blasting ahead of time. There's an announcer from Philly called Gene Kelley who is an exact replica of John Holmes (that is, dig John as a radio announcer), with the same way of *being proud of his verbs*, and so on, like when a groundball is hit, he'll say . . . "a slow, *twisting*, weak roller" as if baseball was the significance of life itself, the things happening in it representing in symbols of action, the symbols of (twisting) despair in the "modern world." . . . Then quickly I turn to old reliable southern-accent Mel Allen, who has that simple back-country mind, like Dean, just pointing out things like . . . "Well, there's Johnny Mize mopping his face with a handkerchief" . . . You can tell Neal, how I dig all this;

my mind, wrapped in wild observation of everything, is drawn, by
the back-country announcer, back to the regular, *brakeman* things
of life. (*Selected Letters* 230–31)

Yet "digging" not only expands the moment, but opens the "digger" up to a
new range of empathetic feelings as well.[6] In his letter to Cassady, Kerouac's
description of Kelley as "being proud of his verbs" is not simply a comment on
his technique. Instead, it demonstrates a desire to understand the announcer
on some sublinguistic level. Kerouac continues to equate Kelley's tendencies
with "life itself" and "symbols of (twisting) despair in the 'modern world.'"
In much the same manner, Allen's "simple back-country" announcing draws
Kerouac to "the regular, *brakeman* things of life." Kerouac thus reinterprets the
announcer's words in his own terms, extrapolating attitudes and feelings that
the two announcers never explicitly verbalize. Marijuana-induced "digging"
is a means of understanding an other and empathizing with their plight. In
On the Road, Sal and Dean smoke "a tremendous Corona cigar of tea" (283),
then proceed to "dig" their newly acquired Mexican friends. Dean exclaims:
"Will you d-i-g that weird brother in the back. . . . And they're talking and
wondering about us, like see? Just like we are but with a difference of their
own" (283–84). Despite the barriers of language and culture, marijuana use
builds a bridge from one self to another. Slowing the world down so that a
moment may be taken in more fully, marijuana-inspired "digging" allows for
a leisurely contemplation of the world around the "digger."

Unsurprisingly, amphetamine use produces the opposite effect. While
marijuana expands the moment and leads to a decelerated reading experience, amphetamines contract the moment, leading instead to a sense of
acceleration. Consider a passage from Kerouac's novel *The Subterraneans.*
Kerouac wrote this work in a Benzedrine-fueled three-day marathon (Charters, *Kerouac* 185), and this often-quoted passage retains the increased energy
that the drug induces:

So there we were at the Red Drum, a tableful of beers a few that is
and all the gangs cutting in and out, paying a dollar quarter at the
door, the little hip-pretending weasel there taking tickets, Paddy
Cordavan floating in as prophesied (a big tall blond brakeman type
subterranean from Eastern Washington cowboy-looking in jeans
coming it to a wild generation party all smoky and mad and I yelled
"Paddy Cordavan?" and "Yeah?" and he'd come over). (13)

Digging involves an attention to a few details within the moment, expanding on them until an empathetic understanding of the object being "dug" is reached. Here, however, Kerouac is obsessed with novelty—his attention continually shifts from character to character as they parade across the room. Even when Kerouac does begin to explicate a character like Paddy Cordavan, he quickly shifts to another facet of the event, explaining how when he "yelled 'Paddy Cordavan?'" Paddy responded "Yeah?" and came over. Rather than dwelling on the inner souls of his characters, Kerouac instead gives quick visual descriptions, then immediately moves on to the next scene or occurrence. By collapsing the present in such a way that more of them can be included in his account, Kerouac provides the reader with a sense of the "acceleration" associated with amphetamine use.

The shortening of the moment that results from amphetamine use is best exemplified in the life of veteran "speed freak" Neal Cassady. As William Plummer notes in *Holy Goof: A Biography of Neal Cassady,* the "raps" and letters of Cassady that would go on to inform Kerouac's prose style were themselves "sped by amphetamine" (129).[7] As a boy, his brother Jimmy would imprison him in a wall-bed, where Cassady experienced a sensation of time having had "gradually apexed to about triple its ordinary speed of passage" (*First Third* 113). Later in life, Cassady was able to control this sensation, "to hold still as death and listen intently for the inner ear to speed up its buzz until, with regular leverlike flips, my mind's gears were shifted by unknown mechanism to an increase of time's torrent that received in kaleidoscopic change searing images, clear as the hurry of thought could make them, rushing so quickly by that all I could do was barely catch the imagery of one before another crowded" (*First Third* 113). This constant "kaleidoscopic change" of "searing images" is an apt description of the type of change in attention that amphetamine enacts. The moment of perception shortens so drastically that Cassady barely had time to perceive an image before "another crowded" to replace it.

The "digging" inspired by marijuana use finds a corollary in the confessional nature of amphetamine consumption. While marijuana use expands the present to allow the "digger" to understand an other more fully, amphetamine use creates an intense desire for personal revelation that finds expression in the hurried pace of the narrative itself. At the beginning of *The Subterraneans,* Kerouac announces that "another confession must be made, as many I must make ere time's sup" (3). As the novel develops, Kerouac continually divulges personal and oftentimes unflattering facts about his life in an effort to tell everything as quickly as possible. In *On the Road,* this desire to "confess" to the Other is tied even more closely to amphetamine use. Carlo (Ginsberg) explains to Sal (Kerouac) that he and Dean (Cassady) "are embarked on a tremendous season together. We're trying to communicate with absolute honesty and absolute completeness everything on our minds. We've had to take benzedrine" (42). Unfortunately for the amphetamine user, however, there never seems to be enough time. Despite conversing the entire night, come daybreak Carlo and Dean's task remains incomplete, and they must meet again to continue their discussion.

Drug-induced writing thus works through the body to inscribe the sensation of the drug state onto paper in order to deliver the "telepathic shock and meaning-excitement" of this state to the reader. *The Subterraneans* offers a frantic cataloguing of doubt that triggers a parallel sensation of acceleration in the reader, while Kerouac's letter to Cassady and *Visions of Cody* slow the reader down into a world constantly expanding with minute detail upon minute detail.

But if writing through the drug state offers a revolutionary means for connection, this technique reaches its limit case with LSD. Experimenting with LSD-25 at Stanford University in 1959, Ginsberg found the type of empathy that he and Kerouac were seeking. In a letter to a relative, Ginsberg claims that he discovered "a sort of identity common with everything" (Schumacher 311). Unfortunately for Ginsberg, this vision was difficult to transcribe into poetry. In "Lysergic Acid," Ginsberg composes under the influence of the drug, but as his biographer Michael Schumacher concludes, the "result was some interesting, though confusing, writing" (312):

> A We
> and that must be an It, and a They, and a Thing with No Answer
> It creepeth, it waiteth, it is still, it is begun, it is the Horns of Battle it
>   is Multiple Sclerosis
> it is not my hope
> it is not my death at Eternity
> it is not my word, not poetry
> beware my Word (*Collected Poems* 232)

Ginsberg is clearly struggling to explain the LSD experience to his readers. But rather than allowing the drug to speak through him onto the page, he instead attempts to reflect on its effects. The poem thus remains mired in negativity, forced to describe what the experience is *not* instead of what it *is*. "Magic Psalm," written after the hallucinogenic experience, takes the opposite tack. Ginsberg writes: "croak my voice with uglier than reality, a psychic tomato speaking Thy / million mouths" (*Collected Poems* 255). Structurally, the lines of this poem follow those of "Howl." But the Benzedrine-inspired format of "Howl" fails to convey LSD's sense of temporality.

Instead of trying to leave the body and meld into the "nonhuman," Ginsberg decides to return to the body as a means of establishing "human relationships rather than relations between the human and nonhuman" (Ginsberg, Interview 314). With this new mind-set, Ginsberg once again took LSD and produced the poem "Wales Visitation." In it, Ginsberg writes: "Bardic, O Self, Visitacione, tell naught but what seen by one man in a vale in Albion, of the folk, whose physical sciences end in Ecology, the wisdom of earthly relations, of mouths & eyes interknit ten centuries visible" (*Collected Poems* 480). Where his earlier LSD poems focused either on explaining the mental conceptions the drug was building or reverting back to earlier forms as a means of making sense of the experience, "Wales Visitation" immerses itself in the objective minutiae of the LSD moment. Drawing on "what seen by one man in a vale," Ginsberg gets back into the body in order to link up with humanity. As Ginsberg claims in Portuges's *The Visionary Poetics of Allen Ginsberg,* "for the first time I was able to externalize my attention instead of dwelling on the inner images and symbols" (122). This "externalization" allows Ginsberg to get outside himself and connect up with the "wisdom of earthly relations" instead of becoming mired in the "nonhuman," abstracted LSD consciousness that allows a user to "enter into alternative universes and with the speed of light" (Ginsberg, "Interview" 315). Ginsberg himself describes the poem as "one giant being breathing—one giant being that we're all part of " (Schumacher 487).

Unfortunately, "Wales Visitation" still fails to convey the LSD experience fully to the reader. The fault lies less with Ginsberg than with the difficult nature of LSD itself. According to a study described by Hartocollis, "At various stages of the experience, subjects typically report that 'time is standing still, racing backwards or forwards, or dragging interminably'" (127). In contrast to a marijuana-induced expansion of the present and an amphetamine-induced contraction of the moment, LSD users undergo a change in attention that cannot be attributed to any particular "speed" at all. The present seems to overexpand to include everything. But the linearity of the written text renders it incapable of holding all of these disparate elements together simultaneously, and thus we get a portrait whose lines run "in time" but whose images cannot possibly do justice to the interconnection LSD inaugurates:

> Valleys breathe, heaven and earth move together,
> daisies push inches of yellow air, vegetables tremble,
> grass shimmers green
> sheep speckle the mountainside, revolving their jaws with empty eyes,
> horses dance in the warm rain,
> tree-lined canals network live farmland,
> blueberries fringe stone walls on hawthorn'd hills,
> pheasants croak on meadows haired with fern—(*Collected Poems* 481)

This passage attempts to present something of the atemporal nature of "peak" moments during the LSD experience. There is certainly an abundance of movement, but at the same time a curious lack of causality. Despite the incessant "breathing" of the "valleys" and the "trembling" of the "vegetables," this parcel of countryside feels strangely divorced from teleological history. Ginsberg likewise avoids the cyclical imagery characteristic of much nature writing. There are no seasons, no seeds, no births, and no decay. We do not transcend, but merely exist a static moment that is nevertheless overflowing with flux. The content of Ginsberg's poem thus leaves the reader with a sense of time "standing still" even as elements within the poem vibrate with life. Yet one wonders if "Wales Visitation" has the formal impact that its imagery suggests. How can you write the feeling of timelessness when the act of writing itself places you squarely back into temporality?

The difficulty Ginsberg encountered in describing LSD sheds light on the limits to which drug temporality can be represented to another. Ginsberg's experience, however, highlights another limit that needs to be addressed when dealing with drug use—dependency. Ginsberg came to believe that he needed drugs in order to perform acts of consciousness-raising, even though they caused him to become physically ill. Deleuze and Guattari are equally aware of the dangers that drug use raises, and they ultimately remain skeptical about their utility: "The line of flight of drugs is constantly being segmentarized under the most rigid of forms, that of dependency, the hit and the dose, the dealer" (284). Imprisoned by the "hit and the dose," the addict spirals downward rather than upward; drug use leads to more drug use, not to a higher plane of understanding or a new "line of flight." This problem is acute in the Beat canon—witness the history of Burroughs's heroin addiction or Kerouac's untimely death due to alcoholism. Such examples lend credence to Deleuze and Guattari's ultimate announcement that drugs fall short of their emancipatory claims. As Deleuze and Guattari explain, "Instead of making a body without organs sufficiently rich or full for the passage of intensities, drug addicts erect a vitrified or emptied body, or a cancerous one" (285). The drugged body may open the user up to new "intensities," but the strict reliance on a chemical substance to effect this change leads to a circular pattern of use, withdrawal, and eventually death.

Despite these reservations, Deleuze and Guattari do not denigrate drug use entirely. Drugs can still show the way. What Deleuze and Guattari are looking for is the point where "drugs have sufficiently changed the general conditions of space and time perception so that nonusers can succeed in passing through the holes in the world" (286). And it is precisely here that Kerouac's and Ginsberg's writing has been successful. By shifting temporal perception through the written word, they have provided the "nonuser" with a means to experience the altered drug reality. This "nonuser" has acquired the insights to be gained from the drug but without facing the negative consequences of drug use that Deleuze and Guattari describe. Kerouac's and Ginsberg's audience is a step ahead. Rather than always starting "over again from ground zero," they are able to "start from the 'middle'" (Deleuze and Guattari 286). These works are thus a blueprint, a launching pad where the reader can shift her or his experience in a fundamental, bodily manner simply by opening a book. Where Henry Miller wanted to "succeed in getting drunk, but on pure water" (Deleuze and Guattari 286), Kerouac and Ginsberg actually achieve such ends, getting the reader "high" off the page.

Notes

1. Who gets to speak about drug use? Certainly not the addict, who is either busy satisfying his or her need for narcotics or repenting in an effort to avoid incarceration. Public rhetoric may have changed from the overly bombastic antidrug campaigns of the Reagan years to the "don't ask don't tell" election strategies of Clinton and Bush, but the notion of handling the question of drugs in an open, honest manner is tantamount to political suicide. And while the scientific community is invested in drug studies, gone are the days when such research meant controlled experiments with individual human subjects. When not in the service of pharmaceutical corporations, research in this field has come to mean highly specific neurological experiments on laboratory animals rather

than investigations of altered states of bodily consciousness. What is missing in all of these forays into the world of drugs is an interest in their possibilities for human existence.

2. Nomenclature creates some difficulty here. In "Sartre and Merleau-Ponty: A Reappraisal," Monika M. Langer explains the distinction between the "prereflective consciousness" and the "ego" that Jean-Paul Sartre describes in *The Transcendence of the Ego:* "In its primary mode (that is, as prereflective consciousness), consciousness is absolute, non-personal spontaneity. . . . The subject, or ego, on the contrary, is an object constituted and apprehended by reflective, or secondary, consciousness" (103). It is this "prereflective consciousness" that Kerouac labels the "subconscious" and that he is trying to tap.

3. This does not mean, of course, that the mind is elided. The point here is that the body should be given equal consideration when discussing the subjective experience of the drug state.

4. What is the exact nature of these "bodily properties" that allows this connection to be established? All of these manifestoes rely on the notion of "energy fields" developed by Alfred North Whitehead. As Charles Olson explains in his "Projective Verse" essay: "A poem is energy transferred from where the poet got it . . . by way of the poem itself to, all the way over to, the reader. Okay. Then the poem itself must, at all points, be a high-energy construct and, at all points, an energy-discharge" (148). Yet the dynamics of this transfer of energy need explication. Does the reader release the writer's latent energy during the act of reading? Or does the artistic work (re)direct the energy that the reader brings to the work?

5. According to Deleuze and Guattari, you never actually reach the "Body Without Organs," but "you are forever attaining it" (150). While the use of the term "limit" appears incongruous with these philosophers' insistence on experimentation and expansion, their deployment of the word circumscribes a space within which there remains infinite possibility. Just as "energy field" poetics bound the interpretive possibilities of a text without reducing it to one final meaning, the "Body Without Organs" seeks to create a bodily container that does not stifle change and adaptation.

6. William S. Burroughs's notion of "digging" is a bit more pejorative. In his introduction to the original *Junky,* Burroughs defines "to dig" as "to size up," a definition that implies an invidious distinction between self and other. In an essay dealing with Beat drug use, Burroughs is conspicuously absent. The reason for concentrating on Kerouac and Ginsberg instead of the more obvious choice of Burroughs is that Burroughs's drug of choice, "junk," is notoriously difficult to represent to another. As Burroughs himself has noted, he produced little while actually under the influence of this drug, and thus for the purposes of this study his contributions are minimal.

7. Culling examples from disparate sources of writing raises the question of genre distinctions. While a letter is not the same as a novel or poem, Beat works tend to conflate such distinctions, viewing all writing as equally literary. In her introduction to *Jack Kerouac: Selected Letters 1940–1956,* Ann Charters rightly observes that Kerouac's "let-

ters bring us closer to the life he actually lived before he turned it into literature" (xxi). Nevertheless, for purposes of exploring writing done under the influence of drugs, such distinctions are unproductive.

References

Belgrad, Daniel. *The Culture of Spontaneity: Improvisation and the Arts in Postwar America.* Chicago: University of Chicago Press, 1998.

Cassady, Neal. *The First Third.* San Francisco: City Lights, 1981.

Charters, Ann. Introduction to *Jack Kerouac: Selected Letters 1940–1956,* xxi–xxiv. New York: Penguin, 1995.

———. *Kerouac: A Biography.* New York: St. Martin's, 1973.

Deleuze, Gilles, and Félix Guattari. *A Thousand Plateaus: Capitalism and Schizophrenia.* Translated by B. Massumi. Minneapolis: University of Minnesota Press, 1987.

Doob, Leonard W. *Patterning of Time.* New Haven: Yale University Press, 1971.

Gale, Richard M. *The Philosophy of Time.* New York: Anchor, 1967.

Gifford, Barry, and Lawrence Lee. *Jack's Book: An Oral Biography of Jack Kerouac.* New York: St. Martin's, 1978.

Ginsberg, Allen. *Collected Poems, 1947–1980.* New York: Harper and Row, 1984.

———. "Improvised Poetics." In *Composed on the Tongue,* by Ginsberg. Bolinas, Calif.: Grey Fox, 1980.

———. Interview by Thomas Clark. In *Writers at Work: The Paris Review Interviews,* 3:279–320. New York: Viking, 1967.

———. "Notes Written on Finally Recording *Howl.*" In *On the Poetry of Allen Ginsberg,* edited by L. Hyde, 80–83. Ann Arbor: University of Michigan Press, 1984.

Hartocollis, Peter. *Time and Timelessness or the Varieties of Temporal Experience.* New York: International Universities Press, 1983.

Kerouac, Jack. "Essentials of Spontaneous Prose." In *Good Blonde & Others,* by Kerouac. San Francisco: Grey Fox, 1996.

———. *Jack Kerouac: Selected Letters 1940–1956,* ed. Ann Charters. New York: Penguin, 1995.

———. *On the Road.* New York: Penguin, 1976.

———. *The Subterraneans.* New York: Grove Weidenfeld, 1981.

———. *Visions of Cody.* New York: Penguin, 1993.

Langer, Monika M. "Sartre and Merleau-Ponty: A Reappraisal." In *The Debate between Sartre and Merleau-Ponty,* edited by J. Stewart, 93–117. Evanston, Ill.: Northwestern University Press, 1998.

McClure, Michael. *Scratching the Beat Surface: Essays on New Vision from Blake to Kerouac.* New York: Penguin, 1982.

Merleau-Ponty, Maurice. *Phenomenology of Perception.* Translated by Colin Smith. London: Routledge and Kegan Paul, 1962.

Olson, Charles. "Projective Verse." In *Poetics of the New American Poetry,* edited by Donald Merriam Allen and Warren Tallman, 147–58. New York: Grove, 1973.

Plummer, William. *The Holy Goof: A Biography of Neal Cassady.* New York: Paragon, 1990.

Portuges, Paul. *The Visionary Poetics of Allen Ginsberg.* Santa Barbara, Calif.: Ross-Erikson, 1978.

Schumacher, Michael. *Dharma Lion: A Biography of Allen Ginsberg.* New York: St. Martin's, 1992.

GENIUS ALL THE TIME

The Beats, Spontaneous Presence, and Primordial Ground

Marc Olmsted

The Beat literary movement cannot be understood in the fullest sense without some examination of Buddhism, particularly in the forms that were available to these mystinauts: explorers of mind and beyond mind to the nature of awareness itself. The poet Anne Waldman, commenting on what constitutes "Beat," perceives "an as-yet unacknowledged body of uniquely articulated and salutary 'dharma poetics'—that derives from Buddhist psychology and philosophy" (Waldman 2009, 164–65). Following Waldman's thinking, one can conclude that the Beat literary movement involved a sacred worldview linked with the aspiration to actualize compassionate and empathetic conduct, an intuitive Tantric Buddhism. While it is Zen Buddhism that is most frequently, and legitimately, associated with the Beat movement prior to the 1960s and 1970s, both Zen and Tantric Buddhism share many philosophical parallels. Simply stated, their highest views regard "enlightenment" as already completely and unshakably present (if obscured), to be realized, rather than polished into existence.

Grasping the connections between Tantric Buddhism and Beat practices can help one understand why the Beat movement continues to draw individuals interested in answering life's Big Questions. The attraction of the philosophy and practice of Tantric Buddhism to many of the Beats lies in Buddhism's exploration of the nature of awareness. As just mentioned, Tantric Buddhism also presents a sacred view of the phenomenal world itself coupled with a deep empathy for all sentient beings that occupy it. Many in the Beat literary movement explored this sacred view with the same empathy or compassion that Tantric Buddhism embodies. But perhaps what is most significant is the light that the Tantric notion of enlightenment sheds on one of the Beat principles of creativity: spontaneity. Indeed, an interesting parallel exists between Buddhist spiritual practice and Beat creative writing. "Mind is shapely, art is shapely" Kerouac said (Kerouac 1992, ii).[1] If the mind is mindful, the art will be mindful—or, in the highest philosophical context of Tantric Buddhism, one just needs to recognize that the mind is already "shapely"; in other words, unclouded awareness itself is naturally mindful, so art is spontaneously "accurate."

There is within Buddhism, and certainly Tantric Buddhism, a place for discipline within spontaneity, or a training that allows spontaneity to surface in a naturally perfected and elegant fashion. Clear mind produces clear art, even if it is the clarity of witnessing the derangement of the senses that, for instance, Arthur Rimbaud pursued. Mind is clear because it is penetrating, not because it is logical or linear. To align oneself by meditation practice can increase awareness of the moment of inspiration. Allen Ginsberg called it "Surprise mind" (Ginsberg 1998, 197), or the mind's ability to surprise the artist with sudden unexpected juxtapositions, such as the surprise of a phrase like "hydrogen jukebox" in "Howl." Trungpa Rinpoche referred to the phenomenon as "magic" or "the total appreciation of chance" (Ginsberg 1998, 197). Expounding on the metaphor, Ginsberg defined magic as "the total delight in accident, the total pleasure of surprise mind, the appreciation of the fact that the mind changes, that one perception leads to another, and that it in itself is a great play of mind. You don't have to go further in order to create a work of art" (Ginsberg 2000, 272). This philosophy of mind, as espoused by Tantric Buddhism, allows the writer to respect the freshness of a first draft and reconsider "mistakes" as *not* accidental.

The earliest origins of Tantric Buddhism, called Vajrayana or "Diamond Vehicle" (or today, often just "Tibetan") are particularly sketchy, since virtually nothing about Tantric Buddhism was written down for hundreds of years from its appearance. According to Tibetan devotional history, Shakyamuni Buddha is said to have begun the teachings of Buddhist Tantra. Its first recorded example stands at the third century C.E. This same history records Buddha also prophesying that another would come and finish what he had barely started. This prophecy is believed only by adherents of Tantric Buddhism, most believing this "other" to be Padmasambhava, an Indian Tantric Buddhist master who established these practices in eighth-century C.E. Tibet. Again, according to devotional history, he is another form of Buddha himself. We know that Tantric Buddhism began in India. Some Buddhists say it influenced the rise of Hindu Tantrism, while Hindu Tantric scholars say the opposite.[2] The word *tantra* itself means *continuity* and refers to the inseparability of the so-called secular world, or world of ignorance, with wisdom and enlightenment. In particular, the emotional poisons of grasping, aggression, and ignorance can actually be brought to the path. Unfortunately, Tantra is now often equated with sexual gymnastics and extended orgasm, but this is a degraded view.

An in-depth discussion of Hindu and Buddhist expressions of Tantra are beyond the scope of this essay, but a brief examination of some significant differences between Hindu and Buddhist thought will facilitate our discussion of Beat Buddhist poetics. Most of these differences can be traced directly to the Pali Canon, a collection of the historical Buddha's teachings recognized by all Buddhists internationally. First, Buddha radically proclaimed *anatta*, which means no atman (soul) or fixed reference of any kind. Second, a creator god was at the very least not a significant issue to entertain. In later written texts from the Mahayana Buddhist tradition (although still attributed to oral teachings of Shakyamuni Buddha in devotional history), such a god was not even regarded as a source of phenomena, for not only was the self regarded as empty, but everything else was as well. Mahayana refers to the "Greater Vehicle" expanding on the Pali Canon, referred to in context as "Lesser Vehicle," or Hinayana, of which Theravada is now the major historical survivor. Both Hindu and Mahayana Buddhist traditions regard the world as like a dream, but drastically depart on who is dreaming it: Hindu deity or one's own mind? Buddhism is unequivocally nontheist. Tantric Buddhism went even further and said the world of form is as sacred as the formless clear open space of the emptiness that is its essence (Dudjom 2009). Appearance is the empty display or "luminosity" of this formless essence.

Chögyam Trungpa Rinpoche, a Tibetan teacher central to Ginsberg's post-1970 work, emphasized being present in one's body, and not attempting to stay high in some psychedelic heaven.[3] Being nontheistic, Trungpa did not so much deny God as deny the individual ego as perceiver of God. In short, the entire issue was moot as long as there was an ego or self attempting to find God.

This nontheist, non-fixed-referential view by its very nature "cuts through spiritual materialism," that is, pursuit of a high as a spiritual antidote that is doomed because this pursuit stems from and reinforces the very craving that has created the illusion of a separate self in the first place. *Cutting through Spiritual Materialism* is, in fact, the title of a series of published talks given by Chögyam Trungpa Rinpoche (who invented this phrase).

The poetry of the mature and spiritually trained Ginsberg shows this influence, exemplified by this passage from the poem "Why I Meditate," dated July 10, 1981:

> I sit because No because
> I sit because I was unable to trace the Unborn back to the womb
> ·
> I sit because I had a vision also dropped LSD
> I sit because I don't know what else to do like Peter Orlovsky (Ginsberg
>   2006, 851)

These lines reveal Ginsberg taking an objectivist perspective—not trying to describe the ineffable but focused instead on the immediate physical reality.

Trungpa Rinpoche suggested the standard breath meditation practice of "calm abiding" as a method to eventually slow down the strobing of thoughts to the point that the gap between them spontaneously stood out and revealed that there were "thoughts without a thinker," as Mark Epstein titled his book on the practice, that is, that there is no solid entity having these thoughts: The belief in a solid thinking entity is the core illusion that causes suffering, the First Noble Truth of Buddhism. In Ginsberg's poetry, the formal training of "calm abiding" breath awareness that he would later undertake with Trungpa Rinpoche is presaged in the following passage from "From Haiku" written in 1955: "Lying on my side / in the void: / the breath in my nose" (Ginsberg 2006, 137). It's likely that Ginsberg may have recalled this expression from a December 1954 letter he received from Kerouac, which he quotes in "Kerouac, Catholicism, Buddhism": "Then you think, 'there is breathing in, there is breathing out,' and soon essential mind will begin to shine." Ginsberg further remarks that when he later reexamined this letter, "I hadn't realized but he [Kerouac] apparently has some idea of sitting, probably from reading" (Corso, Ginsberg, and Holmes 2009, 94).

The practice of sitting leads to realization, and what interested a number of Beat writers is the fact that there is a specific model of Tantric Buddhist realization or enlightenment, similar to Zen, that can be glimpsed again and again, and stabilized with formal practice, a training undertaken in various degrees by Ginsberg, Diane di Prima, Michael McClure, Gary Snyder, and Philip Whalen. An intuited understanding of such practice can also be found in the work of Kerouac and Burroughs. In his praise of Jack Kerouac's *Mexico City Blues,* for instance, Trungpa called Kerouac's spontaneous notations a "great exposition of mind" (Ginsberg 1994b, 14). Whalen, both a Zen master and a poet, used similar language to describe the philosophical foundation of his poetics: "My writing is a picture of the mind moving" (Ginsberg 1998, 197). This exposition of mind is a critical concept when examining the Beat fusion of life and art. Ginsberg, for instance, credited a conversation with Trungpa Rinpoche for his now-famous maxim "First thought, best thought." However, the idea was suggested earlier by Jack Kerouac and even earlier by William Blake, giving credence to the literary lineage of a core Tantric Buddhism principle. Consider, for example, the following declarations:

First thought is best in Art, second in other matters.—William Blake (Ginsberg 1998, 197)

If you don't stick with what you first thought, and to the words the thoughts brought, what's the sense of bothering with it anyway, what's the sense of foisting your little lies on others?—Jack Kerouac (Kerouac 2009, 1)

If you stick with the first flashes, then you're all right. But the problem is, how do you get to that first thought—that's always the problem. The first thought is always the great elevated, cosmic, noncosmic shunyata [emptiness] thought. And then, at least according to the Buddhist formulation, after that you begin imposing names and forms and all that. So it's a question of catching yourself at your first open thought.—Allen Ginsberg (Ginsberg 1980, 117)

Richard Modiano, in "First Thought, Best Thought," a March 2008 editorial that he wrote for poetix.net, lucidly explicates the expression: "This expression is often misunderstood to mean first word, best word by people who believe that thoughts and words are one and the same. Behind first thought, best thought stands a particular epistemology. It's based on a specific practice of observing the rise and fall of thoughts as they occur moment by moment, called by Buddhists *shamatha-vipashyana* in some traditions and *zazen* in others. . . . Practice will reveal that thoughts are not simply words but images and emotions, so to capture that first thought is to be aware of the image/emotion in all its starkness." Ginsberg's own thinking on the approach echoes this epistemological view: He said that it was acceptable to cut, even tinker slightly, in cases where a more specific image, for example, "blue jay" rather than "bird," might strengthen the writing, but the point was to preserve the organic quality (unpublished transcript). So, the "first thought, best thought" summation of spontaneous composition that Kerouac and Ginsberg popularized rests on a down-to-earth, immediate element, but it also points to a Tantric Buddhist view, shared with Zen, that enlightenment already exists. To some extent, there is also a parallel with the Christian maxim "Be still and know" (Old Testament, King James, Psalm 46:10), in the sense of surrendering to a primordial power beyond ego, a beyond within that is here now.

Another Tantric Buddhism principle that was both intuited and embraced by the Beats—and, again, shared with Zen Buddhism—is the notion of the Divine Madman. The drunken saint and the sensuous, earthy Zorba the Greek yogi repeatedly occur in both Buddhist historical canons, where "zen lunatic" and "crazy wisdom"[4] are recurrent phrases. However, what distinguishes them from a hedonistic view is their appreciation without grasping, their lack of attachment that allows sex, alcohol, and passion itself to actually become vehicles for realization. Both Zen and Tantric Buddhist traditions also have their austere monks, but sometimes austerity and wildness find themselves in the same historical personage. Notably, we have multiple accounts of Kerouac's attempts at self-denial as well as his formal embracing of the long, rigorous, and boring practice of sitting, which Ginsberg, Snyder, Whalen, di Prima, and Waldman all practiced under Suzuki Roshi and/or Trungpa Rinpoche, the practice in direct defiance of the need for entertainment or concept-driven revelation.

Even William S. Burroughs pursued the larger intellectual examination of addiction beyond merely heroin, the "algebra of need" itself, a regimen that Ginsberg often called Burroughs's "homemade yankee tantra." Burroughs's approach to Buddhism was complicated, if not seemingly ambivalent, but his letters reveal that he studied Tibetan Buddhism, and in 1954 he recommended to Kerouac that he do the same (Burroughs 1993, 222). In a later letter dated August 18 of that year, while not disavowing Buddhism entirely, he concluded that "Buddhism is only for the West to *study* as *history,* that is, it is a subject for *understanding,* and yoga can profitably be practiced to that end. But it is not, for the West, *An Answer,* not *A Solution*" (Burroughs 1993, 226). His later friendship with Trungpa Rinpoche, even undertaking a solitary retreat in 1975, without his typewriter per Trungpa's instructions, does, however, show a willingness to investigate this further (Burroughs 1976), and his literary practices functioned to effect detach-

ment. For instance, at the end of the 1950s, Burroughs began experimenting with the cut-up method, razoring his and others' texts and rearranging
the sections to get phrases like "dead fingers talk" (Burroughs 2000, 179),
and in the process, Burroughs began to believe that he was cutting through
his own conditioning. In a 1961 letter that he wrote to Ginsberg, Burroughs
explained his process of detachment from the notion of a self:

> I am not talking mystical "greater awareness." I mean complete alert
> awareness at all times of what is in front of you. LOOK OUT NOT
> IN. No talking to SO CALLED SELF. NO "INTROSPECTION."
> Eyes off that navel. LOOK OUT TO SPACE. This means kicking
> ALL HABITS. Word HABIT. SELF HABIT. BODY HABIT. Kick-
> ing junk [a] breeze in comparison. Total awareness = Total pain =
> CUT. (Miles 2000, 240)

Ginsberg later remarked about Burroughs that "he emptied his soul out and
entered at last the open blue space of 'Benevolent indifferent attentiveness'
characteristic of later phases of his art" (Burroughs 1982, 7).

As with every mystical tradition, Tantric Buddhism is no stranger to
the vision and the revelation, but the practice recognizes these as having no
inherent external existence separate from awareness itself. With respect to
Beat writers, one of the more interesting accounts of the visionary experience is Ginsberg's well-known Blakean visions, which John Clellon Holmes
recorded in the first Beat novel, *Go!*, in 1952. In brief, Ginsberg, after mas-
turbating and drowsing off one leisurely afternoon, suddenly heard Blake's
voice reading "Ah Sunflower." Ginsberg himself explained the Blake vision
at length in a 1966 *Paris Review* interview: "and simultaneous to the voice
there was also an emotion, risen in my soul in response to the voice, and
a sudden *visual* realization of the same awesome phenomena. That is to
say, looking out at the window, through the window at the sky, suddenly it
seemed that I saw into the depths of the universe, by looking simply into
the ancient sky. The sky suddenly seemed very *ancient*" (Ginsberg 2001,
17). How did he know it was Blake? It seemed like Blake and was followed
by an epiphany, a non-drug-induced psychedelic experience in which the
cityscape of Harlem lit up with a vibrant and near-microscopic detail. The
experience reoccurred two more times in the same week, once in a bookstore with the same sudden psychedelic brilliance and later on the Columbia
University campus, where the Creator-God seemed to be present as a sinis-

ter, even alien, being who threatened to devour the young poet. After that, Ginsberg turned away from his expanded awareness in a kind of recoiling horror: "And I had a sense of the black sky coming down to eat me. It was like meeting Yamantaka without preparation, meeting one of the horrific or wrathful deities without any realization that it was a projection of myself, or my nature, and I tried to shut off the experience because it was too frightening" (Ginsberg 1994b, 15).

Despite the horrific nature of this visionary experience, he continued his pilgrimage over the years, reading D. T. Suzuki in the early and mid-1950s—he would later visit Suzuki with Kerouac and Peter Orlovsky in 1958 (Fields 1992, 223)—and studying Chinese and Japanese Buddhist painting at the Metropolitan Museum of Art in New York City. He exchanged many letters with Kerouac about Buddhism from 1954 on, his interest at this point appearing largely intellectual, as the following dialogue between the fictionalized Ray Smith (Kerouac) and Alvah Goldbrook (Ginsberg) in *The Dharma Bums* suggests:

> "Well" (sigh), "as for me, I'm just going to go on being Alvah Goldbrook and to hell with all this Buddhist bullshit."
> "You'll be sorry some day. . . . There is no me, no airplane, no mind, no Princess, no nothing, you for krissakes do you want to go on being fooled every damn minute of your life?"
> "Yes, that's all I want, I thank God that something has come out of nothing."
> (Kerouac 1959, 28–29)

By the 1960s, however, he pursued the same experience of expanded awareness with a variety of psychedelic drugs. In 1960, on *yagé* (ayahuasca) in the Amazon, that same sinister God seemed present again: "I began to get high—then the whole fucking Cosmos broke loose around me, I think the strongest and worst I ever had it nearly—(I still reserve the Harlem experience, being Natural, in abeyance)" (Burroughs and Ginsberg 2006, 60). Two years later, a holy man in India told him, "Take Blake for your guru" (Ginsberg 1996a, 3). But it wasn't until that same year in India when he met His Holiness Dudjom Rinpoche, head of the Nyingma School of Tibetan Buddhism, and asked him what to do about the bad drug trips that he kept having that he received sustainable wisdom: "If you see something horrible, don't cling to it. If you see something beautiful, don't cling to it," was

Dudjom Rinpoche's nonjudgmental advice (Ginsberg 1994b, 54). Ginsberg remembered this advice all his life as extremely significant, that is, beyond drugs to an application to phenomena and thought itself. In his poem "The Change: Kyoto-Tokyo Express," written as he returned from India in 1963, he declared his need to return to his own body rather than transcend it: "Come, sweet lonely Spirit, back / to your bodies . . . / . . . Till my turn comes and I / enter that maw" (Ginsberg 2006, 336). This foreshadowed his formal Buddhist sitting practice begun under Trungpa's mentoring in the early 1970s.

Ginsberg's pilgrimage to India[5] was echoed by those of many backpacking youths in the years to come. The endless Kerouacian road now circled the globe, although it must be noted that Kerouac never traveled to India. Still, it was a "rucksack revolution" that both *On the Road* and *The Dharma Bums* helped to ignite. As a result of easily rubbing shoulders with Hindu and Tibetan Buddhist masters, many spiritual seekers, like Ginsberg, would soon expand the alternative Beat culture's philosophical paradigm far beyond the influence of a mostly book-learned Japanese Zen. The increasing use of LSD also made the counterculture zeitgeist of the Beats morph into the hippies, and by the beginning of the 1970s, Tibetan Buddhist teachers were exploring America with the help of some of its world-traveling prodigal students. Ginsberg and Snyder did a benefit for Tharthang Tulku's Nyingma Institute in Berkeley, and Ginsberg himself became involved in formal study with Chögyam Trungpa Rinpoche, as did di Prima and Waldman. Zen students found great parallels and insights in the highest philosophical view of Tibet's Maha-Ati and Mahamudra teaching, and Tibetan Buddhism itself soon was a major influence on American Buddhist students, even if they did not directly embrace it.

Allen Ginsberg's immersion in Tibetan Buddhism led him to create a thesis that combined literary history with Buddhist philosophy to make a case for a lineage of aesthetic and philosophical choices. Ginsberg saw this aesthetic as a writing heritage that includes Beat writers such as Kerouac, Snyder, Whalen, di Prima, and Burroughs, predating them to the objectivist concerns of William Carlos Williams, the visionary romanticism of Blake, all the way back through the spontaneous song-poems of the Tibetan saint Milarepa in the eleventh century C.E. to the cave shaman origins of language and expression itself. In short, it was his own unified field theory that combined everything that made him the poet he finally became.

Critical to this field are the Tantric terms Ground, Path, and Fruition, which Ginsberg used to examine and teach the process of writing, noted particularly in his "Mind Writing Slogans," a collection of quotations already cited here that not only includes the Beat and Buddhist sources, such as Zen koans, Trungpa, and Gelek Rinpoche, but also Frank Lloyd Wright and Plotinus.[6] These slogans essentially align the Tantric terms and composition processes as follows:

> Ground / Inspiration
> Path / Writing Process
> Fruition / Manuscript (including its impact on or perception by the
>   reader).

Ground can be understood as the foundation or source of inspiration, but here one must recognize that Ground is beyond any notion of conceptual or rational mind. It is *Big Sky Mind,* as the Buddhist magazine *Tricycle* chose to call its collection of Beat and Buddhist poems published in 1995. This origin of inspiration, primordial in nature, is without beginning: It is not only before the first dot on paper, but it is also before the paper itself. *Awareness* is probably a less confusing term than *mind* for an analogue of Ground.

The following classical Tibetan poem by Longchenpa may best present the concept of Ground with which Ginsberg worked. Note that the "I" of the text refers to Primordial Awareness itself, Kuntazangpo, a device used in contrast to sentient beings, not a giant Self or God:

> All that is has me—universal creativity, pure and total
>   presence—as its root.
> How things appear is my being.
> How things arise is my manifestation. (Longchenpa 2000, 32)

Not only is the self an illusion, but perception of an outside world as real is also an illusion. In fact, it is empty of any actual substance, apparent but non-existent, like a mirage. There is no ghost in the machine running the show. There is no creator God. Instead, we created the world, we dreamt it, and are dreaming it in karmic agreement. Kerouac expressed this understanding in a short poem: "Mind alone / Introduced the bone" (Kerouac 1997, 229), and in philosophical concert, a fourteenth-century-c.e. Tibetan, Rigdzin Godemchen (literally "Vulture Quilled Awareness Holder"), rendered no solid self and no independently existing world as follows: "May grasping at what seems outer—appearance—be purified. / May fixation on what seems inner—mind's nature—be liberated. / May what lies in the gap—Clear Light—be self-aware" (Zangpo 2002, 237).[7] Rigdzin Godemchen said this came to him as *terma*, that is, from a visionary Padmasambhava.

The first step in this realization is mindfulness, known in Sanskrit as *shamatha*, which means "calm abiding." Buddha pointed out that thoughts strobe so quickly that the sense of a solid self is created much like the spinning spokes of a wagon wheel appear like a solid surface. *Shamatha* slows down the wheel, and the awareness of gaps between thoughts eventually leads to the insight that even the seeming "one who watches" is also without solidity, the insight known as *vipashyana*. The point is not the silence between thoughts, but the awareness of that silence. The goal is not to achieve a blank state, for nonconceptual awareness is present whether there is thought or not. The trick, so to speak, is waking to that awareness, that "essence self-known." The terms *shamatha* and *vipashyana* exist in all three vehicles, or *yanas,* of Buddhism, with corresponding shifts of emphasis on self and perception of phenomena. In the highest view of Tantric Buddhism, waking to the Ground is the Path itself.

In Ginsberg's poetics, the second term, Path, is the process of poetic composition. There are guidelines to this "path" or process, and most revolve around recording the specifics of what is seen, heard, or felt. In a 1999 interview with *Poetry Flash,* Philip Whalen expressed this process through a recollection of hanging out with Kerouac in San Francisco:

> So we would go off into the wild sweet bop neon American Night, run around North Beach, and hang out in Chinatown. And, we'd be out running around, and he'd be writing in his notebook. He was very perceptive. He saw lots of things. His eyes were real good, which mine are not.
>
> But he told me, he said it was out walking with [William Carlos] Williams in Rutherford, and Williams pointed out to him that there was moss growing on the underside of the railroad tracks. And he thought that was kind of wonderful. (Meltzer 1999, 2)

This moment of literary history is a sort of objectivist transmission from Williams to Kerouac, which leads to Ginsberg. It's a process of recognition that can really be the marrow of a great poem, a kind of snapshot precision that recognizes and foregrounds that which to others remains invisible or is erased through editing. Referencing Kerouac as his teacher, Ginsberg remarked in the *Paris Review* article "The Craft of Poetry: A Semester with Allen Ginsberg" by Elissa Schapell that "if the poem, the original skeleton of the poem, retains its integrity, that's it" (Schapell 1995, 135). He acknowledged that he didn't feel as sure of himself as did Kerouac, who came to eschew major revisions, but added that while he didn't "feel the same absoluteness, or courage," he liked that quality in Kerouac: "And what *is* the first thought? The first thought isn't necessarily the first thought you notice. It's the first thought you sub-notice. People edit their awareness of what is underneath their minds," he explained (Schapell 1995, 135). The poet attempts to describe in words the thought in all its vivid particulars, which may involve rewriting in order to retain the originating insight. The point is trust, or confidence that something greater than ego is in operation.

In this process, ordinary moments contain infinity because they are so profoundly and perfectly what is—like a Blakean visionary moment,[8] or as Ginsberg noted by quoting Gustave Flaubert to explain the context of William Carlos Williams's "red wheel barrow," "The ordinary is the extraordinary" (Ginsberg 2000, 269). In other words, everything depends on Williams's "red wheel barrow" because nothing depends on it. Ginsberg tried to honor that picture of the moving mind by not rewriting a text into Apollonian extinction.

The final component of Ginsberg's Tantric Buddhist approach to poetics, Fruition, can be understood as the unobstructed energy of Ground's Realization, often corresponded with Compassion, Conduct, or Action. Ginsberg himself spoke indirectly of this third element in an unpublished letter written to me in June 1994. Referring to Gelek Rinpoche, who had become his teacher after Trungpa's death in 1987, he candidly remarked: "My own practice very lax tho I see Gelek Rinpoche & trust in him—he tells me keep public, keep writing & giving readings—I seem to be causing some lucidity or joy, but don't know how or karmic why, so I do as I'm told by Rinpoche." Ginsberg wondered why he was going to such effort to archive his own work and statements when the possibility of there even being an intact civilization to receive them in one hundred years was hardly guaranteed. Gelek Rinpoche, who had become his teacher after Trungpa's death in 1987, was telling him that the main point was the benefit he brought, however long that would last, in the grand scheme of things.

In other words, as Gelek Rinpoche stated, "to diminish the mass of human and sentient sufferings" (Ginsberg 1998, 201), or as Ginsberg put it:

"The only thing that can save the world is the reclaiming of the awareness of the world. That's what poetry does" (Ginsberg 2001, 173). In 1986, he maintained this belief in slightly different language: "The purpose of art is to provide relief from your own paranoia and the paranoia of others. You write to relieve the pain of others, to free them from the self-doubt generated by a society where everyone is conniving and manipulating" (Raskin 2004, xvi).

As for the manuscript, the chapbook, the webzine, that which is the physical product of the composition process, Ginsberg believed that "poetry can stand out as the one beacon of sanity: a beacon of individual clarity, and lucidity in every direction—whether on the Internet or in coffee houses or university forums or classrooms. Poetry, along with its old companion, music, becomes one mean of communication that is not controlled by the establishment" (Brame 1996).

This is a sentiment that Ginsberg had already summed up in his poem "Memory Gardens," written on the occasion of Kerouac's funeral in 1969:

Well while I'm here I'll
do the work—
and what's the Work?
To ease the pain of living.
Everything else, drunken
dumbshow. (Ginsberg 2006, 542)

The Ground, Path, and Fruit are themselves concisely summed up at the end of a *terma* from H. H. Dudjom Rinpoche: "The essence is original purity beyond rational mind. / The inherent nature is spontaneously self-existing supreme awareness. / Compassionate responsiveness arises as manifold clouds. / May there be the auspiciousness of supreme bliss" (Dudjom 1994, 29–30). The Tibetan word translated as "spontaneously" here, *lhundrup*, is sometimes defined as "spontaneous presence," the nature of the Ground.

Thus, in the end, the poet fulfills the efforts to communicate simply by either sending out the manuscript or self-publishing, the compassionate fruit of inspiration, risen from the ground of primordial awareness and its path of mindfully recorded spontaneity.

Notes

Nancy M. Grace, Virginia Myers Professor of English at the College of Wooster in

Wooster, Ohio, contributed invaluable editorial services to this essay. A deep Buddhist bow of respect.

1. Ginsberg also used the phrase "Art is shapely, Mind is shapely," uncredited as a title of a flyer for San Francisco Poetry Center in 1959 ("Poetics: Mind Is Shapely, Art Is Shapely" [1959], in *Deliberate Prose*). But more often, he attributes to it to Kerouac (both in the introduction cited and in other interviews, as noted by Peter Hale of the Allen Ginsberg Trust), and in 1974, he describes it as something they both "cooked up" ("Towards a New American Poetics," Michael Goodwin et al., in *Spontaneous Poetics*).

2. Herbert Guenther points out that Vedanta, which some say was a response to Tantric Buddhism, still refers to "One," rather than the nondual "zero" language of Buddhism (Guenther and Trungpa 1975, 76).

3. *Allen Ginsberg's Buddhist Poetics,* by Tony Trigilio, also examines Ginsberg's relation with Trungpa Rinpoche and Tantric Buddhism. This essay takes a different approach.

4. *Crazy Wisdom* is a published title of lectures given by Trungpa Rinpoche, who popularized this particular translation of the Tibetan phrase *yeshe cholwa*.

5. Besides the aforementioned *Allen Ginsberg's Buddhist Poetics* by Trigilio, Deborah Baker's *A Blue Hand: The Beats in India* has also examined Tantric Buddhism and the Beats, but it is not a source text for this essay.

6. The slogans first appeared in *What Book!?,* edited by Gary Gach, and not in any primary text of Ginsberg's.

7. This verse has been slightly retranslated from the Tibetan root text here to follow points made by Longchenpa and Dudjom Rinpoche. Ngawang Zangpo has approved our retranslation.

8. In Vajrayana Buddhism, the notion of Sacred View is in many ways similar to Blake's proclamation that if man cleansed "the doors of perception," he would perceive things as infinite (Blake 1958, 101). Again, though, the notion of Sacred View does not include an independent Viewer or an independent object of that View.

References

Blake, William. 1958. *William Blake.* London: Penguin.

Brame, Gloria G. 1996. "An Interview with Poet Allen Ginsberg." *ELF: Eclectic Literary Forum* (Summer). http://gloria-brame.com/glory/ginsberg.htm#elf.html.

Burroughs, William. 1976. *Retreat Diaries.* New York: City Moon.

——. 1982. *Letters to Allen Ginsberg.* New York: Full Court.

——. 1993. *The Letters of William S. Burroughs, 1945–1959.* Edited by Oliver Harris. New York: Viking.

——. 2000. *Word Virus: The William Burroughs Reader.* Edited by James Grauerholz. New York: Grove.

Burroughs, William, and Allen Ginsberg. 2006. *Yage Letters Redux*. San Francisco: City Lights.

Corso, G., A. Ginsberg, and J. C. Holmes. 2009. "Kerouac, Catholicism, Buddhism." In *Beats at Naropa*, edited by Anne Waldman and Laura Wright. Minneapolis: Coffee House.

Dogen, Eihei. 1995. *Moon in a Dewdrop: Writings of Zen Master Dogen*. San Francisco: North Point.

Dudjom, Jigral Yeshe. 1992. *Dudjom Tersar Ngondro*. New York: Yeshe Melong.

——. 1994. *Heart-Essence of the Lake-Born*. Corralitos: Vajrayana Foundation.

——. 2009. "Dzogchen View of Ngondro." jnanasukha.org.

Epstein, Mark. 2004. *Thoughts without a Thinker: Psychotherapy from a Buddhist Perspective*. New York: Basic.

Fields, Rick. 1992. *When the Swans Came to the Lake*. Boulder: Shambhala.

Ginsberg, Allen. 1976. "This Is Allen Ginsberg?" *New Age Journal*, April 22–28.

——. 1980. *Composed on the Tongue*. Bolinas: Grey Fox.

——. 1994a. Letter to Marc Olmsted, June 22.

——. 1994b. "Vomit of a Mad Tyger." *Shambhala Sun*, July, 14–23, 54–55.

——. 1996a. *Indian Journals*. San Francisco: City Lights.

——. 1996b. Unpublished transcript, tape recording, November 17, 1996, Grant Plaza Hotel, San Francisco.

——. 1998. "Mind Writing Slogans." In *What Book!? Buddha Poems from Beat to Hiphop*. Edited by Gary Gach. Berkeley: Parallax.

——. 2000. *Deliberate Prose: Selected Essays 1952–1995*. New York: HarperCollins.

——. 2001. *Spontaneous Mind: Selected Interviews, 1958–1996*. New York: HarperCollins.

——. 2006. *Collected Poems*. New York: HarperCollins.

Guenther, Herbert, and Chögyam Trungpa. 1975. *Dawn of Tantra*. Boulder: Shambhala.

Holmes, John Clellon. 2002. *Go: A Novel*. New York: Thunder's Mouth.

Kerouac, Jack. 1959. *Dharma Bums*. New York: Signet.

——. 1977. *Heaven & Other Poems*. San Francisco: Grey Fox.

——. 1992. *Pomes All Sizes*. San Francisco: City Lights.

——. 1997. *Some of the Dharma*. New York: Viking.

——. 2001. *Old Angel Midnight*. San Francisco: Grey Fox.

——. 2009. *You're a Genius All the Time*. San Francisco: Chronicle.

Lao Tzu. 2003. *Tao Te Ching: The Definitive Edition*. New York: Tarcher.

Longchenpa. 2000. *You Are the Eyes of the World*. Ithaca: Snow Lion.

Meltzer, David. 1999. "Whatnot: A Talk with Philip Whalen." *Poetry Flash* 282 (August–September): 1–5.

Miles, Barry. 2000. *The Beat Hotel: Ginsberg, Burroughs, and Corso in Paris, 1958–1963*. New York: Grove.

Modiano, Richard. 2008. "First Thought, Best Thought." http://whisperdownthewritealley.wordpress.com.

Morgan, Bill. 2007. *I Celebrate Myself: The Somewhat Private Life of Allen Ginsberg.* New York: Penguin.

Raskin, Jonah. 2004. *American Scream: Allen Ginsberg's Howl and the Making of the Beat Generation.* Berkeley and Los Angeles: University of California Press.

Schapell, Elissa. 1995. "The Craft of Poetry: A Semester with Allen Ginsberg." *Paris Review* 135 (Summer): 212–57.

Schumacher, Michael. 1992. *Dharma Lion: A Critical Biography of Allen Ginsberg.* New York: St. Martin's.

Trungpa, Chögyam. 1992. *Transcending Madness.* Boulder: Shambhala.

Waldman, Anne. 2009. "Tendrel: A Meeting of Minds." In *Beats at Naropa,* edited by Anne Waldman and Laura Wright. Minneapolis: Coffee House.

Zangpo, Ngawang. 2002. *Guru Rinpoche: His Life & Times.* Ithaca, N.Y.: Snow Lion.

Spontaneity, Immediacy, and Difference

Philosophy, Being in Time, and Creativity in the Aesthetics
of Jack Kerouac, Charles Olson, and John Cage

David Need

> Time present and time past
> Are both perhaps present in time future
> And time future contained in time past.
> If all time is eternally present
> All time is unredeemable.
> What might have been is an abstraction
> Remaining a perpetual possibility
> Only in a world of speculation.
> What might have been and what has been
> Point to one end, which is always present.
>
> —T. S. Eliot, *Four Quartets*

At the outset of *The Four Quartets* (1936) quoted above, T. S. Eliot takes up
the possibility that the problem of historical conditioning (the limits placed
on human freedom/being by history) might be resolved by drawing a contrast between a processual, which is a historical mode of being limned as
"time present and time past," and a unitive present. This is thought of as "the
still point of the turning world" without which "there would be no dance"
even though "there is only the dance."[1] Although this moment precedes
postwar thematization of immediacy under the tropes of spontaneity and
the popular call to "be here now," the text provides evidence that the new
emphasis on spontaneous praxis in the work of a range of artists was not

simply an expressionist response to the violence of World War II. Rather, this new aesthetic program consistently carried forward an ongoing attempt to address the post-Enlightenment articulation of historical consciousness as a limit condition for awareness and identity.

In what follows, I explore what I call the schematization of being in time in the work of three artists—the writers Jack Kerouac and Charles Olson, and the composer John Cage—all of whom are thought of as introducing foundational frameworks for an emerging aesthetics of spontaneity and immediacy. In each case, I explore the debts the artist owes to one or another of the early-twentieth-century philosophical schemas that directly thematize an account of being in relation to successive moments of time. These include the use Kerouac made of the philosophical/historical schema laid out in Oswald Spengler's *Decline of the West,* Charles Olson's adaptation of key structures and terms used by Alfred North Whitehead in the elaboration of his metaphysics, the influence of the Perennialist philosophy and Vedanta-based aesthetics of Ananda Coomaraswamy on John Cage's understanding of silence as deep measure.

The aim of this essay is to suggest that there are important differences with respect to the ways in which these artists conceptualized the position of the human being in time and that these differences lead to different understandings of the nature and virtues of immediacy and spontaneity. These differences are rooted in their respective philosophical influences and are, in the end, different kinds of arguments about the kinds of freedom one finds in what Eliot called the still point of the present. In delineating influence and borrowing, I have chosen not to address either the truth claims made by a given philosopher or the fidelity of the artist to the philosophical concepts that influenced their compositions or their own versions of such concepts, an undertaking beyond the scope of this forum.

By first exploring the relationship between philosophical discourses and theories of creativity in Kerouac, Olson, and Cage, I aim to show how the differences between their sources and influences lead to very different conceptions of what is at stake in a moment of creative expression. Making sense of these differences allows us to better assess the nuances around the notions of immediacy and spontaneity, which are powerful tropes associated with the 1960s and the Beats in particular.

"Après Moi, Le Deluge": Jack Kerouac and *The Decline of the West*

A key to understanding Kerouac's use of Oswald Spengler's *The Decline of the West* lies in remembering that Kerouac's modernism occurs within the context of a mystically oriented ethnic Catholicism with a stress on the immanent dimensions of the Trinity and the ongoing miraculous action of the Spirit.[2] Kerouac was exposed to Spengler's thought while at Columbia—Spengler was in vogue during the 1930s and 1940s—and *The Decline of the West* was a key shared text in the emerging creative friendships with William Burroughs and Allen Ginsberg.[3] For Kerouac, the text provided a non-Catholic secular and modernist affirmation of a worldview he had first constructed in Catholic Trinitarian terms.

Spengler's account of history was based on the thought that civilizations develop according to an organic model of growth, fruition, and decay. While civilizations differ with respect to the kinds of thought they authorize and privilege, a deep organic pattern is characteristic of all.[4] Thinking in these terms made it possible for Spengler to accommodate Friedrich Nietzsche's influential critique of truth claims as he could differentiate between modes of assertion and knowing characteristics of an epoch (and thus true within context) and knowledge of a deep mode of cultural process characterized by an organic structure of growth and decay. In this way, he could turn Romantic notions of becoming and being to account for the difference between a historically conditioned quotidian consciousness (that lives toward being) and a second fundamentally determinative organic process.[5]

Spengler's account of consciousness and history is similar to other contemporary accounts—including Marx's notion of material relations and Freud's concept of unconsciousness—that attempted to use rationalism to pursue a mode of liberative ideological critique. Each differentiates between a culturally normative mode of awareness/being and a second mode of awareness/being whose structures and entities constitute a deeper, determinative, and rationally discernable mode of being. This basic instinct assumes that culture involves a doubling (at least), and as ever, this mode of thought privileges those capable of intuiting (or being brought in on the knowledge of) that deeper structure.

The basic sweep of Spengler's account led Kerouac and his friends to a series of assumptions about awareness, culture, and their times. According to Spengler's account, the decline of a civilization would be characterized by events and intellectual dead ends that reflected the limits of a given mode of cultural organization. At this time, a *cognizanti* would emerge whose critique of culture and modes of thought would be authorized by recognition of the episodic character of cultural development. This would also authorize otherwise culturally transgressive behavior since extant cultural forms had their day. This paradigm gave Kerouac and his friends a historical mythos by which to understand their position in relation to their times.

Kerouac's first book, *The Town and the City,* had its roots in a more traditional sense of narrative and cultural norms that no longer seemed viable to Kerouac by the time of its publication in March 1950. Kerouac had begun searching for a method suitable for revealing the mode of being in time that he and his friends believed they had intuited. A critical turning point was reached over the Christmas–New Year holidays of 1950–51 and recorded in a series of long letters to Neal Cassady in which Kerouac, for the first time, began the process of recording a confessional stream of consciousness as narrative.[6] He would write the legendary first draft of *On the Road* just two months later in April.

This series of letters begins with the account of an epiphany Kerouac experienced in St. Patrick's Church in New York City in which he saw, at once, both the quotidian event of the evening mass and the fact that this simple set of actions had been going on for hundreds of years. This stereoscopic tableau provided Kerouac with the perceptual touchstone for understanding the relationship of the ordinary, waking thought, and the deep structure of being. Taking off from this, Kerouac began a biographical confession in which he wrote about his brother's death and his childhood, directly, for the first time.

From the very beginning of this account, Kerouac introduces two kinds of awareness—an episodic confessional record of his ordinary childhood memories of people, porches, and casual cruelty. In the midst of this, in a confessional voice, he spoke of an evocation of ecstatic unitive experiences related to the red light of an afternoon that signaled a fundamental good in being. What Kerouac did from this time on was struggle to find ways to create texts that were, on the one hand, phrased in the ordinary speech of his times, about the ordinary things of his times, and that yet somehow provided witness of this deeper and supportive—fated—mode of being in time.

Kerouac's interest in confessional immediacy would continue to develop. In 1953, he would begin the practice of sketching his thoughts in small notebooks, and once exposed to it, he quickly began to compose haiku. By 1956, he regularly composed in episodic, arbitrarily delimited pulses, using the time it took a candle to burn or the length of a page as his measure. This basic approach—the use of an arbitrary measure to parse transcription of vernacular thought—would be the signature method or discipline that he pursued.

For Kerouac, this was not exactly or simply a matter of pure expression or spontaneous shout. Rather, following Spengler, Kerouac took ordinary speech as speech conditioned according to its era, and he used direct transcription and arbitrary measure as a way to signal a deeper structure or rhythm that would be otherwise unrecognizable. In doing so, he hoped to bring the "good news" that the era's absorption in what Kerouac thought of in Spenglerian terms, as Faustian pursuits, was not an apocalyptic end.

There is much more to say about the connections between Kerouac's use of Spengler and both his art and his later turn to Buddhism and then a Buddhist-Christian hybrid religiosity. While the basic structure—a stereoscopic account of knowing in which a deep structure of being in time is found alongside the quotidian—is hardly unique to Spengler. It was Spengler's version of this that framed Kerouac's practice of a confessional realism by which that doubled world could be articulated. Spengler's philosophical history also allowed Kerouac to persist in the heroic conceit that he was a unique figure in mythic time whose art would function as a prophetic call for those with ears to hear. What mattered was not that we ourselves create spontaneously or recover some kind of openness in being; rather what mattered was that from his work, we understood our times and the deeper fact of being by which we were justified. In this sense, spontaneous practice was not a matter of simply transgressing extant norms—it was a discipline to be taken up by those chosen for the work—and, if not led by knowledge of our being in time, it was a practice that would produce only violent self-dramatization and excess. Hence, the difference Kerouac came to maintain at the end of his life between his approach and the more confrontational and politically purposeful transgression of norms in the name of "being here now."

Although Kerouac's sense of our being in time is similar to Eliot insofar as a stereoscopic vision is necessary for knowledge, he does not retain the logical tension between motion and stillness that Eliot assumed. Rather, all being in time occurs against the background of the organic development of cultural forms and is comprehensible in these terms. Spontaneous practice does not depend, in this sense, on theorizing the present or the immediate as a difference; rather, it depends on rethinking being in time as an organic episode within which variation occurs. Under the discipline of that beat—whether established by the limit of a page, the verse frame of a song, or a breath, or a candle's wick—a temporal space is limned within which a gesture freed of normative syntax could take shape. The present was thus not a front wave antithetical to (and thus unknowable for) a reflective self-awareness that seeks to find itself in time; rather *all* being in time was imagined as a *duration,* marked by self-reflection and depth presence in deep form at once.

On Concrescent Shores: Charles Olson's Use of Alfred North Whitehead

Charles Olson's influential essay "Projective Verse" first appeared in 1950 prior to his tenure at Black Mountain College (1951–56).[7] Like Kerouac's letters to Cassady over the 1951 New Year, this essay signaled the turn Olson was taking in his efforts to articulate a meaningful postwar aesthetic program. Olson clearly intended the essay to be canonical—key influences on the essay included William Carlos Williams (who had proposed that a poem be thought of as a "field of action")[8] and Ezra Pound—but the work also made the ambitious effort to ground poetics in modern scientific and secular terms through its use of the ideas and vocabulary of Alfred North Whitehead and Carl Jung. For the purposes of this essay, I focus on the influence of the former.[9]

Whitehead's metaphysics process represents an ambitious attempt to develop an account of being (ontology) that admits change as real without undermining the basis for truth claims. Classical metaphysics located being through a categorical differentiation of being and change; a difference that permitted a strong theory of truth and thus of knowledge. This bifurcation lost its coherence in the face of quantum accounts of the alterity of matter and energy; Whitehead's metaphysics sought to redress this. The key to this lay in explicating what Whitehead called "concrescence," in which a moment of experience "hardens" into a specific and subsequentially determinate quanta of being.

For Whitehead, concrescence is both an all-at-once and analyzable in triadic terms involving: (1) physical prehension or inheritance by which a subject open to being (the actualities formed in past or prior moments of concrescence) mimetically prehends a pattern that produces a secondary, subjective evaluation; (2) a responsive phase of mental prehension, also mimetic in basic structure that is not based on actualities but on eternal forms; and (3) the integration of these as figure and ground. In this structure, what "stands up," as it were, is some figuration that proposes a relation between the eternal forms of the mind and sensed forms.[10]

A difficult aspect of Whitehead's thought lies in his rejection of a classical notion of sequential or serial moments of time in the light of Einstein's proof of relativity. In Einstein's theory, the relationship between entities in time (that is, any form of simultaneity) is relative, and thus there is no absolute present. This makes any assertion of the status of being in time difficult, as occurrences problematically must be thought of in both substantive and relational terms.[11] Attempting to resolve this is well outside the scope of this paper. What matters most for our purposes is to see that Whitehead's speculations set out a basis and a set of terms for attempting to think these issues through, so as to be consistent with Einstein's proof; a mode of being in relational or relative time rather than serial time was imagined.[12]

To understand the use Charles Olson made of the process metaphysics of Alfred North Whitehead in "Projective Verse," it is first necessary to put Olson into his contexts—specifically to explicate his relationship to a group of poets who were loosely allied with William Carlos Williams and sometimes under the flag of "objectivism."[13] The objectivist impulse was a modernist aesthetic that, in the United States, was influenced by an adjacent materialism—often a Marxist-tinted materialism. In broad strokes, the problem taken up by objectivist aesthetics was how to eliminate the influence of an isolated Cartesian or Kantian subject. The goal was the direct presentation of the object world as an aesthetic fact, and the problem was how to get free of the influence of subjective interests (and the historical conditioning of these if this was an issue) or the assumption of a privileged subject (thus the frequent alliance with Marxism). Such art would, furthermore, be consistent with any liberative purpose since it would be a human artifact unconditioned by repressive cultural ideology or moral concerns that modified the private subject.

The influence of the objectivist program has been quite rich—many artists working in relation to Buddhist thought structure the goal of their work in essentially the same terms. Similarly, the politics and aesthetics of the Language poets in the 1970s and 1980s attempt to disarm the influence of ideology according to a postmodern program by collapsing all subjective depth to the single surface of language. In both cases, the assumption is that freedom/good occurs where one can eliminate interiority and reflection, whichever language one uses to speak of such.

Olson's essay "Projective Verse" was intended as a manifesto that would address a basic problem facing any objectivist program. It is actually very difficult to elide the influence of the self—to be selfless according to the ideals of objectivism. By the late 1940s, the limits of doing this through adoption of a social consciousness were beginning to be recognized—it was not liberative to short-circuit the self through subsuming it in a social role—and it was hard for a writer to make his language rich enough to cohere as an aesthetic object without somehow allowing idiosyncratic desire to surface.[14] To use a psychologism, that damned unconscious kept leaking out, and there was no way—Zen hadn't appeared quite yet in the United States—to imagine you could keep that from happening.

What Whitehead supplied to Olson was a metaphysics that presented the subject/object relationship in a way that repudiated the Cartesian subject on the one hand, and on the other showed how the creative actor could be thought to be free of any privilege; even as its influence mattered. Specifically, according to Whitehead's metaphysics, the subject/object dichotomy is folded into the process of concrescence as physical and mental prehension; where physical prehension, far from involving discrete perceptions of particular others, is a mimetic openness to an interconnected field of relations. In this case, the apparent object is not a particular percept—Rilke's panther or Williams's wheelbarrow; it is rather a field of relatively prior occurrences—in other words an actual history—that is prehended and becomes subject to concrescence.

What Olson then speaks of as "projectivist" is taken from the fact that expression—an act of concrescence—*projects* a new figure (a new monad) in the integration of mental and physical prehension. In this way what arises is not a likeness of an object or any other reference or reflection of it; what arises is an expressive realization that becomes an actual fact—because it's concresced—it can then exert its own formative influence. Since this is based on metaphysics, this is the *only* thing that happens.

This is, of course, a very different notion of time and immediacy than we found in either Eliot or Kerouac. The "present" is the all-at-once of concrescence that, however influenced by prehension, is nevertheless fundamentally open in relation to a not-yet-shaped future; an openness in which will-be is literally willed-to-be in the articulation of concrescence. The problem that both Eliot and Kerouac considered—the seeming impossibility of locating an unconditioned locus for the self—is not even on the table because selves are not found by or in their reflections but in the action of making that leaves its trace (or figure or concresced monad). In this sense, creativity is not a *different* mode of practice—it is the only thing that has *ever* been happening. What an artist might do differently would be to develop an intensity of focus that would permit him to develop an immediate relation as a basic line of play.

If there is a connection between Kerouac and Olson, then it lies less in the basic schema by which being in time was understood than in the fact that both writers thought of the artist's actions in muscular and masculine heroic terms. Kerouac's understanding of this is surprisingly undemocratic—meaningful witness of deep being is not simply a matter of applying an arbitrary measure to just anyone's expression; it occurs when a talent or genius applies itself in its time and is, in a sense, destined. For Kerouac, heroism involved his courage in running a great broken field dash with the gift he'd been given. Olson's understanding is, in principle, more democratic—concresced monads are, after all, equally realized—but concrescence is also a battleground in which (and a process by which) worlds are projected. Understanding creative activity as concrescence means that creation is a wresting by which the terms of relation are selected. What occurs is a high-stakes evolutionary struggle in which ideas are realized and gain their pertinence.

To put it another way, both writers offer a response to the problem of human freedom in a historically conditioned consciousness. For Olson, historical conditions are simply facts that have arisen to which we respond from a position of fundamental freedom insofar as in the all-at-once moment of concrescence a person has a fundamental openness toward a field of facts and an unrealized future. Any limit is either imagined or lacks relevance. In Kerouac's hands, we may appear to lack freedom, but we are rescued by the dynamics of deep being since any limits that occur for us when we think according to our times are, in the end, not relevant in terms of such being. The bases for the claim in each case are woven of the liniments of a schema taken from a philosophical discourse—philosophical discourse supplies the assumptions by which a program is thought and an affective project is justified.

With that said, the differences between their sources and influences do lead Kerouac and Olson to very different conceptions of what is at stake in a moment of creative expression. For Kerouac, creative expression occurs within and against a cultural process as a signal of the possibilities in play. New outcomes are not realized—rather an elegiac participatory witness occurs by which a larger structure of being in time is admitted. For Olson, the artist is a Prometheus who forges new individual facts that enter into a larger field of relations. Although constituted in relation to a polis of like individuals, the artist is thought to have the capacity and the heroic opportunity to bring actual *new* things to term. To state this another way, Kerouac accepts that he is involved in a cultural process to which he and his work are subject, while Olson, rethinking the individual as concresced monad, nevertheless retains the notion that the individual has a possible sway in relation to a field of equals. For Kerouac, we understand being in time by adopting a stereoscopic view by which we catch sight of social form against and along the grain of ordinary thought; for Olson, any dualism is collapsed and one exists in a single plane of relations. The conditions of the social and of history—their fact as form is admitted—but the human weight of these vanishes when the individual is thought as stellar monad in what has become a cosmic and thus also ordinary and material and decidedly not a merely social set of relations.

Unstruck Sound: John Cage and Ananda Cooraswamy's Perennialism

The last of the artists considered here is the composer John Cage, an associate of Charles Olson at Black Mountain College and an innovative midcentury composer and theorist. In part because of the connection with Black Mountain, Cage's interests are often considered to be of a piece with (and emblematic of) a broader late-1950s interest in spontaneity and immediacy. However, as we saw with Kerouac and Olson, Cage's approach is shaped by ideas and schemas borrowed from his own philosophical traditions. These influences lead Cage to model the work of the present according to a very different ethic—one in which chance and randomness assumed increased saliency.

Cage himself acknowledges that the writings of the Ceylonese, English-educated philosopher and historian Ananda Coomaraswamy—especially *The Transformation of Nature in Art*[15]—played a significant role in shaping the turn toward his mature aesthetics. Coomaraswamy lived most of his adult life in New York and Boston and was an important contributor to the development of the ties between Indian modernism and European Perennialist philosophy in the twentieth century.[16] At least one of the ideas Cage took from Coomaraswamy—the thought that "the function of Art is to imitate Nature in her manner of operation"—was rooted not just in the Natural Law theories of the Vedic *Dharmashastras* but also in Coomaraswamy's reading (and quotation) of Aquinas. Cage would make a different kind of sense of the dictum.

Natural Law theories presume that there is conformity between the ethical/aesthetic notion of the good and categorical typologies derived in an analysis of natural kinds. The strength of this is the extent to which abstract value—a sense of beauty or the good—appears to be given in a proximate case that can be closely and collectively considered. The problem for Cage, as it was for Kerouac, reflects an awareness that the categorical is actually socially constructed and, furthermore, following the modernist lead of figures like Nietzsche, unsatisfactory. In order to think of the good in relation to Nature, then, a difference needs to be asserted between socially constructed categories and the characteristic order of Nature.

Cage found the basis for asserting that difference in Coomaraswamy's reading of the Upanishads—a collection of heterogeneous sixth-century BCE texts that Indian modernists had taken up as the foundation of Indian metaphysics and religion. The basic move of the Upanishads is to sharply differentiate between appearing form—understood to be illusory or unreal and characterized by change—and being (*brahman*)—understood to be an omnipresent knowing real, characterized as unchanging, lacking form, and so on. Later yogic philosophical traditions developed an account of *brahman* in sonic terms; explicating what was called *sabdabrahman*—the unstruck sound or silence present in, before, and after all sound.

This framework led Cage to focus on the spaces between notes—the rests and subtle gaps between struck sound—as what energized (eroticized) expressive sound. The categorical difference between form (struck sound) and being (thought of as silence) also allowed Cage a way out of the aesthetic limitations he faced in following Coomaraswamy's dictum to conform to Nature's mode of operation. Specifically, Cage could now argue—with the support of any other critique of metaphysics—that Nature's mode of operation was in fact one of randomness, fecundity, and chance, *and not* any socially inflected notion of beauty. He could do this with optimism since all chance rested in a silence that was beyond saying.

Cage's use of chance as a compositional tool in the openness of the present has connections to a modernism that prefers to think of the field of participation in nonhuman, quasi-mechanical terms. At the level of theory, this vision imagines a strong difference between nature and culture and accepts that this difference can be resolved only by turning culture—reflection, language—off. An artist "makes it new" (and Cage was very concerned to present a difference in his work) by giving up intention, by apparently giving up an authorial stake.

In this sense, Cage uses the monist trajectory of Upanishadic thought to license a repudiation of the problem of historical contingency. The conditioning past is asserted to be unreal, a stake extant only as long as one entertains suspect notions of authority, depth (other than silence), and subjectivity. Hence, on this point Cage differs from both Kerouac and Olson—with Kerouac on the matter of dualism vs. monism, and with Olson with respect to the real. That is, like Olson, Cage adopts a monistic perspective (albeit complicated and quantum-plural in Olson's case) as an answer to the problem of historical contingency and cultural influence.[17] This is consistent with the decision each made to repudiate the Romantic subject with its special interiority and depth, a depth Kerouac *does not* repudiate. On the other hand, Cage is a far stronger monist than Olson—historical conditions lack a rootedness attributed only to deep being (*brahman*), while Olson regarded concresced occasions—and thus history—as realized being.

Immediacy and Difference

Kerouac, Olson, and Cage all developed aesthetic practices that aimed to redress the limits set by historical consciousness on creative play. Like Eliot, they did so by borrowing a theory of time and/or of the relationship of the immediate and present to the past. That, however, is where the similarities end; they made use of strikingly different philosophers and traditions, and very different notions of the human and of the artist's act emerged under the broad trope of spontaneity, immediacy, and chance.

At the very least, this suggests we might do well to begin to tease apart assumptions we make about the late 1950s and early 1960s. For instance, Cage and, more recently, Olson are largely seen as critics of American social norms, and yet the metaphysics they rely on and the positions they take ironically retain a place for an atomic individual author—albeit emptied of depth or flattened. Kerouac in many ways goes the furthest in actually supposing a self that is profoundly relational and at stake in being—a notion of self at odds with dominant tropes of individuality in American thought. But Kerouac, again, is widely thought to have missed his own boat in his late-life political conservatism, and thus the potential point of his critique is missed. Hence, general assumptions about the character and cultural position of the aesthetic ethic each advances appear confused.

More generally, this study raises the question whether any of these artists offers sufficient warrant for a spontaneous practice for which prior conditioning is inconsequential. Each uses what can at best be called a speculative metaphysics, and none subjects the desire to be free of conditioning to sufficient critique. That is, each assumes that freedom can be had only by eliding the influence of culture. Olson and Cage go the furthest—each finds a mode of being by which a person stands free, however briefly—Olson in the moment of concrescence where *action* occurs (that is, by escaping into the verb) and Cage by relinquishing intention (at least at the theoretical level).

Kerouac's example is more complicated. On the one hand, he adopted a worldview that admitted a horizon existed with respect to human freedom and creative play—indeed, in his terms, the freedom we have is always subject to a real limit, and being is profoundly relational. The elegiac and confessional character of his work reflects this. On the other hand, Kerouac was not able to live on these terms—he was never successful at managing his own, albeit culturally inflected, desires to be an artist-hero, free of limitations, and the weight of interpersonal relations. To this extent, Kerouac, too, held out for a dream of radical freedom.

What primarily differentiates these accounts of creativity and immediacy is, in the end, quite old—the difference between monist and dualist accounts of being and the different accounts of desire and self that are attendant to such. In this sense, we may think of monism and dualism—beyond any particular example such as Shankara's radically monistic Advaita-Vedanta or Descartes's mind-body dualism—as metaphysical genres characterized by competing commitments. In monism, the commitment is to a radical absolute surety that is realized only by the elision of difference. In dualism, the commitment is to relation (and thus difference) as a primary condition or fact given in being. This difference is of no small matter, as a concomitant difference in ethic subtends as well—reflecting the philosophical materials a person chooses as her or his starting point for thinking about creative work in relation to a notion of being in time. Beat writers and other associated artists serve as recent exemplars relative to our times and to extant ideological systems. Hence, ongoing attraction to, interpretation of, and quarrel with them may well reflect our own metaphysical stakes, commitments, and preferences however these are masked or performed.

Notes

This essay is a revised version of a paper, "The Measure of the Beat: Spontaneous Aesthetics and the Problem of the Open in Kerouac, Olsen, Cage, and Ginsberg," presented at the Louisville Conference on Twentieth-Century Literature, in Louisville, Kentucky, in February 1998, and again given—in altered form under the same title—at the conference Tools of the Sacred, Techniques of the Secular: Awakening, Epiphany, Apocalypse, and Doubt in Contemporary English-Language Verse in Brussels in May 2010.

1. T. S. Eliot, *Four Quartets* (1943; San Diego and New York: Harcourt, 1943, 1971), 15–16.

2. Oswald Spengler, *The Decline of the West,* 2 vols., trans. Charles Atkinson (New York: Knopf, 1926, 1928).

3. For a lengthy discussion of Spengler's influence on Kerouac, Burroughs, and Ginsberg, see John Lardis, *The Bop Apocalypse: The Religious Visions of Kerouac, Ginsberg, and Burroughs* (Chicago: University of Illinois Press, 2001). There is some debate about when Kerouac first found or was given the text. Nicosia has it that Sammy Sampas showed him the book in 1941 (see Gerald Nicosia, *Memory Babe: A Critical Biography* [New York: Grove, 1983], 87). There is also evidence the book was on the syllabus for a class taken at Columbia, and Burroughs is said to have given Ginsberg and Kerouac each a copy of the text at their first meeting. (Ginsberg and Kerouac so embroidered the period of their first meetings that it is difficult to be sure of facts.)

4. It is worth noting that this basic notion is not so different from the much later Marxist French Annales School model of a "world system," with its exposition that any given world system has a characteristic duration (*durée*).

5. Spengler's position can be thought of as an early and influential structuralist intuition. For examples of this influence, see, for instance, Martin Heidegger, *Ontology—The Hermeneutics of Facticity,* trans. John van Buren (Bloomington: Indiana University Press, 1999), 29. Heidegger notes: "The one and only definition of the being of that which comes to expression in cultural forms is: a culture is an *organism,* an autonomous organic life (emerging, blossoming, dying out)"; and "No one prior to Spengler had the courage to actual, without regard for consequences, the definitive possibilities found in the origin and development of modern historical consciousness."

6. Jack Kerouac, *Jack Kerouac: Selected Letters, 1940–1956,* ed. Ann Charters (New York: Viking, 1995), 281ff.

7. Charles Olson, "Projective Verse," in *Collected Prose,* ed. Donald Allen and Benjamin Friedlander (Berkeley and Los Angeles: University of California Press, 1997), 239–49. Other useful essays/essay artifacts in which Olson reveals his debts to Whitehead include: "Human Universe," ibid., 155–66; "Proprioception," ibid., 181–83; and *The Special View of History* (Berkeley: Oyez, 1970).

8. Don Byrd, "The Possibility of Measure in Olson's *Maximus," Boundary 2,* vol. 2,

no. 1/2 (1973–74): 50. Byrd quotes from William Carlos Williams, *Selected Essays* (New York: New Directions 1969), 280–91.

9. A number of essays and monographs have assessed "Projective Verse" and Olson's use of Whitehead, including Shahar Bram, *Charles Olson and Alfred North Whitehead: An Essay on Poetics*, trans. Batya Stein (Lewisburg, Pa.: Bucknell University Press, 2004); Robert von Hallberg, "Olsen, Whitehead, and the Objectivists," in *Boundary 2*, vol. 2, no. 1/2 (1973–74): 85–112; and Rosemary Waldrop, "Charles Olsen: Process and Relationship," *Twentieth Century Literature* 23, no. 4 (December 1977): 467–86. For an analysis of the influence of Jung, see Charles Stein, *The Secret of the Black Chrysanthemum* (New York: Station Hill, 1975). Stein aptly notes the debt Olson bore Jung for his account of the mechanisms of projection.

10. For the sources for this summary, see Thomas E. Hosinski, *Stubborn Fact and Creative Advance* (Lanham, Md.: Rowman and Littlefield, 1993), chaps 2, 3.

11. A good starting place for reviewing these debates is John W. Lango, "The Time of Whitehead's Concrescence," *Process Studies* 30, no. 1 (2001): 3–21. Lango prefers a temporalist account.

12. Whitehead's philosophical program is challenging because of its scope, because of the neologisms he introduced, and because the physics he was influenced by were quite new and hardly completely thought out. A good starting point for tracking the vectors that radiate from his writings are the essays by contemporaries in Paul Arthur Schilpp, ed., *The Philosophy of Alfred North Whitehead* (New York: Tudor, 1941), particularly that by Roy Wood Sellers, "Philosophy of Organism and Physical Realism," (405–34), which offers a good starting point for critique in accounts of sense perception.

13. For good essays on the objectivist impulse in American poetry, see Rachel Blau DuPlessis and Peter Quartermain, eds., *The Objectivist Nexus: Essays in Cultural Poetics* (Tuscaloosa: University of Alabama Press, 1999); and Tim Woods, *The Poetics of the Limit: Ethics and Politics in Contemporary American Poetry* (New York: Palgrave Macmillan, 2002).

14. Objectivism was an aesthetic strategy that many modernist artists adopted according to an idealistic hope that the damaging authority and influence of the subject/self could be subverted. Rainer Maria Rilke's *New Poems* (1907, 1908) represents an important European version, but Rilke presciently, and, in my estimation more honestly, recognized that it was, in fact, not possible. One's own desires leaked out, and neither celibacy nor other disciplines finally silenced them.

15. Ananda Coomaraswamy, *The Transformation of Nature in Art* (Cambridge: Harvard University Press, 1934). For a good discussion of Cage's use of Coomaraswamy, see David W. Patterson, "The Picture That Is Not in the Colors: Cage, Coomaraswamy, and the Impact of India" in *John Cage: Music, Philosophy, and Intention 1933–1950*, ed. Patterson (New York: Routledge, 2002), 177–216.

16. Traditionalism, often loosely allied with Perennialist philosophy, was an influential intellectual movement in the twentieth century—key figures included Coomara-

swamy, René Guénon, Mircea Eliade, Frithjof Schuon, and Seyyed Nasr. Although not among the early figures, D. T. Suzuki, who popularized Zen in the West, also demonstrates a Perennialist perspective. Often associated with the avant-garde, traditionalist thinkers had a disturbing history of political involvement with profoundly authoritarian political movements. Cage's reliance on Coomaraswamy appears ironic in this sense; however, in point of fact, his position vis-à-vis chance is deeply authoritarian. Cage is currently undergoing a revival among writers in their thirties and forties who similarly conflate a critique of authorial intention with freedom. For a good history of this movement (with connections and influence in the Jungian Eranos Foundation among others), see Mark Sedgwick, *Against the Modern World: Traditionalism and the Secret Intellectual History of the Twentieth Century* (Oxford: Oxford University Press, 2004).

17. For a discussion of Cage's monism in relation to diverging trends in American arts and letters, see Christopher Shultis, *Silencing the Sounded Self: John Cage and the American Experimental Tradition* (Boston: Northeastern University Press, 1998).

IV

BEAT POLITICS

Ethics and Affinities

TWO WAYS OF ENDURING THE FLAMES

The Existential Dialectics of Love in Kierkegaard and Bukowski

Andreas Seland

To attempt to place Kierkegaard's and Bukowski's work into the same context may on the face of it seem like an odd, maybe even forced maneuver, something along the lines of a deconstructive tactic. The dialectical complexities of a nineteenth-century dandy-martyr and Romantic, and the crystalline, modern prose of a run-down Los Angeles drunk. That seems like a tough fit. But if one takes time to reflect and look at it from a bird's-eye view, it becomes apparent that they actually share a lot of principal motifs: Both emphasize the solitary individual; both turn their back upon the values and mores of their respective societies and embrace a more elementary view of life, seeing themselves as cutting into life's real core (or lack of such); both focus upon and describe the irrational sides of man; and, as I will argue in this essay, both understand love in a distinct dialectical manner; an understanding that has its roots in Romantic thought.

The Romantics, one has to remember, were a strong influence on the Beats. As Eberhard Alsen has noted, the Beats were part of a wider intellectual movement that in the 1950s reevaluated the notion of the Romantic, a movement that redefined the Romantics' characteristic aloofness and out-of-touchness with common reality, giving this characteristic a new, positive dimension, instead of the negative meaning it had had up to that time.[1] The Beat figure, as we know, is a person who throws himself into the cracks of middle-class morality. He is attached to drugs, booze, and sex, along with Oriental philosophy and jazz, out of a wish to expand his mind—to escape the box, to think, feel, and see differently. "[They] demanded," as John Lardas has noted in regard to the Beats' aesthetics, "that the process of art become a springboard into a world elsewhere."[2]

Bukowski does not quite fit the Beats' mold in this sense. While the archetypal Beats (Kerouac, Ginsberg, and Burroughs) came from relatively affluent backgrounds (middle-class and higher), Bukowski was born into a poor family. He pretty much grew up in the cracks that the other Beats later sought out. Hence, though he shares the proper Beats' preoccupation with the marginal and the immoral, Bukowski has a different orientation from them. This shows itself, for example, in his aesthetics. While the Beats all commonly utilize elements of surrealism in order to short-circuit the flow of thought in their texts and thus open up the reading mind to original aesthetic experiences, Bukowski writes clearly, with a level tone, and a linear narrative structure. While the Beats attack the way in which we commonly think, and break with what they perceive as normality; Bukowski uses ordinary, everyday language, and ordinary, everyday scenes in order to show the extraordinary that lies at the bottom of them.

Still, these differences aside, Bukowski and the archetypal Beats are united in their depiction of man as essentially an outcast and an outsider, and this motif is a proper Romantic one. Moreover, the motif leads us right into the notion of Romantic love mentioned above. For the concept of love developed in the Romantic tradition revolves around the persona of a young, yearning man, somehow set aside in life and full of angst and uncertainty as he doesn't know if he ever will obtain his heart's desire (the typical example being Goethe's Werther).[3] My idea in this essay is to briefly delineate this notion through a recourse to Shelley, Kierkegaard, and Emerson, and then explore aspects of Bukowski's novel *Women* in conjunction with Kierkegaard's philosophical work *Fear and Trembling,* in order to show that their differing treatments of love can be read as variations of the same Romantic thought.

The thought in question is the view that the object of love is really a dialectical entity composed of a subjective/fantasmatic element and an objective/real element, and that, because of this, there exists, *in* the beloved object, an essential gap—a discord between the subjectively projected properties and those that are objectively present. What I aim to show is that Bukowski's and Kierkegaard's treatments of love ought to be read as specific responses to the presence of such an essential discord. And also, in the case of Bukowski, that his response exemplifies the Beats' leitmotif of escaping the box—of not getting caught up in the limited existential horizon of the common man, but instead being able to embrace life in all its variety and complexity, and experience it as a process of continual becoming and change.

Love's Paradox

Love defines. It draws an emotional border, it makes actions and objects take on acute emotional significance, and it puts the world into a definite perspective. I believe Emerson describes it perfectly: "In giving him to another, [love] still more gives him to himself. He is a new man, with new perceptions, new and keener purposes, and a religious solemnity of character and aims. He does no longer appertain to his family and society; *he* is somewhat; *he* is a person; *he* is a soul."[4]

It is one of the main ideas nurtured by the Romantics that the self is grounded in what it loves, and that if it is bereft of this object of love—the self despairs. This grounding, and the following logic of despair, is vividly portrayed in Shelley's poem "Alastor."

At the beginning of the poem, Alastor is shaken in a dream by a vision of "a veiled maid,"[5] and completely in the throes of love, he awakes, and sets out to find this woman, or else all is despair.[6] *He* cannot be without her. And I underscore the "he" here for a reason, for, as Kierkegaard has noted, despair over lost love is not despair over the lost object, but over the loss of the *self* that is defined by its relation to that object.[7] The second Alastor awakens, his self is grounded in his vision of the veiled maid, and, as Emerson notes, "he is a new man." This is shown in the poem by the fact that the poetical grandeur of the earth, "the majesty and the mystery," which Alastor before thrived on, now is gone.[8] All he can think of is the maid. His former self is lost, and a new one gained.

If we step back and take in Alastor's predicament, we can see that the object grounding his self (the beloved) has something of a paradoxical nature. The maid, one has to notice, is a dream object. As she appears to Alastor, she is not real. Though we, the readers, will probably induce that the vision of her has its roots in the form of the young woman who tended Alastor while he was visiting "the ruined temples" in "Dark Æthiopia."[9] To Alastor she comes, nonetheless, as a mental picture, an ideal, an unreal thing imbued with every perfection he can imagine. And he becomes haunted, obsessed. He is not whole without her, and he must find the reality behind *the imago* (in Freudian terms), that is, the internal object is incomplete without its external counterpart.

On the basis of this, we can perceive that the object of love proper is at one and the same time something interior (the imago that came in the dream), and something exterior (a woman that can be seen to fit the internal image). Furthermore, when Alastor becomes driven by his fantasmatic ideal, he lacks a person with whom he can identify it, and so drops into a state of despair. The double aspect of the object of love is, therefore, essential to the emotion. Both ideality and reality are needed. And when reality does not conform to the ideal (because, for example, a concrete object is lacking), despair ensues.

To conclude: The object of love is interior in the sense that it is partly created through the emotions, the dreams, and the imaginations of the one who loves. (This is what Stendhal, in *Love*, speaks of as the *crystallization-process.*)[10] Furthermore, it is interior in the sense that the beloved object is a constituent of the individual's self and self-understanding. It has a highly subjective and existential significance to him (or her). At the same time (if we exclude cases of pathological narcissism), the beloved is an object that is exterior to the self, a real object that stands apart from us and lies outside of our immediate control.

Love, therefore, which is the relationship that grounds our self, and which is, maybe, the emotion that tells the most about who we are, is also the exact point where we are the most violently bound to something that is principally other than ourselves. The paradox being that the object of love is, simultaneously, an interior object in the self, and an exterior object in the world.

The Problem with Love

In his short prose piece on the sentiment of love, Shelley describes the presence of the internal object as follows: "We are born into the world and there is something within us which from the instant that we live and move thirst after its likeness."[11] We have something within us, quoting Shelley again: "a soul within our soul that describes a circle around its proper Paradise which pain and sorrow or evil dare not overleap."[12] A soul within our soul, an immaculate image of human perfection, and we are born into the world with the need to find its proper counterpart, someone we can love.

The problem, of course, is that no one can completely correspond to this image, and that the perfection we find in a person we have deemed worthy of it (probably on the basis of a partial fit) stems from the image itself. We read more into that other person than there is. Again Emerson has a fitting description: "[What] we love is not in your will, but above it. It is not you, but your radiance. It is that which you know not in yourself, and can never know."[13] Hence Slavoj Žižek's famous spin on Lacan's definition of love: "To love is to give something one doesn't have, to someone who doesn't want it."

The object of love is not the other person per se, but an amalgam of our internal object (what the person is *for us*) and what the person is in itself. And this duality of the object forms the basis of a certain essential tension, which again gives rise to an essential insecurity: Is the other really what we think he or she is? Is s/he perfect? Does s/he really love us? Is this *it*?

Apropos this point, we can note that according to Lacanian theory, pathological jealousy, the incessant question of whether the other truly loves you back, and *only* you, and no one else, is purely a paranoid construction—even when well-grounded;[14] that is, it is a problem in the emotional makeup of the one who harbors the jealousy. A problem grounded in the mismatch between the internal object and the external. The incessant skeptical and questioning behavior of the jealous can be seen to be rooted in the fact that the jealous has come to understand, to some degree, that he/she doesn't truly possess the object of love as the object of love doesn't truly exist.

An additional factor regarding this is that when love is confirmed, when we have found the person who responds to our internal object, it is not simply the case that we force an image, a subjective reality upon the other, for by binding the other to our internal object, we also open up toward the other, and respond toward that person in a privileged fashion. When I say that the object of love is a dual, self-contradictory object, something both internal and external, that means that the boundaries that define the object are fuzzy. We see the other for what it is not, but also, when the other acts, no matter what he or she does, the action is done with the authority given to the other by his or her identification with the internal object.

The other, by being loved, becomes an extension of our self, becomes our "better half," the very ground from which our self defines itself. The person becomes a beacon we use to orient ourselves, and, quite commonly, something to remind us that we are safe. This other is an incarnation of what we believe to be the utmost perfection, and what we want to be, maybe even what we understand we never can attain, but nevertheless feel is right, and proper, and so on—in short, our ideal. But the other is still just a person. A person who may very well act out of tune with our dream. This means that when we are in love, we are in a highly delicate position because of our strong emotional dependence upon the other, who must be adequate to our fantasy.

Despair, according to Kierkegaard, is to not want to be what one is, or to want to be what one is not—it is to somehow fail one's ideal, to fail the object that established the self-reflexive relation that is the human self.[15] The ideal here spoken of, is, I believe, part of the internal object that goes into creating the dialectical object of love, and when in love, it is thus not only you yourself that may fail the ideal, but just as much the other. To create a stable definition of oneself—a self that constantly adheres to one's ideal—is therefore as good as impossible when in love, as one is necessarily dependent upon an element—the other person—that is outside of one's control. To Kierkegaard, therefore, love poses a peculiar problem: On the one hand, it is necessary to love in order to have a proper self; on the other, it is necessary not to be attached to an external object in order to have a stable definition of who one is, and thereby secure oneself against despair. As Kierkegaard formulates it in *Fear and Trembling:* "He has grasped the deep secret that even in loving another one should be sufficient unto oneself."[16] My later discussion of Kierkegaard will explore what this means.

Kierkegaard's pessimistic view of love is not the only option, though. If we put aside his principal quest after a well-defined and wholly self-reliant self, we could come to see that the insecurity present in love might actually be part of the very enjoyment of the passion. This is something aptly described in a quote gathered from Stendhal: "Always a little doubt to set to rest—that's what keeps one craving in passionate love. Because the keenest misgivings are always there, its pleasures never becomes tedious."[17] Stendhal's position may be indicative of the healthiest position in regard to love, wherein one accepts the dependence and finds joy in the constant play and struggle into which it casts one.

Kierkegaard's position, then, is that the insecurity and uncertainty inherent in love ought to be avoided (though not love itself). Stendhal's is that it ought be respected and accepted. A logical third position in this little menagerie would be the position wherein the insecurity is sought after in itself. This, I hypothesize, is Bukowski's position.

The Lydia-Object

"Lydia has a grip on me. I can't explain it."
"She's a flirt. She's impulsive. She'll leave you."

"Maybe that's some of the attraction."
"You want a whore. You're afraid of love."[18]

Lydia Vance is the first love detailed in *Women,* the first in a line of women who all share certain definite characteristics, and to simplify matters I will speak of them all as Lydia-objects. The Lydia-object is the kind of object that Chinaski falls for, or rather, Chinaski falls for women that fit with the fantasmatic coordinates of the Lydia-object. So, it is not true, as stated in the introductory quote, that Chinaski is afraid of love. He is afraid of love in its everyday moral, small wooden house with a dog, regular dinners and steady income aspect, but not love itself. It is more a matter of how, and what, and why: "Since I had been born a man, I craved women constantly, the lower the better. And yet women—good women—frightened me because they eventually wanted your soul, and what was left of mine, I wanted to keep. Basically I craved prostitutes, base women because they were deadly and hard and made no personal demands. Nothing was lost when they left."[19] Chinaski wants the wrong kind of love, not unlike the way in which he wants the wrong kind of life. ("I was drawn to all the wrong things.")[20] He wants to write, he wants to drink, to gamble, to fuck, to lie around doing nothing, listen to classical music and stare at passersby, to feel the tremors of the high heels as they bite into the pavement, have working-class epiphanies, then drink some more. He does not want a job, he does want to "make it," as it were, not in the regular fashion. His life draws a line of flight away from the life of his father and mother (as it is described in *Ham and Rye* and Bukowski's numerous poems)—a life defined by the owning of one's own home (Chinaski typically rents a place), by eating hearty dinners, real steaks (Chinaski drinks way more than he eats), by having a proper job, a proper wife, and the appearance of being a proper man (Chinaski gets drunk, gambles, and cares about music and art, throws up into bushes, and is regularly towed away by the police; he fights and starves and laughs and gets poetic in the face of the misery). Love has to be understood in this context. Love is an extension of the personal revolt that defines his life.

The simple kernel of Chinaski's character is this quiet revolt against the establishment. I call it "quiet," because it is neither principled nor political. He never defends it, never argues for it, never says that everybody ought to do as he does, never thinks of himself as superior, or chosen. He simply does not want to be a part of it. As Bukowski fittingly captures the sentiment in his poem "living":

I didn't have any immortal thoughts,
and that was the best part[21]

Chinaski's revolt is choosing to live apart from the establishment, at the margins of it, in a cocoon of the aforementioned elements: writing, music, gambling, drinking—and women. All things that society at large, his father's society, looks down upon as something trivial at best (writing, classical music), or straightforwardly immoral (senseless drinking binges, no-good whores). Hence, because it is an element belonging to the same fantasmatic cocoon, love has to follow the same logic. Chinaski loves something in the face of what one *ought* to love: "Lydia jumped up on the coffee table. Her bluejeans fit tighter than ever. She flung her long brown hair from side to side. She was insane; she was miraculous."[22]

Madness and insanity are the key. Girls that are *out there*. Unmarred by the stifling and prosaic order of things. As Chinaski says about another girl: "Valerie was 22, absolutely lovely, with long blond hair, mad blue eyes and a beautiful body. Like Lydia, she had also spent some time in a madhouse."[23] The Lydia-object is partly defined by a lack of normality. She is not a "good woman." And it is the negative property that here draws Chinaski in. The fact of the irregularity, not what she is, but what she is not. But with the irregularity, the madness, also comes an additional, positive characteristic: namely, vitality and passion. An excess of emotions that form a stark contrast to the seclusion and apathy characteristic of Chinaski himself. And this excess is equally important. The women bring him life and youth, pulling him out of himself: "Why did I do these things? I didn't want her now. And Mindy was flying all the way from New York City. I knew plenty of women. Why always more women? What was I trying to do? . . . I was old and I was ugly. . . . By being with young girls did I hope I wouldn't grow old, feel old? I just didn't want to age badly, simply quit, be dead before death itself arrived."[24] It is not simply old age talking. As is apparent if one reads the aforementioned poem "living" (written when Bukowski himself was about forty-five—younger than Chinaski is in *Women*), life to Bukowski (ergo to Chinaski), if he is left to himself, curls up into an apathetic cradle position. He sleeps, dreams, and observes. Drinks and distances himself. Refuses to partake. What is important to him is the deep rift between himself and the everyday world of work and house loans. Curiously, as we now see, the women he falls for, picked because they enforce the barrier in question, also break it down. They bridge the rift and force him out of himself, force him to socialize, force him to feel. ("Lydia liked parties. And Harry was a party-giver. So we were on our way to Harry Ascot's.")[25] As his biographer Barry Miles states in the foreword to *Women*: "His relation to women had to be tempestuous in order to be real."[26] They have to pull him into motion.

In the object of love, as it is part ideal, part real, there is a gap, and one has to somehow respond to it in one's emotional makeup. Ignoring the gap, as, for example, Don Quixote does in Cervantes's novel, will lead to a nasty break-down when it eventually is discovered that a perfect unity doesn't exist between the subjective belief and the objective state of affairs (as occurs in the novel).

To Chinaski, the gap in question is actually part of the fantasmatic makeup that attracts him. His women, as I have attempted to show, namely have a dual role. Partly, they enforce the distance between Chinaski and the world. The distance that is his ideal, and that defines his *wrong kind of life*. His women are not "good women." Yet, at the same time as they form part of his cocoon (by force of what they are not), they simultaneously have the positive characteristic that they are vital and without inhibitions, that they enliven him, that they draw him out of himself and force the world upon him in measured strokes. They are there because Chinaski doesn't want to "be dead before death itself arrives." So, the Lydia-object is a clear-cut unstable object. The gap and instability (and the following insecurity) is part of what attracts. It is an object that both belongs to Chinaski's cocoonist ideal, while at the same time directly goes against this ideal—and this double movement is what defines it. The Lydia-object itself perfectly exemplifies the Romantic understanding of love for which I here argue; it is a perfect example of the contradictory nature of the beloved object. Chinaski has come to love the contradiction itself.

And, because of this, do we not see here a sort of absolute realization of the Beat spirit, wherein Chinaski not only loves the wrong women according to society's standards, but loves the wrong women per se? He loves those he cannot possibly have—loves, really, against himself as much as against the establishment. Thereby, ultimately, he draws a line of flight not only away from the life of his parents and what is considered "right," but, more crucially, away from himself, giving himself over to a continual process of becoming and change.

Well, You Can't Have Her Anyway

If Bukowski's position is to seek out the instability inherent in love, Kierke-gaard's position is the exact opposite. While Bukowski submits to the externality in the beloved object and needs the element that he is unable to control, Kierkegaard's position is an attempt to wholly assimilate the beloved object into the subject itself and eliminate what cannot be controlled. Thus, while Bukowski invariably breaks the cocoon, Kierkegaard makes it perfect. Consider the following scenario from Kierkegaard: "A young lad falls in love with a princess, the content of his whole life lies in this love, and yet the relationship is one that cannot possibly be brought to fruition, be translated from ideality into reality."[27] It is a worst-case scenario. A case in which the gap between the internal object and the external is plainly insurmountable. Part of Kierkegaard's motivation for picking this scenario in his most lucid treatment of how a Knight of Faith loves is, I believe, his awareness that the gap in question is principally insurmountable. The subjective ideal is never fully translatable into reality. There will always be a difference, a remainder of something other, and the world will never dance in perfect tune with one's fantasies (one's inward being is always at odds with the exterior). This is what I earlier spoke of as "the problem with love." Hence, he underscores the point in the very structure of the example. Anyway, it must be kept in mind that what he says about love here is his ideal no matter what circumstances. It is the following maneuvers that give Abraham his absolute emotional autonomy in regard to Isaac, and that enables him to obey the imperative to kill, yet also to immediately stay his hand when asked to stop, and that without the least bit of either confusion or regret.

After introducing the scenario, Kierkegaard proceeds to describe a series of mental acts that the Knight of Faith must perform. These are, more or less, aimed at clearing the Knight's mind and making room for the central double movement of infinite resignation and absurd faith that will come. The initial maneuvers consist in a thorough self-analysis, through which one must become certain that the princess truly is "the content of one's life," that it truly is impossible to win her, and, furthermore, to honestly take in over oneself the magnitude of the predicament. Then, at the exact moment when one faces the princess's absolute importance and, simultaneously, the absolute impossibility of ever gaining her ("this moment is life and death"),[28] that is, in the moment where one faces head-on the gap in the object of love, one performs the movement of infinite resignation:

> So the knight makes the movement, but what movement? Does he want to forget the whole thing? . . . No! . . . [The] Knight will remember everything. . . . His love for the princess [will] take on

for him the expression of an eternal love, [will] acquire a religious character, be transfigured into a love for the eternal being which, although it [is] denied fulfillment, still [reconciles] him once more in the eternal consciousness of his love's validity in an eternal form that no reality can take from him.[29]

The object of his love is now wholly ideal, and the Knight cuts off the connection to the real, to the exterior object, and resigns himself to the interior object, to his love *in itself.* "From the moment he made the movement the princess is lost."[30] What happens instead is that "the desire which would convey him out into reality, but came to grief on an impossibility, now bends inwards but is not lost thereby nor forgotten. . . . He keeps this love young, and it grows with him in years and beauty."[31] The love becomes wholly fantasmatic, not delusional, but consciously interior. At this level, the Knight is in an emotional autonomous state vis-à-vis the object he loves, but he is neither happy nor content. He is conscious of his internal object *as* an internal object, that is, of how his own psychic apparatus functions when it comes to love, and therefore "reconciled in the eternal consciousness of his love's validity in an eternal form," but he has nothing that fits the coordinates of his fantasy. He just has his fantasy *as a fantasy,* and is reconciled to that.

The next movement, the movement of faith, is to ground the now free, interior object in God's omnipotence. It is to be infinitely resigned, resigned unto the eternal image of the beloved (the internal object), but nonetheless able to say with a full heart: "I nonetheless believe I shall get her, namely on the strength of the absurd, on the strength of the fact that for God all things are possible."[32] It is to win her on the same infinite plane that one has erected "the eternal form of the love that no reality can take away." It is *not* to come to believe that one will eventually win the actual princess. It is to win her *interiorly,* on a different plane than the real—on the fantasmatic one. Hence, it is to come to exist in a thoroughly dialectical manner, with an interior that moves along one axis (the princess is mine, I am the luckiest guy in the world), and an exterior that moves along a different axis (the princess is lost, I accept it). It is "[to] exist in such a way that my opposition to [real] existence expresses itself every instant as the most beautiful and safest harmony."[33]

The further details of Kierkegaard's concept of the religious will not be explored here. The point at hand is to see the way in which the religious is a response to the gap inherent in the object of love, a way to master the insecurity, tension, and possibility of despair that lies in love. Also, it is to see how the subject, through the final movement of faith, actually comes to re-create the very gap that originally defined the beloved object, inside itself. The Knight of Faith exists, as I said, in a thoroughly dialectical manner. His self revolves around the gap between the fantasmatic/the internal (where he has won the princess), and the real/the external (where she is lost). This shows that the Knight has internalized the tension, and, thereby, comes to be fully in control of himself and the situation. ("[It] is only lower natures who have the law for their actions in someone else, the premises for their actions outside themselves.")[34] But by doing this, the Knight also comes to live in an eternal leap over the gap that now separates the two antithetical planes that define him. And, in its existential aspect, this is what Kierke-gaard's *leap of faith* actually amounts to.

At the end of *Women,* Chinaski buys a whore. Afterwards he convinces him-self that he ought to stick with Sara, that he has "straightened himself out"[35] and found himself a good woman for a change (though she is not really, not in the traditional sense: hers is just a more placid, benign form of madness, and she still confirms Chinaski's marginal character and still, in subtle ways, breaks it down). He even goes on to turn down the usual phone call from the next unstable woman. But we still get the distinct impression that his ordeal with women isn't over. It lies partly in his insistence that he really is a good guy: "I was a good guy and he knew it. Animals knew things like that."[36] With such an insistence there open few rooms for change.

But, additionally, we have grounds for thinking that it isn't over, because the ordeal itself is the manner in which Chinaski responds to the gap inher-ent in the object of love. By loving he lives out the vacillation between the fantasmatic and the real. He picks women who simultaneously fit with his fantasy, and go against it—who express in their very nature the gap formally present in the object of love.

The Knight of Faith, on the other hand, responds differently to love. He internalizes the gap and severs the connection to the real, thereby making the vacillation the motion of an internal leap, living in his own dream (or heaven).

The point is that both Bukowski and Kierkegaard can be read as for-mulating responses to the problem stated through Shelley's poem. Alastor's tragedy is that he kills himself because he cannot find an object that fits the coordinates of his fantasy—because he cannot handle the presence of the gap, and he doesn't dare break out of himself and his solitude and accept something lesser. His dream object drives him to his own destruction. The Knight of Faith solves this by removing the need for an external object—the very need for breaking out. Bukowski solves it by living through the break, by seeking it—again and again. As the title of one of his poetry collections state: What matters most is how well you walk through the fire.

Notes

1. Eberhard Alsen, *The New Romanticism: A Collection of Critical Essays* (New York: Garland, 2000), 3.

2. John Lardas, *The Bop Apocalypse: The Religious Visions of Kerouac, Ginsberg and Burroughs* (Urbana: University of Illinois Press, 2000), 171.

3. For a detailed discussion of the role of gender in Romantic love, see Sharin Elkholy's article: "What's Gender Got to Do with It? A Phenomenology of Romantic Love," in *Athenäum: Jahrbuch für Romantik* (Paderborn: Yearbook, 1999), 121–61.

4. Ralph Waldo Emerson, *Essays and Lectures* (New York: Library of America, 1983), 331.

5. Percy Bysshe Shelley, *Shelley's Poetry and Prose* (New York: Norton, 2002), 78.

6. Ibid., 79.

7. Søren Kierkegaard, *The Sickness unto Death* (London: Penguin Classics, 1989), 50.

8. Shelley, *Shelley's Poetry and Prose*, 79.

9. Ibid., 77. More precisely, the dream image is a conglomeration of the girl and of "the secrets of the birth of time" that Alastor uncovered in the temple—a metonymic figure, in the Lacanian sense.

10. Stendhal, *Love* (London: Penguin Classics, 1975), 45.

11. Shelley, *Shelley's Poetry and Prose*, 504.

12. Ibid.

13. Emerson, *Essays and Lectures,* 333.

14. Slavoj Žižek, *The Sublime Object of Ideology* (London: Verso, 2009), 49.

15. Kierkegaard, *The Sickness unto Death*, 43.

16. Søren Kierkegaard, *Fear and Trembling* (London: Penguin Classics, 1986), 73.

17. Stendhal, *Love*, 126.

18. Charles Bukowski, *Women* (London: Virgin, 2009), 61.

19. Ibid., 76.

20. Ibid., 104.

21. Charles Bukowski, *Burning in Water, Drowning in Flame* (New York: Ecco, 2003), 118.

22. Bukowski, *Women*, 3.

23. Ibid., 29.

24. Ibid., 73.
25. Ibid., 17.
26. Ibid., viii.
27. Kierkegaard, *Fear and Trembling,* 70.
28. Ibid., 71.
29. Ibid., 72.
30. Ibid., 73.
31. Ibid.
32. Ibid., 75.
33. Ibid., 78.
34. Ibid., 73.
35. Bukowski, *Women,* 303.
36. Ibid., 304.

Anarchism and the Beats

Ed D'Angelo

The first problem that we seem to be confronted with when we try to compare the philosophy of the beats to the philosophy of anarchists is that the beats were poets, not philosophers, and do not seem to have had a "philosophy." But things are not as they seem.

Following Oswald Spengler's idea of a second religiosity that arises out of the primitive elements (the "fellaheen") of a declining civilization, the beats understood themselves to be religious prophets of a new form of liberated consciousness. Poetry was both a means to achieve this new form of consciousness and a means to express that consciousness once it was achieved by other means including travel, drugs, sex, or meditation. The transformation of consciousness sought by the beats was therefore primarily religious in nature, not political or ideological. Kerouac was especially careful to distance himself from an aesthetics that might subordinate art to political ideology. But that does not mean that the beats believed that the transformation of consciousness they sought had no political or social implications. It merely means that, for them, political ideology follows consciousness, not the reverse.

In an author's note he wrote shortly before his death in 1997 to a 1961 essay titled "When the Mode of the Music Changes, the Walls of the City Shake," Ginsberg wrote: "It seemed to me the breakthroughs of new poetry were social breakthroughs, that is, political in the long run. I thought and still think that the bulwark of libertarian-anarchist-sexualized individual poems and prose created from that era to this day—under so much middle-class critical attack—were the mental bombs that would still explode in new kid generations even if censorship and authoritarian (moral majority) fundamentalist militarily-hierarchical 'New Order' neoconservative fascistoid creep Reaganomics-type philistinism took over the nation. Which it nearly has. Thus the title—Poetics and Politics, out of Plato out of Pythagoras—continuation of Gnostic—secret politically suppressed—liberty of consciousness and art—old bohemian—tradition."[1] Ginsberg here locates the beats within the Platonic philosophical tradition, but he identifies with Plato the mystic, not Plato the rationalist.

The irony of the fact that Plato banished the poets from his ideal city is that Plato was himself a great poet. The *Republic* is a work of fiction written with poetic skill and replete with rhetorical devices including metaphor and allegory. The rationalist Plato's argument against the poets is that they are two steps removed from the absolute truth of the ideal forms. Perceptual objects are already mere shadows of the forms, but the images concocted by poets are mere shadows of perceptual objects meant to stir up the basest part of the soul, the appetites. Philosophers, Plato believes, should rely only on reason to apprehend the truth. But yet, Plato recognizes that not everyone in his ideal city will be a philosopher. For those who are not capable of reason, it will be necessary to guide and persuade them with poetry and fiction—hence Plato's notion of the "noble lie." However, poetry is dangerous. Because it has the power to alter people's beliefs, perceptions, and emotions, it has the potential to disrupt the state and make the "walls of the city shake." Therefore, according to Plato, poetry must be controlled by the philosophers, who will craft fictions that maintain justice and harmony. Imagination serves a purpose, but it serves a just purpose only when controlled by reason.

The beats invert the rationalist Plato's hierarchy of imagination and reason by grounding reason in imagination and in the body's rhythms and emotions. Like the romantic anarchist poet William Blake, who warned of an excessive capacity to reason in the "dark satanic mills" of England's industrial revolution, Ginsberg warned of an excessive capacity to reason relative to imagination and emotion in the nuclear age. Ginsberg warned that reason had become a "horrific tyrant" in Western civilization and "created the nuclear bomb which can destroy body, feeling, and imagination."[2]

The transformation of consciousness sought by the beats was not a mere change in the ideas or ideology contained within consciousness, but a transformation of consciousness itself entailing the psychological death and rebirth of the ego.[3] The radical psychiatrist R. D. Laing and the Jungian analyst John Weir Perry understood madness and mysticism in the same way, as a journey to the underworld where the ego—burdened by the outmoded norms of its society—was torn asunder and reassembled, as in the ancient Egyptian shamanic myth of Osiris, who is torn apart in the night sea and reassembled by the goddess Isis, before rising again as Horus, the morning sun, which sets the measure, the law, the rhythm for a new day and a new social order. In this respect, the beats were in tune with primal (and stateless) society, the original hunter-gatherer society, that was led, not by warriors, not by philosopher-kings, and certainly not by capital, but by the ecstatic shamans, whose tales of their journeys to the underworld were told in song and dance, poetry and chant.

It is in terms of the hero's journey to the underworld that Ginsberg would like us to understand the apparent criminality, nihilism, and madness of the beats. Ginsberg's own journey to the underworld seems to have begun during the period 1944–46, when he established contact with the founding members of the beat generation. He emerged from this period a different man, with a transformed sense of self and a new set of moral and aesthetic values.

Ginsberg met Lucien Carr in 1944 in the Union Theological Seminary dormitory, which was being used as a residence for Columbia students. Carr's friend Edie Parker introduced him to Jack Kerouac. Carr then introduced Kerouac to Ginsberg, and both of them to his older friend from St. Louis, William Burroughs. By August 14, 1944, Carr had killed David Kammerer, a mutual friend of Carr and Burroughs from St. Louis, creating the first of many media spectacles that portrayed members of the beat generation as criminals, nihilists, and madmen.

Neal Cassady arrived in New York City in December 1946 and established friendships with Kerouac and Ginsberg, for whom Cassady was an authentic fellaheen of the American West. As Ferlinghetti said in his editor's note to the 1981 printing of Neal Cassady's autobiography, *The First Third*, Cassady was "an early prototype of the urban cowboy who a hundred years before might have been an outlaw on the range. (And as such Kerouac saw him in *On the Road*.)"[4] Cassady was a hustler, a car thief, a womanizer, and a small-time drug dealer. But it was Cassady's fast-paced, free-associative, run-on sentences—in addition to bebop jazz, the music of the African American fellaheen—that inspired Kerouac's and Ginsberg's notions of spontaneous prose.

In 1948 during a time of quiet meditation and simple living, Ginsberg heard Blake's voice in his Harlem apartment: "Ah, sunflower. . . ." Then, in 1949, Ginsberg was arrested for helping Herbert Huncke store stolen goods in Ginsberg's apartment. He subsequently spent eight months at the Columbia Psychiatric Institute, where he met Carl Solomon, to whom he dedicated "Howl." The tabloids covered the story and added to the emerging image of the beats as criminals, nihilists, and madmen. According to Ginsberg, fellow beat writer John Clellon Holmes's 1952 *New York Times* article "This Is the Beat Generation" reinforced the earlier media image of the beats with an "overtone in terms of violence and juvenile delinquency, i.e., mindless protest."[5] Indeed, his novel *Go* was originally titled *The Daybreak Boys,* after a river gang from the 1840s. In an interview with John Tytell, Holmes explained that "our attraction to criminality, mostly crimes without a victim like drugs, fit with our feeling that the definition of man's nature was inadequate. And we were interested in excessive experiences, in the extreme, because a man who puts himself outside the law is a man who is putting himself into himself."[6]

After Ginsberg's 1955 reading of "Howl" at the Six Gallery, poetry readings became popular at cafés and nightspots in San Francisco and Greenwich Village. By the late 1950s, the beat generation had been transformed from a small circle of bohemian writers to a popular social movement among alienated and rebellious young people. In 1958 following the successful launch of *Sputnik,* the Soviet spaceship, the San Francisco columnist Herb Caen dubbed the new rebels "beatniks," adding the suffix "-nik" to "beat" from "Sputnik," thereby associating the beats with communism. Caen's appellation was also intended to allude to derogatory Yiddish words that end in "-nik," such as "nudnik," meaning "someone who is a boring pest."[7] That's why Ginsberg refers to "beatnik" as a "foul word" constructed by "industries of mass communication which continue to brainwash Man and insult nobility."[8]

On the right end of the political spectrum, Norman Podhoretz turned the popular image of the beats against them in his 1958 essay "The Know-Nothing Bohemians," arguing that the "spirit of hipsterism and the Beat Generation strikes me as the same spirit which animates the young savages in leather jackets who have been running amuck in the last few years with their switch-blades and zip guns."[9] On the left end of the political spectrum, the former Trotskyite Norman Mailer became interested in the new "hip" culture as a potentially oppositional force in modern society and declared that the difference between hip and square culture would be the major problem facing Americans for the next twenty-five years. In his 1959 essay "The White Negro," Mailer repeated the popular image of hipsters as criminals and psychopaths but turned it around by arguing that in a society verging on totalitarianism, only criminals and psychopaths have the courage to act with existential authenticity. Mailer—like Paul Goodman and William Burroughs—sensed that the bureaucratic workplace and the suburban nuclear family threatened the nineteenth-century ideal of American manhood represented at its extreme by the image of the western outlaw. In 1981, Mailer helped win the release of the writer Jack Abbott from prison. Abbott's fatal stabbing of Richard Adan shortly after his release from prison seemed to confirm Podhoretz's worst fears about Mailer's notions of literary genius just as American society was taking a sharp turn to the right in reaction against the beat-inspired counterculture of the 1960s and 1970s.

But Ginsberg and Kerouac saw things differently than either Mailer or Podhoretz. Although Ginsberg acknowledged in a 1989 interview that Mailer had a good grasp of the "goof that middle-class white culture was making" and that he had a sense of a "transcendent change of consciousness," he and Kerouac rejected Mailer's macho and violent notion of hipsterism. Kerouac, Ginsberg said, didn't like Mailer's essay because he "saw beat as Christ-like; the Lamb, the emergence of the lamb, not the emergence of the grand criminal savants." Ginsberg, who described himself as a "delicate artistic fairy," agreed with Kerouac that Mailer's notion of beat was too violent and macho.[10]

Nor did Ginsberg believe that the beats could be understood in sociological or ideological terms: "That's some hangover from class war. Kerouac's whole point was that 'beat' went beyond the old Marxist ideological battle of class warfare and into some *practical* attitude of transcendence. Practical had to do with, I mean, like dropping LSD or learning meditation techniques. It's like the bomb, you know. It's not cleansing yourself of the middle class, it's cleansing the doors of perception themselves; in which case middle-class notions and ego notions and everything else gets cleansed."[11] The underworld into which Ginsberg and Kerouac descended was not the criminal underworld, but that of the unconscious, which also exists beyond the social rules and conventions of ordinary waking consciousness. The beats, in this respect, resemble shamans or mystics who transgress the bounds of social rules and conventions in their lonely journey beyond the walls of the city, into the forest, up the mountain, and into the belly of the beast. When they return to the city, they may be condemned as criminals, or they may be welcomed as prophets of a new law.

According to the Manichean logic of the Cold War era, you were either a good American or an evil communist. There was little recognition of any third alternative or middle ground. Since the beats were not considered to be "good Americans," they were often accused by their critics of being communists. But the beats were not communists—at least not in the sense that America's Cold War enemies were communists. Ginsberg saw little difference between capitalist or communist governments because they both rely on violent police bureaucracies to enforce their will both domestically and internationally. So little do they contradict one another, according to Ginsberg, that they could not exist without each other: "They need each other, feed on each other, and often make their living from each other's mythical existence."[12]

The beats were the latest incarnation of romantic bohemian anarchism dating back to the early nineteenth century. Their political philosophy contradicted orthodox Marxism as well as certain aspects of the Bakuninist anarchist tradition in at least three respects. First, the beats did not believe that the working class or the industrial proletariat is the historical agent of change that will bring about a communist society. Second, they were not materialists. They did not believe that consciousness is a superficial structure built upon the social relations of the means of production. Third, they did not believe that history is a dialectical process that proceeds by way of negation. As a consequence of these points, they did not believe in class struggle. As pacifists they were especially opposed to class warfare and any other type of violent social action.

A bohemian community began to develop in Greenwich Village as early as the 1860s, when Henry Clapp founded the *Saturday Press,* which published Walt Whitman, Mark Twain, and William Dean Howells. Members of the literary magazine congregated at Pfaff's basement tavern at 653 Broadway. Throughout the late nineteenth century as more Italian, Irish, and German immigrants arrived in Greenwich Village, the bohemians followed, attracted by cheap rents and their fellow bohemians.[13] The golden age of Greenwich Village bohemia occurred between the fin de siècle and World War I, when modernist art combined with anarchism in what the historian John Patrick Diggins called the "Lyrical Left."[14] After World War I, Greenwich Village underwent a period of gentrification. The bohemian community became a popular tourist attraction that, like Coney Island, provided a temporary escape from the increasingly mechanical routine of the bureaucratic workplace. Although a circle of Greenwich Village bohemian anarchists survived the period between the world wars, most leftists abandoned anarchism for communism following the apparent success of the Russian Revolution. In 1934, the Marxist Cowley looked back at the Greenwich Village bohemians of 1919 with contempt: "The New York bohemians, the Greenwich Villagers, came from exactly the same social class as the readers of the *Saturday Evening Post.* Their political opinions were vague and by no means dangerous to Ford Motors or General Electric: the war had destroyed their belief in political action. They were trying to get ahead, and the proletariat be damned. Their economic standards were those of the small American businessman."[15]

Cowley argued that the bohemians were revolting against the puritanical, production-oriented values of an earlier, accumulative phase of industrial capitalism. Their values—which resemble the values of the post–World War II beats—included the romantic belief that children naturally possess special potentialities that are crushed by a repressive society, and that liberated children can save the world; the idea of free and unhindered self expression; the idea of paganism, that the body is a temple of love; the idea of living for the moment; the idea of female equality; the idea that we can be happy by psychological rather than political means; and the idea of travel or a change of place. But World War I increased productive capacity so much that when the war ended it became necessary to stimulate consumer demand. Bohemian values, Cowley argued, became useful for the new consumer capitalism: self-expression and paganism stimulated consumer demand, living for the moment meant buying on the installment plan, and female equality doubled demand. The Socialist Michael Harrington made a similar argument about the hippies of the 1960s in his 1973 book *The Death of Bohemia*. Ginsberg, he said, had literary standards and political commitments comparable to the pre–World War I bohemians, but the mass counterculture of the post-Beatles era was "a reflection of the very hyped and videotaped world it professed to despise."[16]

But are bohemian values really so easily co-opted by the capitalist system? The history of the United States after 1973 would suggest not, because the system found it necessary to crush those values. Daniel Bell, for example, agreed with the Marxists that the counterculture was a product of consumer capitalism, but in his 1976 book *The Cultural Contradictions of Capitalism*, he warned that the counterculture could undo the productive capacity that made consumer capitalism possible in the first place.

Anarchists, too, were accused of being petty bourgeois at least since the release of Marx's 1847 book *The Poverty of Philosophy*, in which Marx accused the anarchist Pierre-Joseph Proudhon (1809–1865) of being a petty bourgeois. Indeed, Proudhon's anarchism is the anarchism of the small farmer and artisan class who envision a world not of communism but of an equal exchange of labor. Proudhon's mutualist economics was already anticipated by Josiah Warren (1798–1874) in the United States. The Marxist accusation that bohemians are petty bourgeois is similar. Marxists accuse bohemians of being petty bourgeois because they are individualistic and do not seek social change through collective or political means.

There is another thread of anarchist thought, however, that does not yield to this particular line of Marxist criticism. Like other young Russian aristocrats of his generation, Michael Bakunin (1814–1876) became disenchanted with the tsar's regime, especially after serving in the tsar's army, and sought answers in romanticism and German Idealism. Because the study of philosophy was banned in Russian universities, radical young people formed their own study groups. The two most important were one headed by Nicholas Stankevich and another headed by the socialists Alexander Herzen and Nicholas Ogarev. Bakunin joined both and soon thereafter became Russia's leading Hegelian. However, Bakunin radicalized Hegel. Whereas Hegel's dialectic retains and conserves the past as it negates and supersedes it, Bakunin's dialectic was a revolutionary force that negates the past without conserving it, thus creating an entirely new future. In his immortal words, "the passion for destruction is a creative passion."[17]

In 1844, Bakunin went to Paris where he met Proudhon and Marx. Bakunin's collectivist anarchism combined Proudhon's rejection of centralized authority with Marx's class analysis and critique of capitalism. Bakunin envisioned a society without a state in which workers would collectively own and operate the means of production. In 1848, Bakunin's revolutionary passion was devoted to the cause of Slavic nationalism. In 1849, he fought on the barricades alongside the romantics Richard Wagner and Wilhelm Heine against Prussian troops. In 1868, Bakunin joined the First International and led the anarchist faction until the anarchists were expelled by Marx in 1872. Thus began the long-standing feud between Marxists and anarchists. Bakunin warned that the state was antithetical to socialism and predicted that a communist state would turn workers into herd animals. A later generation of communist anarchists including Emma Goldman, Alexander Berkman, and Peter Kropotkin were among the first to recognize the failure of the Russian Revolution.

Communist anarchism gradually replaced Bakunin's collectivism in the European anarchist movement of the late nineteenth century. Communist anarchism was first proposed by the Italian anarchist section of the First International, but the Russian scientist Peter Kropotkin (1842–1921) later became its leading theoretician. Like Bakunin, the communist anarchists were revolutionaries engaged in class warfare. But whereas Bakunin, following Proudhon, believed that the product of labor should be distributed to workers according to the amount of labor they expended, the communists believed that the product of labor should be distributed according to need. The communists argued that the unequal distribution of wealth to workers would ultimately produce a class-stratified society and a state to defend the interests of the wealthy.

Kropotkin envisioned a decentralized society of cooperative farms and workshops, as well as neighborhood and village councils, each operating on the principle of mutual aid and voluntary cooperation. He argued that humans had evolved to voluntarily cooperate with one another in small, face-to-face communities. He decried large urban factories that produced for export or trade rather than for local use because they created economic inequality and degraded the quality of work. His model was instead the medieval village commune in which skilled artisans and small farmers produced for utility rather than exchange value and derived aesthetic enjoyment from their work. Kropotkin lived in England from 1886 until 1917, when he returned to Russia. During his time in England, he befriended the romantic socialist William Morris, who, like Kropotkin, envisioned a decentralized society of cooperative labor and drew on medieval models for inspiration.

Although most of the beats envisioned a decentralized society of cooperative communities similar to that envisioned by the communist anarchists, they did not believe that workers were the agents of change who would usher in such a society. Nor were they interested in waging class warfare. In fact, the bohemians of the postwar years had an uneasy relationship with the American working class. In Greenwich Village, bohemians were violently assaulted by Italian and Irish American workers because they were black or gay or were believed to be communists. The anarchist beat poets Diane di Prima and Tuli Kupferberg both reported such incidents.[18] Michael Harrington reported that Jimmy Baldwin was beaten for sitting with a white woman.[19] Harrington discussed socialist politics with his friends at the White Horse Tavern, where he says they were frequently raided by fist- and chair-swinging Irish kids who accused them of being communists and faggots. One night the owner of the tavern asked Harrington and his friends to sing their songs of solidarity with the workers in a foreign language so the workers at the tavern wouldn't understand what they were saying and start a fight.[20] The beat writer Seymour Krim said that when he moved to the Village he was "scared of the Italian street-threat that used to psychically de-ball all us violin-souled Jewish boys."[21] According to Ronald Sukenick, the Italian hoods in Greenwich Village represented a leitmotif of fear for bohemians in Chandler Brossard's *Who Walk in Darkness* (1952). "This accurately reproduces the feel of the streets at the time," Sukenick wrote, "and in retrospect I see it corresponds to the situation of the cultural underground in the forties and fifties, with its hostility toward the middle class and its ideological divorce from the working class in consequence of the failed socialist movements of the thirties."[22]

In a 1960 letter to Peter Orlovsky, Ginsberg complained that the communists had taken over a conference he attended in Santiago, Chile, and that most everybody was unpoetic. Everybody "got up and made fiery speeches about the workers. Everybody wanted revolutions." He expected Peter to be in a labyrinth of worries, but said that he was in "a labyrinth of communists which is just as bad."[23] In a 1960 letter to Ginsberg, Gary Snyder said that there was "no longer a problem of helping out American workers, but of giving up national comfort for whole world welfare" and added that communism "confuses the cures of economic suffering with the cures of illusion-bound ego." Snyder felt that American workers had been bought out with "bread and circuses."[24]

In a January 22, 1968, letter to Snyder, Ginsberg reported that he had sung a tribute of Guthrie folk songs and was pleased to see a return of that anti-authoritarian tradition, adding that it was "nice to see all the hippies in bells at concert applauding 'Union Maid,' union this time the community (in my head) rather than UAW NMU."[25] Thus Ginsberg placed more hope in hippies than in workers and their large industrial unions. Gary Snyder agreed with him in spite of the fact that one of the sources of Snyder's own anarchism was his early exposure to the anarcho-syndicalist Wobblies in the Pacific Northwest. In an interview with *Playboy* after the 1968 Chicago DNC, Ginsberg complained about "two different versions of communism: the Russian and American police states." Again he placed hope in the new hip consciousness, which realized that "authoritarianism of any nature is a usurpation of human consciousness," and warned that the problem now would "be how to transform the 'greasers'—the blue-collar class which is always in favor of a strong police force and the persecution of minorities." He hoped that rock 'n' roll and psychedelics might transform their consciousness. In the same letter, however, he mentioned with approval Thomas Parkinson and Kenneth Rexroth, two San Francisco bohemian anarchists more to his liking.[26]

One of the sources of the beats' rejection of Marxism was its materialism. In a 1972 interview, Ginsberg said that Kerouac "was very overtly com-

munistic for several years, from '39 to '41, '42," and read some *Das Kapital,*
Communist Manifesto, and the *Daily Worker.* But Kerouac came to dislike
Marxism because "at the time there was a large attack by the left against the
idea of revolution of consciousness, sexual revolution particularly, and psychedelic revolution." By the 1940s, the beats had already read Artaud and
Huxley's *Doors of Perception.* By 1952, they had experimented with peyote.
Kerouac objected to the fact that the Marxists rejected his bohemianism
as "petit bourgeois angelism" and attempted to make the cultural revolution the beats "were involved in, which was a purely personal thing, into a
lesser political, mere revolt against the temporary politicians, and to lead
the energy away from a transformation of consciousness to the materialistic level of political rationalism." Ginsberg felt that it would have been pre-
mature to speak about politics at that time. Before political issues could be
adequately addressed, it was necessary to "get back to Person, from public
to person. Before determining a new public, you had to find out who you
are, who is your person. Which meant finding out different modalities of
consciousness."[27]

In 1963 Ginsberg flew to Saigon and questioned journalists about the
American role there. Deeply disturbed by what he found, he participated in
his first political demonstration upon his return to San Francisco, a demonstration against Madame Nhu, the wife of Vietnam's chief of secret police. In
an interview that took place during the demonstration, Ginsberg said that
he attended the demonstration to be tender to Madame Nhu. He explained
that hostilities would end only when everyone's blocked-up feelings of
tenderness for one another were released from their bodies. He said that
tenderness is a normal instinct and that it was Whitman who first exposed
tenderness as the unconscious basis of American democracy. He supposed
that "some form of community sharing or communism is appropriate to
the future State of Man." But he didn't see how that could work "without
first a sharing of feelings. Then material arrangements will fall into place."[28]

Ginsberg's rejection of the state was based in a personalist metaphysics
that held that only persons are real. Since the state is not a person, it is not
real. Whitman had said all along "that the State doesn't exist (as a living Person), only people exist through their own private consciousness. So we realized we were in the midst of a vast American hallucination" constructed by
the mass media and paid for by the CIA.[29] The state appears to be necessary
only when our natural feelings of tenderness for one another are blocked
and we are separated from one another in a competitive struggle for wealth

(Locke) or honor (Hobbes). Therefore the state may be overcome through a revolution in consciousness that liberates our feelings of tenderness.

Daniel Belgrad argues that the American avant-garde of the 1940s was built upon the automatic techniques of the surrealists to create a new "culture of spontaneity" that was intended to undermine the abstract rationalism of the new bureaucratic order. Charles Olson's "projective verse" offers an example that is particularly relevant to the beats. Olson's experience of government and industry during the war convinced him that a new personalism that went beyond the politics of both Left and Right was necessary to overcome the dehumanizing effects of modern bureaucratic organization. Following Carl Jung, Olson believed that social repression is mediated by the ego operating at the level of consciousness. Direct access to the unconscious through spontaneous expression therefore offered a means of liberation.[30] Charles Olson taught his theory of spontaneous projective verse at Black Mountain College, where he influenced an entire generation of American poets, including Robert Duncan, Allen Ginsberg, and the beats.

Yet another source of the idea that society could be changed by cultural means was the circle of radical pacifists around Dave Dellinger. Radical pacifists in the War Resisters League gradually moved toward an anarchist position during and after World War II as they adopted methods of nonviolent direct action inspired by Gandhi and Thoreau. Dellinger enjoyed a lifelong friendship with the anarchist David Wieck, who like him had also served time at Danbury and practiced nonviolent direct action against Jim Crow rules in prison. Anarchists had long promoted direct action as a nonpolitical means of changing society.

After the war and his release from prison, Dellinger and fellow conscientious objectors established a magazine, *Direct Action,* with the belief that America was ripe for radical change. Lewis Hill wrote a "Call to a Conference" in the first issue of *Direct Action* that led to a meeting of radical pacifists in Chicago in 1946 and the establishment of the Committee for Non-Violent Revolution (CNVR). By 1947, however, the mood of the country became more conservative. World War II accelerated the trend toward efficient bureaucratic organization and scientific management of work. When the war ended, the trend continued, "but with mass consumption— 'a higher standard of living'—replacing wartime urgency as its primary justification."[31] The working class accepted the new bureaucratic order in return for a consumer lifestyle. As CNVR member Lewis Hill commented regarding the Marxist preoccupation with the proletariat, "When one is looking for the proletariat one looks for chains; but in the industrial class in America what one sees is bathtubs and credit-plan refrigerators, with a heavy sprinkling of life-insurance investments."[32] Hill concluded that the cultural basis for a nonviolent social revolution did not yet exist in the United States.[33] He detached himself from the CNVR to pursue his dream of an FM radio station in Berkeley that could contribute to the needed cultural transformation. Pacifica station KPFA was finally established in 1949 and became an important platform for beat and anarchist voices in the early postwar period.

In the 1960s, the possibility of a mass movement reappeared, although it was no longer organized around the working class or labor issues. Dellinger served as chairman of the National Mobilization Committee to End the War in Vietnam (MOBE), a coalition of groups including the emerging counterculture, which staged mass protests between 1966 and 1970. It was Dellinger who asked Jerry Rubin to be project director for the October 21, 1967, march on the Pentagon at which Abbie Hoffman led a chant to levitate and exorcise the building. In a similar vein, Ginsberg led a chant to calm police and protesters in Lincoln Park at the 1968 Democratic Convention in Chicago. Ginsberg corresponded with Dellinger throughout the 1960s and testified on his behalf at the trial of the Chicago Seven. Thus, during the 1960s, anarchist pacifists collaborated more effectively with the bohemian counterculture than with workers.

David Thoreau Wieck (1921–1997), an anarchist philosopher and the editor of *Resistance,* wrote in regard to his encounter with the bohemian anarchist Kenneth Rexroth: "I'm not sure I have him right about this, but I feel that the only philosophy he trusted was the poets' and the mystics." According to Wieck, Rexroth's anarchism combined the principles of Alexander Berkman's communist anarchism with Gustav Landauer's mystical, pacifist, bohemian anarchism. The state, Landauer famously wrote, is not an institution to be confronted by violent force from without, but "a certain relationship between human beings, a mode of human behavior; we destroy it by contracting other relationships, by behaving differently." The state is therefore primarily a cultural phenomenon. And so, Landauer concluded, only poets acting as revolutionary prophets can sweep away the state.

In 1953, Ginsberg met Rexroth on a visit to San Francisco with the help of a letter of recommendation from William Carlos Williams. In 1954, Ginsberg moved to San Francisco and began attending Rexroth's Friday-night gatherings. He and Rexroth got along well. Rexroth introduced Ginsberg to the major figures in the San Francisco Poetry Renaissance, including Robert Duncan and Jack Spicer. It was Duncan who introduced Ginsberg to the beat writer Michael McClure.

In December 1952, Duncan and his partner Jess Collins opened the King Ubu art gallery for only one year to eliminate the risk of it becoming co-opted for commercial purposes.[34] The King Ubu was named after an absurdist play by the French satirist Alfred Jarry (1873–1907) whose theme was the repression of individual expression by the state. Jarry was an anarchist who carried a pistol on his hip and offended the French government by speaking the forbidden Breton dialect. Rexroth, Spicer, and Lamantia all read poetry at the King Ubu.

In mid-1954, the King Ubu was reopened under the name the Six Gallery by a cooperative of artists including Spicer and Wally Hedricks. It was Hedricks who in 1955 proposed to Rexroth that they set up a group poetry reading at the Six Gallery.[35] Rexroth passed the idea on to Ginsberg and referred him to Gary Snyder, who recruited Philip Whalen for the reading. Ginsberg recruited Lamantia and McClure. Rexroth served as the master of ceremonies.

And thus the beat movement was born in the context of Rexroth's circle of anarchist poets when on October 13, 1955, Ginsberg performed his famous reading of "Howl" at the Six Gallery. As Rexroth said, Ginsberg "inhaled the libertarian atmosphere and exploded."[36]

Notes

1. Allen Ginsberg, *Deliberate Prose: Selected Essays 1952–1995,* ed. Bill Morgan (New York: Harper Collins, 2000), 253.

2. Allen Ginsberg, *Allen Ginsberg Spontaneous Mind: Selected Interviews 1958–1996,* ed. David Carter (New York: Perennial, 2001), 431. See also Ginsberg, *Deliberate Prose,* 279–83.

3. See Gregory Stephenson, *The Daybreak Boys: Essays on the Literature of the Beat Generation* (Carbondale and Edwardsville: Southern Illinois University Press, 1990).

4. Neal Cassady, *The First Third & Other Writings,* ed. Lawrence Ferlinghetti (San Francisco: City Lights, 1981), vi.

5. Ginsberg, *Allen Ginsberg Spontaneous Mind,* 514.

6. John Tytell, "An Interview with John Clellon Holmes," in *The Beats: A Literary Reference,* ed. Matt Theado (New York: Carroll and Graf, 2001), 409.

7. Bent Sorensen, *An On & Off Beat: Kerouac's Beat Etymologies,* www.arts.usyd .edu.au/publications/philament/issue3_Critique_Sorensen.htm.

8. Allen Ginsberg, *The Letters of Allen Ginsberg*, ed. Bill Morgan (Philadelphia: Da Capo, 2008), 222–23.

9. Norman Podhoretz, "The Know Nothing Bohemians," in *The Beats*, ed. Seymour Krim (Greenwich, Conn.: Gold Medal, 1960), 123.

10. Ginsberg, *Allen Ginsberg Spontaneous Mind*, 514.

11. Ibid., 515.

12. Ginsberg, *Letters of Allen Ginsberg*, 359–61.

13. June Skinner Sawyers, ed., *Greenwich Village Reader: Fiction, Poetry, and Reminiscences, 1872–2002* (New York: Cooper Square, 2001), xxvii.

14. John Patrick Diggins, *The Rise and Fall of the American Left* (New York: Norton, 1992). See also Allan Antliff, *Anarchist Modernism: Art, Politics, and the First American Avant-Garde* (Chicago: University of Chicago Press, 2001).

15. Sawyers, *Greenwich Village Reader*, 286.

16. Ibid., 475.

17. Mark Leier, *Bakunin: The Creative Passion* (New York: St. Martin's, 2006).

18. Sawyers, *Greenwich Village Reader*, 436–37, 529.

19. Ibid., 472.

20. Ibid., 472, 605.

21. Ibid., 605.

22. Ibid., 529.

23. Ginsberg, *Letters of Allen Ginsberg*, 226.

24. Allen Ginsberg and Gary Snyder, *The Selected Letters of Allen Ginsberg and Gary Snyder*, ed. Bill Morgan (Berkeley: Counterpoint, 2009), 31.

25. Ibid., 101.

26. Ginsberg, *Allen Ginsberg Spontaneous Mind*, 186.

27. Ibid., 285–87.

28. Ibid., 13.

29. Ibid., 282.

30. Belgrad, *Culture of Spontaneity: Improvisation and the Arts in Postwar America* (Chicago: University of Chicago Press, 1998), 29.

31. Daniel Belgrad, "The Transnational Counterculture: Beat-Mexican Intersections," in *Reconstructing the Beats*, ed. Jennie Skerl (New York: Palgrave Macmillan, 2004), 31.

32. Quoted in Scott H. Bennett, *Radical Pacifism: The War Resisters League and Gandhian Nonviolence in America, 1915–1963* (Syracuse, N.Y.: Syracuse University Press, 2003), 148.

33. James Tracy, *Direct Action: Radical Pacifism from the Union Eight to the Chicago Seven* (Chicago: University of Chicago Press, 1996), 51–52.

34. See Allan Antliff, *Anarchy and Art: From the Paris Commune to the Fall of the Berlin Wall* (Vancouver: Arsenal Pulp, 2007), 128. See also Patrick Frank, "San Francisco

1952: Painters, Poets, Anarchism," in *Drunken Boat #2,* ed. Max Blechman (Brooklyn, N.Y.: Autonomedia; Seattle: Left Bank, 1994), 146–52.

35. Linda Hamalian, *A Life of Kenneth Rexroth* (New York: Norton, 1991), 242.

36. Quoted in Frank, "San Francisco 1952: Painters, Poets, Anarchism," 152.

Between Social Ecology and Deep Ecology

Gary Snyder's Ecological Philosophy

Paul Messersmith-Glavin

Gary Snyder is not a philosopher, nor does he "consider himself particularly a 'Beat.'"[1] Snyder is a poet, an essayist, an outdoorsman, and a practitioner of Buddhism. But despite his reluctance to identify with the Beat title, he has been an undeniable influence on the Beat generation and its writers. He was fictionalized as the character Japhy Ryder in Jack Kerouac's *The Dharma Bums*,[2] and helped initiate the San Francisco Renaissance by organizing poetry readings with his close friend Allen Ginsberg, among others, thus ushering in the Beats as a recognized social force. Although not a philosopher in the traditional or academic sense, his writings contain a very complex treatment of modern society's relationship to the natural world. Snyder's chief concerns are protecting nature from the ravages of civilization, putting humans back in touch with our "wild" selves, and returning us to a sense of self-contemplation, community, and embeddedness in nature.

Snyder puts his philosophical views into practice in the foothills of the Sierra Nevada Mountains, where he has made his home since 1970. Eschewing publicity, he sits *za zen* every day, and is a lifelong proponent of ecological thinking. Snyder also draws from Mahayana Buddhism, bioregionalism, and social anarchism in developing his perspective and philosophical orientation. Snyder most clearly spells out the beliefs he conveys through his poetry and practices in his essay work and interviews.

Because Snyder's views are so nuanced, it's possible for various schools of thought to adopt him as their own. Despite being claimed by proponents of deep ecology, and finding his place within this school of thought, Snyder's background, his reading of Marx and anarchism, and his philosophical and political concerns align him also with social ecology, making him an appropriate bridge between these two polarized nature philosophies. The debates between social ecology and deep ecology characterized the emergent Green movement in the 1980s and 1990s and had a tremendous influence within the Earth First! movement. They reverberate today as we face an increasingly dire ecological future. Social ecology is primarily concerned with the dialectic between forms of domination in the human world, and how this leads to the domination of nature. It is a view that emphasizes that the solution to humans' destruction of nonhuman nature is a social one. Deep ecology is more concerned with changing human consciousness, drawing from religious and philosophical perspectives. Snyder acknowledges both, emphasizing the need to change consciousness, while advocating for social changes to reharmonize humanity's relationship to nonhuman nature.

Snyder's Early Life and Influences

Snyder's biography is key to understanding his philosophical impulses. He spent most of his early years in rural Washington state, and then moved with his mother, following a divorce, to Portland, Oregon. Snyder first developed an appreciation for nature at a young age: "I found myself standing in an indefinable awe before the natural world. An attitude of gratitude, wonder, and a sense of protection especially as I began to see the hills being bulldozed down for roads, and the forests of the Pacific Northwest magically float away on logging trucks."[3] Yet observing these realities, Snyder did not have the tools at hand to apprehend them. He explains that his parents were Wobblies, members of the Industrial Workers of the World (IWW), but he could find nothing in their politics to help him understand what was happening. For that he needed imagination and reading Marx and anarchist texts.[4]

Snyder's radical parentage, working-class childhood, and early grounding in Marxism and anarchism come across quite clearly in his essays and interviews. As he points out, "One of the most interesting things that has ever happened in the world was the Western discovery that history is arbitrary and that societies are human, and not divine, or natural, creations—that we actually have the capacity of making choices in regard to our social systems."[5]

Snyder was also exposed to local native Coast Salish people at a young age. They influenced his views of how it was possible to exist in the world, resulting in a lifelong fascination with Native American beliefs and rituals. As we will see, it is Snyder's understanding of Native American views and customs that ultimately rounded out his reading of Marx. Snyder criticizes Marxists both for looking down upon so-called primitive people, and for not sufficiently understanding the effects of capitalism upon nature and the destruction of wilderness.

In the exerpt from this poem Snyder reflects on his predecessors, the men he grew up with:

> you bastards
>
> > my fathers
> > and grandfathers, stiff-necked
> > punchers, miners, dirt farmers, railroad-men
>
> > killd off the cougar and grizzly
>
> > nine bows. Your itch
> > in my boots too,
>
> —your sea roving
> tree hearted son[6]

Poets and Poetry

Snyder's love of poetry began in his childhood. At the age of seven, Snyder was bedridden for weeks as a result of an accident. During this time his parents checked out books for him at the Seattle library, and from that he developed a voracious appetite for reading. By his early teens, Snyder was reading poetry, particularly that of Carl Sandburg and Edgar Lee Masters, and at the age of seventeen, D. H. Lawrence and Walt Whitman.

Although a prolific essayist, Snyder's primary medium of expression became poetry. He won the Pulitzer Prize for his book *Turtle Island* in 1974, and went on to write sixteen books of poetry. For Snyder, the poet plays an essential role in society, laying the foundation for people's self-understanding and connection to tradition and place. Snyder sees poets as transmitting the "complex of songs and chants" that "a whole People sees itself through." In the West, he sees this role filled initially by "Homer and going through Virgil, Dante, Milton, Blake, Goethe, and Joyce. They were the workers who took on the ambitious chore of trying to absorb all the myth/history lore of their own past traditions, and put it into order as a new piece of writing and let it be a map or model of the world and mind for everyone to steer by."[7]

For Snyder there are at least two levels of poetic expression. The first is that which seeks to show the "implicit potentials of the language," making language work better and bring more "delight," since language is primarily a means of communication. Thus, increasing the clarity, playfulness, and interest in communication is one level of expression. But for Snyder, his primary focus is on another level, that in which "poetry is intimately linked to any culture's fundamental worldview, body of lore, which is its myth base, its symbol base, and the source of much of its values—that myth-lore foundation that underlies any society."[8] Poetry, ideally, holds a society together by giving it shared meaning. Despite his reading of Marx, and his anarchism, Snyder does not see poetry as "the work of prophecy. Nor is it, ultimately, the work of social change." While admitting that it can play this role in a minor capacity, poetry is really meant to bring "us back to our original, true natures from whatever habit-molds that our perceptions, that our thinking and feeling get formed into. And bringing us back to original true mind, seeing the universe freshly in eternity."[9] This perspective echoes Snyder's interest in Buddhism, particularly Zen of the Mahayana tradition. For Snyder, the gifted poets speak not for themselves, but for everyone: "And to express *all* of our selves you have to go beyond your own self. Like Dogen, the Zen master, said, 'we study the self to forget the self. And when you forget the self, you become *one* with all things.' And that's why poetry's not self-expression in those small self terms."[10] Snyder seeks to express the importance of nature, beyond the concerns of humans, even adopting wild nature's standpoint, in his poetry.

While looking to poets to express the myth and lore that underlie any civilization, Snyder insists on staying in touch with the simple things, and not forgetting his roots. Snyder advises poets, and people generally, to "get back in touch . . . with ordinary things: with your body, with the dirt, with the dust, with anything you like, you know—the streets. The streets or the farm, whatever it is." He expresses what might be misinterpreted as a kind of anti-intellectualism, suggesting that we "get away from books and from the elite sense of being bearers of Western culture and all that crap. But also, ultimately, into your mind, into *original mind* before any books were put into it, or before any language was invented."[11] This kind of celebration of "ordinary folks" and anti-elitism characterizes Snyder's work. Here he also echoes Zen Buddhism, emphasizing the importance of self-understanding, of knowing one's mind.[12]

Western philosophers from the Sophists on may differ with Snyder here, saying it is impossible to achieve such a state of mind. In an interview with Paul Geneson in 1976, for instance, Snyder was asked to respond to Jean Paul Sartre, who, upon approaching a tree, thinks: "'I feel in an absurd position—I cannot break through my skin to get in touch with this bark, which is outside me,' the Japanese poet would say what?" Snyder responds: "Sartre is confessing the sickness of the West. At least he's honest." He goes on to say: "The Oriental will say, 'But there are ways to do it, my friend. It's no big deal.' It's no big deal, especially if you get attuned to that possibility from an early life . . . to learn about the pine from the pine rather than from a botany textbook. . . . They also know that you can look at the botany textbook and learn a few things too."[13] Here Snyder draws from his experience in nature. He spent much time hiking trails and breathing fresh air to counter an urban-based perspective that may not be able to imagine embracing, let alone understanding, a tree. Because he is a poet, Snyder injects some levity and playfulness into the discussion. For Snyder, the poet plays the part of the Trickster, opening minds and considering fresh perspectives. Here he suggests, contrary to Sartre, that we really can understand the pine, that we can know the natural world beyond ourselves.

Plato would probably have little patience for Snyder. But as Snyder points out, Plato's "*The Republic* is a great myth, a totalitarian vision that nobody took seriously until the twentieth century. The ideas were disastrous, whether they came through Hitler or Stalin." In contrast to this, Snyder says that poets "stay with the simple old myths that are clearly just plain stories, and don't presume (as a rule) to try and formulate public policy. Poets' lies are easily seen through and not dangerous because they promise so little. Plato's Big Lie is sinister because it promises control and power to the leaders."[14] Snyder is suspicious of leaders, and of the state. Although Snyder accuses Plato of providing a justification for the crimes of Hitler and Stalin, he also writes that "the Tragedians asked Plato to let them put on some tragedies. Plato said, 'Very interesting, gentlemen, but I must tell you something. We have prepared here the greatest tragedy of all. It is called The State.'"[15] Snyder categorizes the state as being part of what he calls "biosphere culture," the global organization of the planet along totalitarian lines. Snyder sees that biosphere culture began with "early civilization and the centralized state; [they] are cultures that spread their economic support system out far enough that they can afford to wreck one ecosystem, and keep moving on. . . . It leads us to imperialist civilization with capitalism and institutionalized economic growth."[16]

Here Snyder reflects on what poets need:

> As for poets
> The Earth Poets
> Who write small poems,
> Need help from no man.[17]

Snyder's Mahayana Buddhism

As should be clear from Snyder's views on the role of poets and poetry in society, one of the biggest influences on his work is the philosophy of Buddhism. Like Alan Watts, Snyder has done a great deal to popularize Buddhism in the West, both by explicitly talking about it and by presenting a Buddhist perspective in his poetry. Snyder first read Ezra Pound's and Arthur Waley's translations of Confucius, the *Tao Te Ching*, and Chinese poetry. He read the *Upanishads, Vedas, Bhagavad-Gita,* and other Chinese and Indian Buddhist classics. He explains: "The convergence that I found really exciting was the Mahayana Buddhist wisdom-oriented line as it developed in China and assimilated the older Taoist tradition. . . . Then I learned that this tradition is still alive and well in Japan. That convinced me that I should go and study in Japan."[18] In a certain sense, Snyder is right to reject a Beat identity. He spent six years in Japan when the Beats were making a name for themselves in the United States, and he was not a part of the original New York circle. Through much of the mid-1950s until the late 1960s, when the Beats were in their heyday, Snyder was shuttling back and forth between California and Japan as a practicing Buddhist.

Deep ecologists, such as George Sessions and Bill Devall, authors of *Deep Ecology: Living as if Nature Mattered,* draw a great deal from this tradition as well. In a chapter entitled "Some Sources of the Deep Ecological Perspective," Sessions and Devall state that "contemporary deep ecologists have found inspiration in the Taoist classic, the *Tao Te Ching,* and the writings of the thirteenth-century Buddhist teacher, Dogen." For these authors, "Eastern traditions express organic unity, address what we have called the minority tradition, and express acceptance of biocentric equality in some traditions."[19] Sessions and Devall dedicate their book to Snyder, and state "among contemporary writers, no one has done more than Gary Snyder to shape the sensibilities of the deep ecology movement."[20] So what is the significance of Buddhism to Snyder, and to deep ecologists?

The Buddhist teachings, or Dharma, are separated into three schools, associated with the spread of Buddhism to different countries. These three schools are often referred to as "Turnings of the Wheel." The early Buddhist school of thought is the Hinayana, originating in India. It puts emphasis upon individual enlightenment or an end to personal suffering through the achievement of nirvana. As C. W. Huntington Jr. points out: "Release from fear and suffering can be achieved only by learning to see completely through this illusory appearance of a self, and beyond even death, to the underlying collocation of perceptual and conceptual data responsible for the illusion. This is defined as 'wisdom.'"[21]

The second "Turning of the Wheel" is the Mahayana, which developed in Japan as Zen, and in China as Chan. The Mahayana represents an internal self-critique of the Buddhist tradition. Practitioners of the Mahayana believed that the Hinayana emphasis upon wisdom, or insight into the nature of suffering, was insufficient, and elevated compassion to the same level as wisdom. Concurrent with this development was the introduction of the Bodhisattva ideal, in which Buddhist practitioners were instructed to postpone individual enlightenment until all can be freed of suffering. Thus compassion for the suffering of others became of prominent importance.

The third and final "Turning of the Wheel" occurred with the development of Buddhism in Tibet, ushering in the Vajrayana, which saw the mixing of indigenous Tibetan religious beliefs with Buddhism, and an emphasis upon visualization techniques and rituals. About the Vajrayana, Snyder says, of "all the sophisticated and learned religious traditions in the world today, [Vajrayana] seems to be the only one that has traditional continuous links that go back to the Stone Age. . . . These are the religious insights and practices that belonged to the Paleolithic hunters at the beginning. This is the real nature mysticism."[22]

Of the three "Turnings of the Wheel," Snyder, while appreciative of the Vajrayana, is most immersed in the Mahayana. Despite his fascination with "primitive" cultures and shamanism, Snyder says: "There is nothing in primitive cultures that is at all equivalent to Mahayana philosophy or logic. There is a science and true sophistication of certain states of mind and power that can come through shamanism but the shaman himself doesn't understand the power. Buddhism and yoga have been gradually evolving as a true science of the mind and science of the nature of things but of a different order from the physical sciences we've had so far."[23]

After spending the better part of six years in a Japanese Zen monastery, Snyder returned to the United States. Since then, he has attempted to bring his meditation practice into everyday life. For Snyder, what we need to do "is to take the great intellectual achievement of the Mahayana Buddhists and bring it back to a community style of life which is not necessarily monastic."[24] For Snyder, Zen is

> a way of using your mind and practicing your life and doing it with other people. It has a style that involves others. It brings a particular kind of focus and attention to work. It values work. . . . At the same time it has no external law for doing it. So you must go very deep into yourself to find the foundation of it. In other words it turns you inward rather than giving you a rulebook to live by. Zen is practice that is concerned with *liberation,* not with giving people some easy certainty.[25]

Thus for Snyder, the "real work" is to achieve liberation for all sentient beings, working alongside others to make the world a better place: "The poet is right there . . . in the area that says 'Let the shit fly,' which is different from the religious person in civilized times, who is operating in the realm of control, self-discipline, purity, training, self-knowledge."[26] This position may reflect Snyder's decision to leave the Japanese monastery and rejoin the world, with all its troubles and difficulties. It also represents an attempt to live up to the Bodhisattva ideal, to work alongside others to help everyone end suffering together. As Snyder notes: "The mercy of the West has been social revolution; the mercy of the East has been individual insight into the basic self/void."[27]

Buddhists have an expansive concept of the self. It is an anti-essentialist philosophy, rejecting both the idea of a "soul" and of God. A central principle in Mahayana is that of "emptiness," which is a dialectical concept. Emptiness, or *Sunyata,* posits that nothing has an essential nature, and all things can only be understood in relationship to their context. As Huntington explains: "As components of worldly experience all elements of conceptualization and perception come into being through an unstable conjunction of the requisite circumstances, and cease to be through disjunction of these same circumstances: Their intrinsic nature is like a bundle of hollow reeds."[28]

This insight leads Snyder to quote Dogen, in saying, "in his funny cryptic way . . . 'whoever told people that "Mind" means thoughts, opinions, ideas, and concepts? Mind means trees, fence posts, tiles, and grasses.'"[29] Buddhism allows Snyder to see human mind in nature, and nature in the human mind. And it provides an alternative philosophical framework for deep ecologists disillusioned with the West.

Here Snyder speaks to tradition in his work, and the place of those who came before him:

> Out there somewhere
> a shrine for the old ones,
> the dust of the old bones,
> old songs and tales.
>
> What we ate—who ate what—how we all
> prevailed.[30]

Deep Ecology

Arne Naess coined the term "deep ecology" in his 1973 article, "The Shallow and the Deep, Long-Range Ecology Movements."[31] According to Sessions and Devall: "Naess was attempting to describe the deeper, more spiritual approach to Nature exemplified in the writings of Aldo Leopold and Rachel Carson. He thought that this deeper approach resulted from a more sensitive openness to ourselves and nonhuman life around us. The essence of deep ecology is to keep asking more searching questions about human life, society, and nature as in the Western philosophical tradition of Socrates."[32] Deep ecology had a major influence on the Earth First! movement in the 1980s and 1990s, and today has helped shape the perspectives of primitivists and anticivilization advocates.[33] Deep ecology, in addition to drawing from Buddhism, Taoism, and Native American traditions, also draws from Western philosophy, what it calls the "minority tradition." This includes the anarchists Peter Kropotkin and Murray Bookchin and "such diverse individuals as Thomas Jefferson, Henry Thoreau, Walt Whitman, Woody Guthrie and Carl Sandburg, as well as Paul Goodman, and in the novels of Ursula Le Guin," among others.[34]

The Western philosopher who most impresses Sessions is Spinoza. For Sessions, "Spinoza's metaphysics is a conceptualization of the idea of unity; there can be only one Substance or non-dualism which is infinite, and this Substance is also God or Nature. What we experience as the mental and the physical have no separate metaphysical reality, but rather are aspects or attributes of this one Substance. Individual things, such as Mt. Everest, humans, trees, and chipmunks, are temporary expressions of the continual flux of

God/Nature/Substance."[35] For Sessions, Spinoza's position here echoes the insights of Buddhism. Sessions points to the Norwegian philosopher Jon Wetlesen's "meticulous comparison of Spinozism and the ways of enlightenment of Mahayana Buddhism" to support his claims.[36]

Deep ecology developed as a critique within the environmental movement confronting what were seen as the reformist shortcomings of mainstream environmental activists. Mainstream environmental organizations are criticized by deep ecologists for sharing an industrial paradigm with polluters. Snyder says the debate "within environmental circles is between those who operate from a human-centered resource management mentality and those whose values reflect an awareness of the integrity of the whole of nature. The latter position, that of deep ecology, is politically livelier, more courageous, more convivial, riskier, and more scientific."[37] For Sessions and Devall, "deep ecology goes beyond a limited piecemeal shallow approach to environmental problems and attempts to articulate a comprehensive religious and philosophical worldview." They quote the Australian philosopher Warwick Fox, who "expressed the central intuition of deep ecology: 'It is the idea that we can make no firm ontological divide in the field of existence: That there is no bifurcation in reality between the human and the nonhuman realms . . . to the extent that we perceive boundaries, we fall short of deep ecological consciousness.'"[38] It is this lack of differentiation between the human and the nonhuman, between humans and nature, which is one of social ecologists' many problems with deep ecology.

Here Snyder reflects on the passing of time, and offers advice to future generations:

> The rising hills, the slopes,
> of statistics
> lie before us.
> the steep climb
> of everything, going up,
> up, as we all
> go down.
>
> In the next century
> or the one beyond that,
> they say,
> are valleys, pastures,

we can meet there in peace
if we make it.

To climb these coming crests
one word to you, to
you and your children:

stay together
learn the flowers
go light[39]

Social Ecology vs. Deep Ecology

Social ecology's fundamental premise is that the ecological crisis is rooted in the social crisis, and that social hierarchies lead to the attempt to dominate nature. Therefore, according to social ecologist Murray Bookchin, in order to solve the ecological crisis, we must resolve the social crisis, which leads some humans to dominate others. Thus the ecological crisis is rooted in a class-based, hierarchical, patriarchical society.

The failure to make a distinction between human and nonhuman nature, and the general tendency to emphasize "oneness," is a chief concern of social ecologists in their debates with deep ecologists. As Janet Biehl and Bookchin argue: "Deep ecology . . . views first nature, in the abstract, as a 'cosmic oneness,' which bears striking similarities to otherworldly concepts common to Asian religions. In concrete terms, it views first nature as 'wilderness,' a concept that by definition means nature essentially separated from human beings and hence 'wild.' Both notions are notable for their static and anticivilizational character." Biehl and Bookchin continue, arguing, "Deep ecologists emphasize an ungraded, nonevolutionary continuity between human and nonhuman nature, to the point of outright denial of a boundary between adaptive animality and innovative humanity."[40]

Murray Bookchin was undoubtedly deep ecology's leading critic in the 1980s, when this nature philosophy was gaining traction within the emergent Green movement. In 1987, at the first national gathering of the Greens, Bookchin launched his first polemic, entitled "Social Ecology versus Deep Ecology: A Challenge for the Ecology Movement." Bookchin was addressing the new movement that was "looking for an ecological approach, one that is rooted in an ecological philosophy, ethics, sensibility, and image of nature, and ultimately for an ecological movement that will transform our domineering market society into a nonhierarchical cooperative society—a society that will live in harmony with nature because its members live in harmony with one another."[41] Bookchin proposes social ecology, a view he began to develop in the early 1960s.[42]

Bookchin viewed the differences between social and deep ecology as being of the utmost importance, saying that they "consist not only of quarrels with regard to theory, sensibility, and ethics. They have far-reaching practical and political consequences. They concern not only the way we view nature, or humanity; or even ecology, but how we propose to change society and by what means."[43] Bookchin brings a Left perspective, and a social orientation to ecological issues.

Rather than taking on deep ecology through an immanent critique in which he would explore deep ecology from the inside out, drawing out its implications to show its limitations, Bookchin chose a polemical approach, taking deep ecology head-on, in a polarizing fashion. Bookchin's approach presented two starkly different nature philosophies, one (his) leading to human liberation and reconciliation with nature, and the other (deep) leading to a wishy-washy kind of liberal reformism at best, and eco-fascism at worst.[44] This style of debate led Snyder to say that Bookchin "writes like a Stalinist thug."[45] Yet Bookchin raised many essential issues confronting deep ecology. For instance, he criticized Edward Abbey, a revered figure to members of Earth First!, for the racism of his views on non-European immigrants, however couched in ecological terms they were; he denounced a writer in the *Earth First!* journal who, using the pseudonym "Miss Ann Thropy," welcomed the AIDS virus as a necessary population control (along with "war, famine, humiliating poverty"); and he took on Dave Foreman, at the time an Earth First! spokesman and de facto leader, who said in an interview that "the worst thing we could do in Ethiopia is to give aid—the best thing would be to just let nature seek its own balance, to let the people there just starve."[46] However polarizing Bookchin's debate style was, he raised essential problems with many positions taken by deep ecologists. The lack of a social analysis, informed by the values of the Left, led many prominent proponents of deep ecology to embrace profoundly racist political positions. While Snyder did not support these views, neither did he publicly condemn them, largely staying out of the fight.

Bookchin's central philosophical problems with deep ecology stem from both its tendency not to make distinctions within human society, to blame "humanity" in general rather than specific human rulers, for instance, and also its ahistoricism:

Deep ecology contains no history of the emergence of society out of nature, a crucial development that brings social theory into organic contact with ecological theory. It presents no explanation of—indeed, it reveals no interest in—the emergence of hierarchy out of society . . . in short, the highly graded social as well as ideological development that gets to the roots of the ecological problem in the social domination of women by men and of men by other men, ultimately giving rise to the notion of dominating nature in the first place.[47]

This observation leads Bookchin to accuse deep ecology of viewing nature as being what one sees looking through a "picture window." He argues that deep ecologists maintain a strong distinction between humans and nature, between the city and "the wild."

The political theorist Tim Luke engages in a more sympathetic, immanent critique than does Bookchin. Yet he arrives at many of the same conclusions concerning deep ecology's flaws. Luke writes: "Nature in deep ecology simply becomes a new transcendent identical subject-object to redeem humanity. By projecting selfhood into Nature, humans are to be saved by finding their self-maturation and spiritual growth in it. . . . Nature, then, becomes ecosophical humanity's alienated self-understanding, partly reflected back to itself and selectively perceived as self-realization, rediscovered in biospheric processes."[48] But what of Snyder, the appointed poet laureate of deep ecology? Does he share the views of other deep ecologists such as Sessions and Devall?

Here, Snyder relates a hike, and some words he encountered:

> Fifteen years passed. In the eighties
> With my lover I went where the roads end.
> Walked the hills for a day,
> looked out where it all drops away,
> discovered a path
> of carved stone inscriptions tucked into
> the sagebrush
>
> "Stomp out greed"
> "The best things in life are not things"
> words placed by an old sage.[49]

Nature/The Wild/Wilderness

In contrast to the views of other proponents of deep ecology, in which nature is a static concept, outside of human culture, Snyder's understandings are far more nuanced. When speaking of nature, Snyder proposes three categories: nature, the wild, and wilderness. Bookchin and Snyder would be in agreement in defining nature. Bookchin, drawing from Hegel, sees human culture as a second nature, as nature rendered self-conscious.[50] Thus both humans and the nonhuman are expressions of nature. Similarly for Snyder, nature is "the physical universe and all its properties."[51] The second category is the wild, which is the organic process and essence of nature. The wild is the ongoing process of the evolution of nature. Finally, wilderness is that aspect of nature that exists outside of the human world. Wilderness "is simply topos—its areas where the process is dominant."[52]

Human society is an expression of nature; it is natural; "we can say that New York City and Tokyo are 'natural' but not 'wild.'"[53] So there is nothing unnatural about New York City, "or toxic wastes, or atomic energy, and nothing—by definition—that we do or experience in life is 'unnatural.'"[54] Thus, for Snyder, "civilization is part of nature . . . our body is a vertebrate mammal being."[55] In contrast to civilization, wilderness "is a part of the physical world that is largely free of human agency. Wild nature is most endangered by human greed or carelessness. 'Wild' is a valuable word. It refers to the process or condition of nature on its own, without human intervention. It is a process, a condition, not a place. 'The wilds' is a place where wild process dominates."[56]

We thus have nature, which includes human culture, and the wilderness, which is outside of human society. And we have the wild, which is a complex process of becoming. For Snyder, "'ecology' is a valuable shorthand term for complexity in motion."[57] Humans can become more wild by getting in touch with nonhuman nature. By spending time in the wilderness, discovering aspects of themselves outside of human culture, humans can reconnect with their biological selves, better understanding their place in the world.

Snyder's view of nature is neither romantic nor one-dimensional. Having spent a great deal of time hiking trails, and working as a fire lookout for months at a time deep in the wilderness, Snyder has developed a healthy appreciation for the complexity of the natural world: "Life in the world is not just eating berries in the sunlight. I like to imagine a depth ecology that would go to the dark side of nature, the ball of crunched bones in a scat, the feathers in the snow, the tales of insatiable appetite." Hence, for Snyder, in addition to being beautiful, fecund, and alive, wild nature is "also nocturnal, anaerobic, cannibalistic, microscopic, digestive, fermentative, cooking away in the warm dark."[58]

Snyder's multidimensional definition of nature, and his three categories, brings an interesting perspective to discussion of the ecological crisis, in which toxic waste, industrial pollution, and the continuing emission of greenhouse gases into the atmosphere threaten human life. In this context, Snyder points out that "nature is ultimately in no way endangered; wilderness is."[59]

This poem represents a kind of manifesto:

We look to the future with pleasure
we need no fossil fuel
get power within
grow strong on less.[60]

The War against the Wild

Snyder's insights concerning wilderness and human society's destruction of it come at a critical time in human evolution. Since the Industrial Revolution, the capitalist mode of production has been polluting the air, land, and water at an alarming rate. The problems of deforestation, water and air pollution, and chemicals in the food supply may only be overshadowed by the effects of catastrophic climate change. The increasing presence of greenhouse gases such as carbon dioxide and methane in the atmosphere threatens to raise global temperatures by as much as nine degrees Fahrenheit by the end of this century if business as usual continues. At this date, rather than reducing emissions, capitalism is, in fact, increasing them. This will truly be disastrous for humanity, affecting the Southern Hemisphere more than the Northern, but wrecking civilizations across the globe.[61] Snyder speaks to the starkness of the situation: "What we are witnessing in the world today is an unparalleled waterfall of destruction of a diversity of human cultures; plant species; animal species, of the richness of the biosphere and the millions of years of organic evolution that have gone into it."[62]

Like social ecology, which links the domination of humans by humans with the attempt to dominate nature, Snyder draws a similar parallel: "A society that treats its natural surroundings in a harsh and exploitative way will do the same to 'other' people. Nature and human ethics are not unconnected. The growing expansion of ecological consciousness translates into a deeper understanding of interconnectedness in both nature and history, and we have developed a far more sophisticated grasp of cause and effect relationships."[63] Bookchin implores the ecological movement to examine the nature of hierarchy in society, and to explore dominant power relations in order to understand the root causes of ecological destruction. He is quick to point out that it is not science or technology per se that is the problem. Snyder concurs, calling these things "straw men," and asks the question, "Who is being served by them?" He answers, "A small number of owners who have centralized it, production, the banks, and even the government so to speak." Like Bookchin's advocacy of a libertarian technology, one that serves human needs in harmony with nature, Snyder asks if it is possible to have a "technology that is bioregionally appropriate and serves the needs of the people at the same time?" Snyder offers the opinion that a libertarian technology "would have developed considerably longer ago if it had not been to the disadvantage of centralized economies to explore solar technologies. . . . A decentralized energy technology could set us free. It's only the prevailing economic and government policies that block us from exploring that further. There is a people's technology."[64] A "people's technology" would serve human needs, rather than corporate profit. For Snyder, the centralization of power is a central problem. The decentralization of energy production would shift power back to the people from the hands of corporations. A "people's technology" would also work with, rather than against, the processes of the natural world.

In contrast to many advocates of deep ecology who, as Luke points out, mostly want to preserve nature for field trips, with deep ecology "a philosophy for properly outfitted mountain climbers, backpackers, and field biologists,"[65] advocates of environmental justice, those who advance the interests of the poor, would find an ally in Snyder. According to Snyder: "Environmental concerns and politics have spread worldwide. In some countries the focus is almost entirely on human health and welfare issues. It is proper that the range of the movement should run from wildlife to urban health. But there can be no health for humans and cities that bypasses the rest of nature. A properly radical environmental position is in no way anti-human. We grasp the pain of the human condition in its full complexity, and add the awareness of how desperately endangered certain key species and habitats have become."[66] Thus the attempt to separate the concerns of the city from those of the wild must be fought. As Snyder points out: "It's all one front ultimately. It only serves the interests of the industrial capitalist cancer to have people think it's two fronts, that environment is white people's concern and jobs poor people's and black people's concern. . . . The natural world, as anyone should see, is being ripped off, exploited, and oppressed just as our brothers and sisters in the human realm are being exploited and oppressed."[67] Thus Snyder joins social concerns with the effort to stop the destruction of the natural world.

A kind of pessimism, or perhaps realism, infuses the excerpt from this poem:

> And when humanity is laid out like coal
> somewhere some earnest geologist
> will note them in his notebook.[68]

Bioregionalism and Reinhabitation

As we have seen, Snyder is a critic of the state. But what would he propose to replace this mode of social organization? For Snyder, and the larger bioregional movement in general, the answer is obvious: the bioregion. A bioregion is an area defined by its natural boundaries that is "posited on the idea that the human community is only one of the communities on any given part of the planet, and that the other communities—plant life, animal life, mineral life—inside the landscape with its watershed divisions, its soil types, its annual rainfall, its temperature extremes, all of that constitutes a biome, an ecosystem, or, as they like to say, a natural nation."[69] In getting to know one's bioregion, one can better understand the natural context within which we live. We can learn where our water comes from, where our waste goes, and how best to live within our surroundings. For Snyder, "the ethics or morality of this is far more subtle than merely being nice to squirrels."[70] This is a huge undertaking, and it is the task that awaits us: "We haven't discovered North America yet. People live on it without knowing what it is or where they are. They live on it literally like invaders. You know whether or not a person knows where he is by whether or not he knows the plants. By whether or not he knows what the soils and waters do."[71] In contrast to being stewards of the land, understanding where we really are, in Americans, Snyder sees "a nation of fossil fuel junkies, very sweet people and the best hearts in the world. But nonetheless fossil fuel junkies of tremendous mobility zapping back and forth, who are still caught on the myth of the frontier, the myth of boundless resources and a vision of perpetual materialistic growth."[72] Reorganizing society along bioregional lines alone is not enough. We would also need to incorporate social ecology's emphasis on confronting human forms of domination, such as racism, sexism, and hetero-patriarchy, for this to really approximate a liberatory alternative to the state. History is littered with examples of cultures that were bioregionally defined, but that maintained internal hierarchies and forms of domination.

Many so-called primitivists such as John Zerzan advocate for a return to hunter-gatherer societies to solve the problems of civilization and reconcile humans' relationship with nature. Snyder advocates for learning from primitive cultures. Quoting the economic anthropologist Marshall Sahlins, he says that "the upper Paleolithic was the original affluent society, and he estimates that they worked an average of 15 hours a week. . . . There is no class of landless paupers in "primitive culture." Landless paupers belong to civilization."[73] In an echo of the myth of the fall from grace, Snyder quotes the anthropologist Claude Levi-Strauss, who "says that civilization has been in a long decline since the Neolithic,"[74] but he believes that "we cannot again have seamless primitive cultures, or the purity of the archaic, we can have neighborhood and community."[75] In response to criticisms, and in contrast to other advocates of primitivism, Snyder says, "It isn't really a main thrust in my argument or anyone else's I know that we should go backward."[76] But how do we move forward?

Snyder here relates the difficult tasks of a pragmatic politics:

> September heat.
> The Watershed Institute meets,
>   planning more work with the B.L.M.
> And we have visitors from China, Forestry guys,
>   who want to see how us locals are
> doing with our plan.
> Editorials in the paper are against us,
> a botanist is looking at rare plants in the marsh.[77]

Ecologizing the Dialectic

For Snyder, the bringing together of social and ecological concerns is the best way to address the ecological crisis: to understand the roots of the destruction of wilderness in the hierarchies inherent in capitalist, patriarchical culture. For Snyder this means "supporting any cultural and economic revolution that moves clearly toward a free, international, classless world."[78] Marxists, and leftists generally, understand the divisions within human society but often fail when addressing ecological issues. For Snyder, this is because they "have been unable to bring themselves to think of the natural world as part of the dialectic of exploitation; they have been human-centered—drawing the line at exploitation of the working class." Snyder believes that his "small contribution to radical dialectic is to extend it to animals, plants: indeed, to the whole of life."[79] In addition to not understanding the import of ecological issues, and of the necessity of developing an ecological consciousness, Marxists have also fallen short in their appreciation for so-called primitive peoples. For Snyder, "Marxists, granted the precision of their critique on most points, often have a hard time thinking clearly about primitive cultures, and the usual tendency is to assume that they should become civilized."[80] Rather than primitive peoples becoming civilized, Snyder advocates that civilized people learn from the wisdom of the "non-civilized."

Snyder says that when he first went to college, he felt a contradiction being a member of a society that was destroying "its own ground." This led him to a lengthy political analysis, and "the discovery of Marxist thought." While recognizing that capitalism is a large part of the problem of the destruction of nonhuman nature, believing as he does that "pollution is somebody's profit,"[81] Snyder thinks there is more to it than that: "For a long time I thought it was only capitalism that went wrong. Then I got into American Indian studies and at school majored predominantly in anthropology and got close to some American Indian elders. I began to perceive that maybe it was all of Western culture that was off the track and not just capitalism—that there were certain self-destructive tendencies in our cultural tradition." This led him to study the traditions of Native Americans, to Japan to study Buddhism, and ultimately to go "back to the land," reinhabiting the foothills of the Sierra Nevada Mountains.[82] It also led him to a lifetime of critiquing contemporary society, advocating the development of an ecological consciousness, and to try and change society. Since human activity can in fact change social relations, we have a responsibility to act. Even the most seemingly innocent activity can make a difference: "Without knowing it, little old ladies in tennis shoes who work to save whooping cranes are enemies of the state."[83]

In contrast to Western critics of Buddhism and Asian philosophies in general, including Bookchin, who say that these worldviews lead to a passive acceptance of the way things are and a kind of quietism, Snyder posits that "to act responsibly in the world doesn't mean that you always stand back and let things happen: you play an active part, which means making choices, running risks, and karmically dirtying your hands to some extent. That's what the Bodhisattva ideal is all about."[84]

Part of getting his hands dirty has involved being on the California Arts Council, shaping policy for the arts in California, and doing local ecological organizing, including the unglamorous work of arguing in city council meetings: "I've spent years arguing the dialectic, but it's another thing to go to supervisors' meetings and deal with the establishment, to be right in the middle of whatever is happening right here, rather than waiting for a theoretical alternative government to come along."[85]

All this is in sharp contrast to Luke's criticism of deep ecology as being "in the last analysis 'utopian ecologism.' As a utopia, it presents alluring moral visions of what might be; at the same time, it fails to outline practicable means for realizing these ecologically moral visions."[86] While this may be true for the deep ecology of Sessions and Devall, who advocate an incoherent ensemble of consciousness change, reformism, and "direct action" to reconcile our relation to the rest of nature, Snyder is quite explicit about the need to replace capitalism as an economic system, the state as a form of social organization, and to reintegrate humans into their natural environment. He advocates developing a new sense of human community, extending the notion of community to the nonhuman, and reinhabiting the land along bioregional lines:

> Whatever sense of ethical responsibility and concern that human beings can muster must be translated from a human-centered consciousness to a natural-systems-wide sense of value. First, simply because such a bighearted sense of the world seems right, but also to help avert the potential destruction of even the very processes that sustain most life on earth. . . . Such an extension of human intellect and sympathy into the nonhuman realms is a charming and mind-bending undertaking. It is also an essential step if we are to have a future worth living. It was hinted at in our ancient past, and could, if accomplished, be the culminating human moral and aesthetic achievement.[87]

The danger, as Luke points out, is that "to evoke such religious outlooks in post-industrial America, on one level, may promote maturity and forsaking consumerist illusions." But on another level, it can provide "an ineffectual opiate for the masses as their current material standard of living disappears in deep ecological reforms."[88] To counter this danger, we need a revolutionary movement with a social consciousness, a clear understanding of what we are up against, and the will to radically restructure and transform society from the ground up. Snyder advocates utilizing "civil disobedience, outspoken criticism, protest, pacifism, voluntary poverty, and even gentle violence if it comes to a matter of restraining some impetuous redneck,"[89] to bring about a new society. As Snyder's life and philosophy point out, drawing as it does from Zen, bioregionalism, and social anarchism, nothing short of this will solve the deep ecological crisis in which we find ourselves. Exemplifying the best of both social ecology, with its commitment to ending social domination to halt humanity's destruction of wild nature, and deep ecology, drawing as it does from Asian philosophies such as Buddhism and Daoism, Native American traditions, and the examples of "primary peoples," Snyder is positioned perfectly to help us achieve the seemingly impossible task of harmonizing our relationship with the rest of nature before it is too late.

Notes

1. Jann Garitty, assistant to Gary Snyder, e-mail to author, October 29, 2010.

2. Jack Kerouac, *The Dharma Bums* (New York: Viking, 1958).

3. Gary Snyder, *The Old Ways* (San Francisco: City Lights, 1977), 15.

4. Ibid., 16.

5. Gary Snyder, *The Real Work: Interviews and Talks 1964–1979* (New York: New Directions, 1980), 101.

6. Gary Snyder, *Turtle Island* (New York: New Directions, 1974), 75.

7. Snyder, *The Real Work,* 171.

8. Ibid., 70.

9. Ibid., 72.

10. Ibid., 65, emphasis in original. The concept of "original true mind" (*honshin* in Japanese) is central to Zen.

11. Ibid., 64, 65, emphasis in original.

12. Snyder is obviously well read, and works in the medium of intellectual expression. His point here is that we should not take ourselves too seriously, and that it is important to take a step back from reading and writing to better understand ourselves.

13. Ibid., 67.

14. Gary Snyder, *Back on the Fire* (Berkeley: Counterpoint, 2007), 44.

15. Snyder, *The Old Ways,* 15.

16. Ibid., 21.

17. Snyder, from "Dusty Braces," in *Turtle Island,* 87.

18. Snyder, *The Real Work,* 94, 95.

19. Bill Devall and George Sessions, *Deep Ecology: Living as if Nature Mattered* (Salt Lake City: Peregrine Smith, 1985), 100.

20. Ibid., 83.

21. C. W. Huntington Jr., *The Emptiness of Emptiness: An Introduction to Early Indian Madhyamika* (Honolulu: University of Hawaii Press, 1989), 87.

22. Snyder, *The Real Work,* 176.

23. Ibid., 15.

24. Ibid., 16.

25. Ibid., 153.

26. Ibid., 177.

27. Gary Snyder, *Earth House Hold* (New York: New Directions, 1969), 92.

28. Huntington, *The Emptiness of Emptiness,* 91.

29. Gary Snyder, *The Practice of the Wild* (San Francisco: North Point, 1990), 20.

30. Gary Snyder, from "Old Bones," in *Mountains and Rivers Without End* (Washington, D.C.: Counterpoint, 1996), 10.

31. Arne Naess, "The Shallow and the Deep, Long-Range Ecology Movements," *Inquiry* 16 (1973).

32. Devall and Sessions, *Deep Ecology,* 65.

33. Jason McQuinn, "Why I Am Not a Primitivist," www.insurgentdesire.org.uk/notaprimitivist.htm.

34. Devall and Sessions, *Deep Ecology,* 18. While pointing to this list of sometimes contradictory authors as a source of inspiration, Devall and Sessions do not really integrate their thoughts into a coherent philosophy.

35. Ibid., 238.

36. Ibid.

37. Snyder, *The Practice of the Wild,* 181.

38. Devall and Sessions, *Deep Ecology,* 66, quoting Warwick Fox, "Deep Ecology: A New Philosophy of Our Time?," *Ecologist* 14, no. 5–6 (1984). Devall and Sessions both deny an ontological division between the human and the nonhuman and, at the same time, posit nature as distinct from the human realm, as being "out there."

39. Snyder, "For the Children," in *Turtle Island,* 86.

40. Janet Biehl and Murray Bookchin, "Theses on Social Ecology and Deep Ecology," Institute for Social Ecology website, 1995, www.social-ecology.org/1995/08/theses-on-social-ecology-and-deep-ecology/.

41. Murray Bookchin, "Social Ecology versus Deep Ecology: A Challenge for the Ecology Movement," *Green Perspectives: Newsletter of the Green Program Project,* no. 4–5 (Summer 1987).

42. Murray Bookchin, *Our Synthetic Environment* (New York: Harper and Row, 1962);

Murray Bookchin, "Ecology and Revolutionary Thought," in *Post-Scarcity Anarchism* (Berkeley: Ramparts, 1971).

43. Bookchin, "Social Ecology versus Deep Ecology," 3.

44. Ibid., 5.

45. Bob Sipchen, "Ecology's Family Feud: Murray Bookchin Turns up the Volume on a Noisy Debate," *Los Angeles Times*, March 27, 1989.

46. Murray Bookchin and Dave Foreman, *Defending the Earth: A Dialogue between Murray Bookchin and Dave Foreman* (Boston: South End, 1999), 123–24. The author writing under the pseudonym "Miss Ann Thropy" is reported to be Christopher Manes.

47. Ibid., 9.

48. Tim Luke, "The Dreams of Deep Ecology," *Telos*, no. 76 (Summer 1988): 81.

49. Snyder, from "Finding the Space in the Heart," in *Mountains and Rivers Without End*, 150.

50. Murray Bookchin, *The Philosophy of Social Ecology* (New York: Black Rose, 1990).

51. Snyder, *The Practice of the Wild*, 9.

52. Paul Ebenkamp, ed., *The Etiquette of Freedom: Gary Snyder, Jim Harrison, and The Practice of the Wild* (Berkeley: Counterpoint, 2010), 73.

53. Snyder, *The Practice of the Wild*, 11.

54. Ibid., 8.

55. Ibid., 181–82.

56. Snyder, *Back on the Fire*, 25, 26.

57. Ibid., 31.

58. Ebenkamp, *The Etiquette of Freedom*, 77.

59. Snyder, *The Practice of the Wild*, 181.

60. Snyder, from "Tomorrow's Song," in *Turtle Island*, 77.

61. "Contributions of Working Groups I, II and III to the Fourth Assessment Report of the Intergovernmental Panel on Climate Change," IPCC, Geneva, Switzerland, 2007, www.ipcc.ch/publications_and_data/ar4/syr/en/main.html.

62. Snyder, *The Old Ways*, 17.

63. Snyder, *Back on the Fire*, 23.

64. Snyder, *The Real Work*, 147.

65. Luke, "The Dreams of Deep Ecology," 86.

66. Snyder, *The Practice of the Wild*, 181.

67. Snyder, *The Real Work*, 144, 145.

68. Gary Snyder, from "The Politicians," in *The Back Country* (New York: New Directions, 1968), 145.

69. Ebenkamp, *The Etiquette of Freedom*, 42.

70. Snyder, *The Old Ways*, 63.

71. Ibid., 69.

72. Snyder, *The Real Work*, 9.

73. Snyder, *The Old Ways,* 34.

74. Ibid., 61.

75. Snyder, *The Real Work,* 161.

76. Ibid., 111.

77. Gary Snyder, from "What to Tell, Still," in *danger on peaks* (Washington, D.C.: Shoemaker Hoard, 2004), 41.

78. Snyder, *Earth House Hold,* 92.

79. Snyder, *The Real Work,* 130.

80. Snyder, *The Old Ways,* 25.

81. Snyder, *A Place in Space,* 36.

82. Snyder, *The Real Work,* 94.

83. Ibid., 160.

84. Ibid., 107.

85. Ibid., 117.

86. Luke, "The Dreams of Deep Ecology," 90.

87. Gary Snyder, *A Place in Space: Ethics, Aesthetics, and Watersheds* (Washington, D.C.: Counterpoint, 1995), 210.

88. Luke, "The Dreams of Deep Ecology," 79.

89. Snyder, *Earth House Hold,* 92.

WILLIAM BURROUGHS AS PHILOSOPHER

From Beat Morality to Third Worldism to Continental Theory

Jones Irwin

> I thought philosophically: isn't life peculiar?
>
> —William Burroughs, *Naked Lunch*

The literary oeuvre of William Burroughs occupies an enigmatic position both in relation to the aesthetic movements of his time and the wider philosophical thematics of this period. In this essay, I want to focus especially on the latter problematic—the question of "Burroughs as philosopher." Even on a superficial inspection, it is clear that Burroughs's work is significantly concerned with philosophical issues such as the relationship between the social and the individual, the experience of mortality, the nature of artistic integrity, and the distinction between morality and immorality. In relation to the question of morality, for example, Burroughs certainly sees a moral vision as central to his thinking and art. Despite all the appearances to the contrary, Burroughs consistently views his art as "telling the truth," or, in commentator Mitch Tuchman's phrase, as an "impassioned moralism" (qtd. in Rodley 1997, 157). In this essay, I will first look at how this moral dimension of Burroughs's work can be traced from the influence of the wider Beat movement. Second, I will explore how J. G. Ballard's reading of Burroughs can help us explore a more sociopolitical emphasis in Burroughs's work, which culminates in a relentless critique of contemporary society (a critique that has connections, as we will see, to the Third Worldist movement, as well as to critical theory). As the influential Slovenian philosopher

Slavoj Žižek has observed, "the Freudian image of a society and social norms which repress the individual's sexual drives no longer seems a valid account of today's predominant hedonistic permissiveness" (Žižek 2006, 2). It is with such an explanatory vacuum in mind that we can best see the renewed relevance of Burrough's sociopolitical critique.

Burroughs and a Beat Morality and Politics

In order to look at Burroughs's connections to philosophy, it is useful to see him in the context of perhaps the most significant postwar literary avant-garde in America, the Beats. Although Burroughs is often categorized as unequivocally a Beat writer, it should be said at the outset that this perception is not wholly correct. The Beats were a distinct American group of writers, evolving from the 1950s, including Allen Ginsberg, Jack Kerouac, and Gregory Corso. As the historian of the Beat movement Ann Douglas has noted, Burroughs was "a leader of postmodern literary fashion in the 60s" (Douglas 1999, xxvi). His work led him to "discard the humanistic notions of the self . . . human is an adjective not a noun . . . his starting point [being] the place where the human road ends" (Douglas 1999, xxvi). If humanism is the philosophy which optimistically places the human, rational, moral individual at the center of the universe, Burroughs's work rejects what it sees as the hubris of such a philosophical position. This antihumanism distinguishes Burroughs from any of the other Beat writers. Burroughs's antihumanism was initially directed against the humanism of Allen Ginsberg, linking Burroughs to a different and distinctive tradition within American modernist writing. As Douglas notes: "While he is part of the Beat movement, he also belongs to another literary tradition of *avant-garde* novelists headed by Nabokov, Pynchon, John Hawkes, William Gaddis, John Barth and Don DeLillo" (Douglas 1999, xxvi).

While the emphasis on a fractured personhood and self links Burroughs very obviously to postmodernism, a connected emphasis on moral responsibility in his work marks him out from many other postmodern writers and philosophers. Mitch Tuchman has paradigmatically noted this important aspect of Burroughs's work in referring to his "impassioned moralism." This "morality" is perhaps best understood as Burroughs's own, independent of his association with the ethics of the Beat movement, but it nonetheless also connects to Burroughs's involvement in the latter. In her text *Reconstructing the Beats*, Jennie Skerl tries to put the Beats in some kind of contemporary context: "The Beats were an *avant-garde* arts movement and bohemian subculture that led an underground existence in the 1940s and early 1950s, gaining public recognition in the late 1950s with the publication of *Howl* (Ginsberg 1956), *On the Road* (Kerouac 1957), *Naked Lunch* (Burroughs 1959) and the new American poetry (Donald Allen, 1960)" (Skerl 2004, 1). In many respects, the Beats were part of a global counterculture or avant-garde: "a transnational counterculture organised against the corporate capitalist postwar order" (Skerl 2004, 3). Here, Skerl explicitly makes the connection between the Beats and the respective movements of surrealism and Dada. The Beats were an "arts community . . . who sought to create a new alternative culture, as a critique of mainstream values and social structures, as a force for social change and as a crucible for art" (Skerl 2004, 2). Like the Dadaists and surrealists before them, the Beats sought to erase the boundaries between art and life, to create art that "could organise a new life praxis from a basis in art. . . . They fashioned a role as poet-prophets who sought a spiritual alternative to the relentless materialist drive of industrial capitalism" (Skerl 2004, 2).

Burroughs is certainly paradigmatic in the Beat movement, although he later declaimed affinity in terms of literary style with them (despite the obvious personal connections). In many respects, one of the key elements of Burroughs's work, and more generally that of the Beats, which we can connect to a philosophical thematic, relates to the whole political-philosophical dimension of their critique of the contemporary American society in which they found themselves. Key to this critique was the concept of *alienation,* which they inherited from a Marxist tradition but which also connected to concepts of alienation in a thinker like Freud, and which were developed by neo-Marxist thinkers of the time such as Herbert Marcuse (Marcuse 2002). As Skerl notes, the Beats were in countercultural resistance to what Robert Holton called the "centripetal cultural logic of postwar America . . . [which] was ubiquitous from childhood on. This was summarized in the phrase 'you must adjust,' and the Beats' mantra might rather be described as 'break out of the cage'" (qtd. in Skerl 2004, 15). At root, the Beats were in revolt against what they perceived as the fundamental values of conservative America. Skerl refers here interestingly to Herbert Marcuse's seminal text *One Dimensional Man* (Marcuse 2002). Paraphrasing Marcuse, she asks whether alienation becomes obsolete when the individuals of a society identify with the life that is imposed upon them. Her answer is in the negative: "The result of this identification is not the loss of alienation though but actually constitutes a more progressive stage of alienation characterized by the loss of ability to imagine alternatives" (Skerl 2004, 17). The resultant task of the Beats, according to Skerl, was a moral and ethical one, and this is where we see Burroughs's affinity with the Beats over the postmodernists. Here, she quotes Chandler Brossard: "Their task—experienced, really, as an aesthetic/moral obligation—was to create a new sensibility and a new language with which to illuminate the existential crisis of the postwar American in conflict with his society's values" (qtd. in Skerl 2004, 17). The ultimate aim of such a sense of moral and aesthetic obligation was personal and cultural "renewal."

If this is a sociological crisis of the middle classes, it is also a philosophical and existential crisis more generally, and it is not difficult to also see affinities between Burroughs, the Beats, and the existentialist movement. As with many of the existentialists, most especially Jean-Paul Sartre and Albert Camus, there is a spirit of revolt in the Beats, and we can speak of both Burroughs and the Beats as trying to "redefine the world" in a way which connects to Sartre's declaration in *Existentialism and Humanism* that "existence comes before essence" (Sartre 2001). That is, for Sartre, as against the previous "essentialist" definitions of human nature, existentialism asserts the absolute independence of the individual subjectivity who is "thrown" into the world without a prior definition or identity. The figure of the existentialist can be seen as relating to the figure of the "hipster" in the Beat movement. Quoting Brossard, Skerl notes that "because he was opposed in feeling to those who owned the machinery of recognition . . . and thus defined legitimate space . . . the hipster was really nowhere . . . but longed from the very beginning to be somewhere" (qtd. in Skerl 2004, 18). Of course, for both the Beats and the existentialists, this longing to be somewhere was ultimately a question of personal responsibility, which could not be abdicated onto the wider society. Renewal, whether individual or societal, could come about only through the creation of new identities, in effect ex nihilo. In Kerouac's paradigmatic *On the Road,* for example, Sal Paradise announces: "rising from the underground, the sordid hipsters of America, a new beat generation" (qtd. in Skerl 2004, 26). This constitutes an unequivocal call to arms, for existentialists and hipsters alike. While, in Burroughs's fiction, everyone is in conflict, everyone is also responsible, for everyone is capable of resistance: "There are no victims, just accomplices; the mark collaborates with his exploiter in his own demise." For Burroughs, every individual is responsible for his or her own fate, and, in contemporary society, those who claim to be victims must face up to their own complicity in their oppression. This strong notion of responsibility, based on a complicity, is quintessentially Burroughsian (and also resonates with Sartre's existentialist conception of "bad faith"). As Ann Douglas notes, Burroughs was a lifelong critic of power, and the misuse of power, perhaps going back to his early understanding of Hitler's regime, and his realization that "everything that Hitler had done was legal" (Douglas 1999, xvi). For Burroughs, we are everywhere complicit with power, "to speak is to lie—to live is to collaborate" (Douglas 1999, xvi).

One of the most interesting issues in relation to the whole political dimension of this problematic relates to the possibility of identifying where the Beats can be placed politically on the spectrum of Right to Left? Skerl foregrounds this in terms, first, of the conflict between the political claims of the Beat movement and the political claims of the more established Left. This conflict is described as "a long-standing discursive battle between the countercultural and the scientific socialist points of view. Whereas the socialists advocated rational bureaucracy in the name of the proletariat, the counterculture grounded their vision of liberation in the 'magical' worldview of the non-Western world, which the socialists considered superstitious, ignorant and harmful" (Skerl 2004, 33). This is a very interesting perspective as it also allows us to broaden out the whole problematic beyond a simply Westernized perspective to embrace the very conflict between East and West, and this seems wholly appropriate given Burroughs's own connections to Morocco and Tangiers. Indeed, this is less an exclusively East and West problematic and more a question of what the Brazilian philosopher of education Paulo Freire has called the distorted relationship between the "metropolitan" societies and the Third World, which Freire refers to as "dependent societies" (Freire 1977, 14). Freire's understanding of the complex dynamics both between and within these societies is worth quoting here: "In the relationship between metropolitan and dependent societies, the alienation of the latter corresponds to the lordly manner of the former. In either case however, one must refrain from absolutising the statement for just as, among the alienated, there are those who think in a non-alienated manner, there are unlordly denizens of the metropolises. In both cases, for different reasons, they break with the norms of their respective contexts" (Freire 1977, 14).

Burroughs's work can thus be said to embrace a certain Third Worldism. What this also clarifies, however, is that the Left were ambiguous in their relation to Third Worldism and especially the vision of this put forward by the counterculture, which they regarded as "bourgeois." Freire, for example, is very critical of what he sees as a "sectarianism" common to certain aspects of both Right and Left on this issue (Freire 1977, 12). Ginsberg himself refers to this as "the tendency among the Marxists to deplore our bohemianism as some sort of petit bourgeois angelism" (Ginsberg qtd. in Skerl 2004, 33). This also connects our thematic more broadly to the whole edifice of Latin American fiction, which has a paradigmatic affinity to the Beat movement. For example, Skerl cites Octavio Paz in this context. Paz, in his native Mexico, offers a different vision or diagnosis of the problem from that offered by the scientific socialists. Third Worldism, on his terms, is understood from a spiritual rather than an economic perspective, and the reference here is to the 1950s: "We are facing obstacles that will not be economic but spiritual . . . in an industrial society that we are beginning to glimpse" (Paz qtd. in Skerl 2004, 33). What is required, according to Paz, is the "invention of a new vision of man" (Paz qtd. in Skerl 2004, 33).

It is certainly arguable that the Beats, and thus Burroughs himself, are connected more readily to the Magical Realist counterculture than to any other strand of thinking. This, in fact, for Skerl, is what makes the Beats identifiable as a "third force": "The Beat/Magical Realist counterculture thus constituted a 'third force' in the hemispheric cultural politics of the 1940s. Neither corporate-capitalist nor state-socialist, but with strong ties to indigenous ways of thinking and being" (Skerl 2004, 33). This is their integral Third Worldism, and it also connects them to Frantz Fanon's work most paradigmatically, in his *The Wretched of the Earth* (as well as to Albert Memmi's *The Colonizer and the Colonized* and to Freire's work). Here, Skerl is connecting Burroughs most especially to Kerouac and Ginsberg as the high trinity of the Beats. She delineates their common themes with a thinker such as Paz, and indeed the wider Magical Realist tradition, as "pre-Columbian myths and symbols, a nonlinear approach to time; open or dialogical forms; a faith in drug-induced insight; a turn to Eastern religions; and finally an imagery of nakedness and communion" (Skerl 2004, 33).

This Third Worldism, or "transnational perspective," represents an intervention in the dominance of a certain kind of capitalistic or "corporate liberalism" after 1940. One answer to this hegemony was of course the answer of the more traditional Left, that of what Skerl calls a "scientific socialism." Often the Beats would be placed precisely in this very space of opposition on the Left, but here Skerl reads the signs rather differently. This involves a discarding of the traditional Left position, and this discarding also has connections to the politics of the avant-garde, most notably to dissident sur-realists such as Georges Bataille and Pierre Klossowksi, and looks back to Arthur Rimbaud, among others. We can also see the emphasis on eroticism in Burroughs and the Beats more generally as connected to this thematic. Here, Mexico becomes paradigmatic: "The transnational counterculture constructed Mexico—with its rich cultural heritage of religious symbol-ism, indigenous ways of life and interpersonal (rather than bureaucratic) social relations—as a site of opposition to the corporate liberal version of modernity" (Skerl 2004, 40).

"A Cautionary Warning?"—On Burroughs and Ballard

In trying to understand Burroughs and his relation to philosophy, J. G. Ballard is a useful interlocutor. Ballard is in no doubt as to the quality of Burroughs's fiction, his specific place in the canon of experimental writing and writers: "a novel [*Naked Lunch*] that I believe to be the most important and original work of fiction by an American writer since World War II" (Ballard 1993, i). This can be said to connect Burroughs and our analysis of his work to the metalevel history of literature, and especially as we start to think about or introduce the concept of a philosophical literature, which tends to be associated almost exclusively with the existentialist movement. What I want to claim, in this context, is that Burroughs is most deserving of this title: his work is a philosophical fiction par excellence. Ballard is also revealing in his analysis of what the term "Naked Lunch" actually means: "Naked Lunch is both the addict's fix, the rush of pure sensation through the brain, and also the stark and unsentimental truth about ourselves, our self-delusions and deceits, served with a dressing of the spiciest humour" (Ballard 1993, i). Finally, there is a reference to the very process of charac-terization which Burroughs uses which again can be seen as quite specific: "Here, you will find a host of hilarious characters, led by the gregarious Dr. Benway, the most corrupt and charming physician in twentieth century lit-erature" (Ballard 1993, iii).

There is a proximity between Ballard and Burroughs and the philosophi-cal significance of their shared perspective on the contemporary world. Bal-lard speaks of an "ever more ambiguous world" and the "spectres of sinister technologies . . . an overlit realm ruled by advertising and pseudo-events, science and pornography" (Ballard 1990, 9). Citing the more optimistic tenor of Marshall McLuhan's readings of new media (Ballard 1990, 8), Ballard warns that we must, perhaps, pay more attention to Sigmund Freud's profound pessimism in *Civilisation and Its Discontents:* "Voyeurism, self-disgust, the infantile basis of our dreams and longings—these diseases of the psyche have now culminated in the most terrifying casualty of the century, the death of affect" (Ballard 1990, 9). For Ballard, this "demise of feeling and emotion" is linked intrinsically to the framework of "sex as the perfect arena; like a culture bed of sterile pus; for all the veronicas of our own perversions" (Ballard 1990, 9). The tone here is decidedly moral and impassioned, while obviously recognizing both the lure and the inherent ambivalence of meaning associated with many of these contemporary phenomena.

The philosophical resonances with Burroughs's work are clear. Taking *Naked Lunch* as an example, we can say that this novel eschews the usual psychological or realistic profiles of character or place. Instead, we are presented with a delirious and apocalyptic drama in which the boundaries between fiction and reality are radically blurred. Two such scenes are "Bradley the Buyer" and "AJ's Annual Party" in *Naked Lunch*. In the first case, we are presented with an apparently real character, Bradley, who in his work as a narcotics agent ("the best in the business") infiltrates the drug underworld. His espionage is so good that he is described as the "the only completeman in history" (Burroughs 1993, 27). However, Bradley falls victim to the lure of drugs himself: "A yen comes on him like a great black wind through the bones." The poetry of Burroughs's prose here is utterly distinctive and beautiful. But what one also gets is a move from a seemingly real situation to a delirious denouement, a radical surrealism. Bradley's addiction becomes so bad that he becomes a liability to the narcotics agency and so he is "destroyed with a flame thrower. The court of inquiry ruled that such means were justified in that the buyer had lost his human citizenship and was in consequence a creature without species" (29).

This delirious surrealism then moves back to what appears to be a more realist or sociopolitical critique, highlighting once more the hybridized nature of Burroughs's text. Burroughs describes the nature of drug addiction in sociological or psychological terms: "The junky's shame disappears with his non-sexual sociability which is also dependent on libido; the addict regards his body impersonally as an instrument to absorb the medium in which he lives; evaluates his tissue with the cold hands of a horse trader" (63). From surrealism back to social psychology, and then again the book reverts to the original surrealism with perhaps the most famous and grotesque of the scenes of *Naked Lunch,* that of "AJ's Annual Party." As Edmund

White has observed, *Naked Lunch* is a "delirious exploration of sexual violence," and this is nowhere more apparent than here. What this scene also demonstrates is a very radical blurring of the distinction between reality and fantasy. AJ is described as "that international-known impresario of blue movies and short wave tv" (79), and we have thus an initial ambiguity which runs throughout the scene—is what is being depicted real or simply a film or television fantasy? The reference to "blue movies" also anticipates the deeply pornographic nature of the scene. The extremism of the approach is not in doubt—"Cunts, pricks, fence straddlers, tonight I give you" (79). Who, we might ask, are the fence straddlers? Is this the fence between good and evil, or between what is real and merely delirious?

This ambiguity is exacerbated by the reference to "on screen"; "On Screen; Red-haired, green-eyed boy, white skin with a few freckles . . . kissing a thin brunette girl in slacks" (79). Here, we have Johnny and Mary, how very conventional. But it is Mary who asks Johnny to strip and not vice versa, and when he seeks to grope her breasts, she "stops his hands." She wants to "rim him": "she pushes his cheeks apart, leans down and begins licking his anus, moving her head in a slow circle" (80). Next she sucks him and then "straps on a rubber penis" (79). At this point, a hardly conventional scene is intensified in its radicalism. Mary works "the [rubber] penis up his [Johnny's] ass" (80), and next, they are joined by "Mark" in the doorway and become a threesome. Johnny is led by Mark and Mary into another room, and now it is Mark "who pushes his cock up Johnny's ass. . . . Mark's liquid spurts through Johnny" (80). From unconventional heterosexuality to a seemingly conventional homosexuality, although all in the context of an enigmatic threesome. But this is no final climax.

Next Mark and Johnny sit facing each other in a "vibrating chair" and "Johnny impaled on Mark's cock" (80). The scene abruptly shifts to becoming a "gallows" (80). Johnny's hands are tied behind his back. And it is Mark who ties the noose around Johnny's neck and who first moves to push Johnny off the platform, in an ultimate connection between sex and death, but Mary intervenes "Mary: No, let me" (85). Mark concurs, and it is thus Mary who pushes Johnny off the platform. As Johnny's neck is snapped, his "cock springs up and Mary guides it into her cunt," in a perfect orgasm of murder and coitus (85). The rope is cut, but Mary is still impaled. However, all is not yet over. As the scene becomes ever more extreme (or absurd), Mary begs to hang Mark but it is Mark who hangs her, tightening the noose around Mary's neck. He pushes her off the platform and her neck snaps: "Wheee, he [Mark] screams, turning into Johnny. Her neck snaps. A great fluid wave undulates through her body. Johnny drops to the floor and stands poised and alert like a young animal" (86). Thus we have sex, murder, identity metamorphosis, and identity transfer all in one go. In the finale, the surrealist and staged element is stressed, but there is also an important ultimate reinstantiation of the very distinction between the movies and how the actors are in "real life," between fantasy and reality: "Neon—chlorophyll green, purple, orange—flashes on and off. . . . FADEOUT. Mary, Johnny and Mark take a bow with the ropes around their necks. They are not as young as they appear in the Blue Movies. . . . [T]hey look tired and petulant" (89).

This extraordinary scene and finale of "AJ's Annual Party" can be connected in different ways to contemporary philosophy, and in the concluding section, I will draw out some of these connections.

In regard to contemporary philosophy, Burroughs's work can be especially connected to a strand of thinking which extends from French surrealism to Jacques Derrida (Derrida 1972), in the Continentalist philosophical tradition. Early surrealists such as Antonin Artaud and his "Theatre of Cruelty" (Artaud 1970) have connections to Burroughs here, especially in the concept of what Artaud calls the "body without organs, a pure body," in effect the authentic self who breathes for him/herself, and who can inspire cultural and social revolution. As with Burroughs, what Artaud is attacking here is the societal "organisation" of the body. Burroughs would seem to be aiming at something similar, a performed body which is both very real and intensely fictive or hallucinated. Artaud speaks of a nonphonetic, "hieroglyphic" *writing of the body* to bring about "*the alienation of alienation*" (Irwin 2010, 14). Certainly, Burroughs writes in a stylistic form which can border on the hieroglyphic, especially in scenes like "Bradley the Buyer" and "AJ's Annual Party" in *Naked Lunch,* as we have seen above. We have also seen how crucial the concept of alienation is for his work, and the attempted overcoming of such alienation. We might equally link Burroughs here to the work of the French Sadean tradition (derived from the work of the Marquis de Sade), and especially the writings of Georges Bataille (Bataille 1985). In this alternative tradition, the obscene is a primary notion of human consciousness, human sexuality is a highly questionable and contested phenomenon, and there are extreme and demonic forces in consciousness which are linked to the desire for death (cf. Irwin 2010).

In his consistent (if delirious) avowals of "eros" and embodiment, we might also connect Burroughs to Jacques Derrida's work on embodiment and sexuality. Derrida sets out to critique the disavowal of embodiment and sex in Plato's *Phaedo,* a view which Derrida sees as dominating much of the history of philosophy insofar as "Plato dismissed the senses" (Derrida 2005, 120). There is also "the prefiguring of touch" (Derrida 2005, 120), by which Derrida means the construction of a prefigured or preformed discourse which would subordinate touch first within the hierarchy of senses (to vision most especially but also to hearing). This will then be exacerbated by a hierarchy of sense subordinated to the intelligible or the rational. Derrida thus presents Plato here (or at least this singular version of Plato's) as "anti-tactile" (Derrida 2005, 120). Even in recent phenomenological discourse on the body, Derrida traces a limit which reaches a certain "anthropological limit of phenomenology" (Derrida 2005, 220). Phenomenology would still be too humanistic.

Derrida speaks of "amorous bodies, wrestling in the sheets of the internet's webs" (Derrida 2005, 301) and the whole image of virtual sexuality (or what Luciana Parisi has called "abstract sex" [Parisi 2004]) looms large, which Burroughs very obviously anticipates. This revolutionizes what we mean by touching, beyond an anthropological limit: "The sense of touch is the sense of the electronic age" (Derrida 2005, 354). This is "distance touching" (Derrida 2005, 301). Here, we reach the "limit of sense" (Derrida 2005, 308). Our senses would now become "spaced out" into an "areality"; "sight becomes distended" (Derrida 2005, 309), and this would be something to affirm for Derrida: "the oui that jouit" [le oui qui jouit] (Derrida 2005, 347). This is a reference to the "yes that plays" in Hélène Cixous's discourse (Cixous 1994, xviii), and it would all come back to the deconstructed I: "as in je/jeu" (Cixous 1994, xviii). This is the "I" that plays or the self which is also a "game," or "in the game," "en jeu," in Artaud's sense of "on stage." This joyous (and somewhat raucous) element in deconstruction specifically reminds one of Burroughs. In *Naked Lunch,* as we have seen, the "I" is played out in a kind of frenzied abandon of self and integrity, with the limits of morality and relationality (and indeed of life and embodiment per se) constantly being penetrated and transgressed by a radical movement of desire and writing. In this precise sense, we can say that Burroughs's work prefigures some of the most radical aspects of Derrida's deconstruction as well as, more generally, the movement of Continentalist philosophy itself.

But if there is a Rimbaudian "derangement of the senses" in Burroughs's writing, there is also a vehement political critique which extends beyond a mere decadence for the sake of decadence aesthetic. This dimension becomes clearest when we look at Burroughs's aforementioned connections to Third Worldism. Burroughs seeks, as Ann Douglas observes, to "punch a hole in the big lie" (Douglas 1999, xxii), and we can see this, among other places, in his return to animistic values, a literary and mystical move which attacks the basis of Western modernity and indeed the very self-justification of the West itself. For Burroughs, much of human life and human action can best be understood in terms of a demonology and a thematic of possession which bears little relation to post-Cartesian thinking in the West. However, as Freire has shown, reductionist readings of animism and magic in non-Western societies apply an externalist logic which fails to understand the inner coherence of the magic system (Freire 1977). The genius of Burroughs's work is not simply to avoid such reductionist readings of so-called primitive or Third World magic, but to actually harness the resources of the magical universe to bolster the power and articulacy of literature itself. In this, we can say that Burroughs practiced literature as magic while simultaneously thematizing a fundamental misunderstanding between East and West. In this, he was perhaps the least likely Third Worldist.

As with Deleuze and Guattari's *Anti-Oedipus* (Deleuze and Guattari 2004), as Foucault (Foucault 2004) notes, Derrida's texts are also always directed against a certain kind of "fascism"; "the fascism in us all, in our heads and in our everyday behaviour . . . the tracking down of all variations of fascism, from the enormous ones that surround us and crush us to the petty ones that constitute the tyrannical bitterness of our everyday lives" (Foucault 2004, xiv). We have seen that Burroughs's work vehemently operates on an analogous trajectory.

References

Artaud, Antonin. 1970. *The Theatre and Its Double.* Translated by Victor Corti. London: Calder.

Ballard, J. G. 1990. Introduction to the French edition of *Crash.* 1974. Reprinted in his *Crash.* Triad Paladin: London.

———. 1993. Introduction to *Naked Lunch,* by William Burroughs. London: Flamingo.

Bataille, Georges. 1985. *Visions of Excess: Selected Writings 1927–1939.* Edited by Allan Stoekl. Minneapolis: University of Minnesota Press.

Burroughs, William. 1993. *Naked Lunch.* London: Flamingo.

———. 1999. *Word Virus: The William Burroughs Reader.* Edited by James Grauerholz and Ira Silverberg. London: Flamingo.

Cixous, Hélène. 1994. *The Hélène Cixous Reader.* Edited by Susan Sellars. London: Routledge.

Corso, Gregory. 1970. *Elegiac Feelings American.* New York: New Directions.

Deleuze, Gilles, and Félix Guattari. 2004. *Anti-Oedipus.* London: Continuum.

Derrida, Jacques. 1972. *Writing and Difference.* Chicago: University of Chicago Press.

———. 2005. *On Touching—Jean-Luc Nancy.* Stanford: Stanford University Press.

Douglas, Ann. 1999. "Punching a Hole in the Big Lie: The Achievement of William S. Burroughs." In *Word Virus: The William Burroughs Reader,* edited by James Grauerholz and Ira Silverberg. London: Flamingo.

Ferlinghetti, Lawrence. 1958. *A Coney Island of the Mind.* New York: New Directions.

Foucault, Michel. 2004. Foreword to *Anti-Oedipus,* by Gilles Deleuze and Félix Guattari. London: Continuum.

Freire, Paulo. 1977. *Cultural Action for Freedom.* Translated by J. da Veiga Coutinho. London: Nicholls.

Irwin, Jones. 2010. *Derrida and the Writing of the Body.* Surrey: Ashgate.

Kerouac, Jack. 2002. *On the Road.* London: Penguin.

Marcuse, Herbert. 2002. *One Dimensional Man.* London: Routledge.

Parisi, Luciana. 2004. *Abstract Sex.* London: Continuum.

Plato. 1961. *Phaedo.* London: Penguin.

Rodley, Chris, ed. 1997. *Cronenberg on Cronenberg.* Rev. ed. London: Faber.

Sartre, Jean-Paul. 2001. *Existentialism and Humanism.* London: Methuen.

Skerl, Jennie, ed. 2004. *Reconstructing the Beats.* London: Palgrave, 2004.

Žižek, Slavoj. 2006. *Lacan.* London: Granta.

CONTRIBUTORS

CHRISTOPHER ADAMO is assistant professor of philosophy at Centenary College. He has published articles on phenomenology and existentialism in *Philosophy Today* and *Graduate Faculty Philosophy Journal*. His recent work focuses on religious pluralism and the conditions for genuine interfaith respect. Adamo's research interests have also turned toward utopian studies, specifically, the history of utopian literature and its social and political functions. His most recent article, "One Ring or Many? Lessing's Nathan the Wise and Religious Pluralism," appears in *Philosophy and Literature*.

MICHEAL SEAN BOLTON teaches at East Tennessee State University. His research focuses on the application of critical theory in the interpretation of experimental and postmodern U.S. literature with particular interest in poststructuralist, cybernetic, and posthuman theoretical interpretation. He is currently at work on a book-length study of William S. Burroughs's experimental novels. He is also a poet and a musician working on nonstructural and ambient music

ANN CHARTERS is emerita professor of English at the University of Connecticut in Storrs. A preeminent authority on the Beat writers, she wrote the first biography of Jack Kerouac; compiled *Beats and Company,* a collection of her own photographs of Beat writers; and edited the best-selling *Portable Beat Reader.* Charters also edited *The Portable Kerouac Reader; Selected Letters of Jack Kerouac, 1957–1969; Beat Down to Your Soul; The Portable Sixties Reader;* and several textbooks, including *The Story and Its Writer.* With Samuel Charters, she coauthored *Brother-Souls: John Clellon Holmes, Jack Kerouac, and the Beat Generation.*

ED D'ANGELO studied anarchism with David Wieck and taught philosophical psychology and political philosophy at Rensselaer Polytechnic Institute before turning to library science. He is currently a supervising librarian at the Brooklyn Public Library. D'Angelo has published a series of political essays in anarchist magazines that culminated in his analysis of the war on drugs in "The Moral Culture of Drug Prohibition" in the *Humanist* (1994). He was a member of the founding collective that opened the anarchist bookstore Blackout Books in New York's Lower East Side. He examines the decline of American culture as reflected in its public libraries in his most current book, *Barbarians at the Gates of the Public Library: How Postmodern Consumer Capitalism Threatens Democracy, Civil Education and the Public Good* (2006), and in "The Public Library, Commercialized" in the *American Dissident* (2008).

SHARIN N. ELKHOLY is assistant professor of philosophy at the University of Houston–Downtown. Her research interests are in the intersections of phenomenology, ontology, and existentialism. Elkholy's *Heidegger and a Metaphysics of Feeling: Angst and the Finitude of Being* (2008) establishes a framework for understanding the ontological dimensions of community and the foundations of a prereflective mode of intersubjective recognition. She is author of "Friendship Across Differences" (*Janus Head*, 2007); "What's Gender Got to Do with It: A Phenomenology of Romantic Love" (*Athenäum: Jahrbuch für Romantik*, 1999); and "Feminism and Race" for *The Internet Encyclopedia of Philosophy* (forthcoming).

JANE FALK is senior lecturer at the University of Akron. Her areas of research and interest include the work of Joanne Kyger, Philip Whalen, Lew Welch, and Gary Snyder, as well as the influence of Zen Buddhism on writers associated with the Beat movement. She has contributed an appreciation of Philip Whalen's "The Diamond Noodle" to *Continuous Flame,* a tribute volume to Whalen, as well as biographies of Whalen to the *Encyclopedia of Beat Literature* and other works. Her essay on Zen influences on Whalen's poetry appears in *The Emergence of Buddhist American Literature*, and her review of Joanne Kyger's collected poems, *About Now,* appears in the online magazine *Jacket.*

JOSH MICHAEL HAYES is lecturer in Philosophy at Santa Clara University. He was previously visiting assistant professor of philosophy at Loyola Marymount University, and a postdoctoral Fellow in the Humanities at Stanford University. He specializes in the history of philosophy with an emphasis upon the intersection between ancient Greek philosophy and environmental ethics. His articles have appeared in numerous philosophy journals, including the *Review of Metaphysics* and *Philosophy Today*. His most recent research explores the influence of Aristotle upon pragmatic naturalism and contemporary American literature.

JONES IRWIN is lecturer in philosophy at St. Patrick's College, Dublin City University. His monograph *Derrida and the Writing of the Body* was published in 2010, and he has a forthcoming book on Paulo Freire's philosophy of education. He has a long-standing interest in philosophy of literature and the writings of William Burroughs, and has published extensively on avant-garde writings from Bataille to Pasolini. His next project is a book of interviews assessing the relationship between the Slovenian psychoanalytical philosopher Slavoj Žižek and the Slovenian context of independence from Yugoslavia and the art, punk and political movements (NSK), which contributed significantly to this process.

A. ROBERT LEE, formerly of the University of Kent, U.K., has been professor of American literature at Nihon University, Tokyo, since 1997. His publications include *Designs of Blackness: Mappings in the Literature and Culture of Afro-America* (1998); *Multicultural American Literature: Comparative Black, Native, Latino/a and Asian American Fictions* (2003), which won the American Book Award for 2004; *Japan Textures: Sight and Word*, with Mark Gresham (2007); *Gothic to Multicultural: Idioms of Imagining in American Literary Fiction* (2008); *Modern American Counter Writing: Beats, Outriders, Ethnics* (2010); and the four-volume *Native American Writing* (2011). He is editor of *The Beat Generation Writers* (1995) and has written on Burroughs, Ted Joans, LeRoi Jones/Amiri Baraka, Bob Kaufman, Oscar Zeta Acosta, Diane di Prima, Joanne Kyger, Anne Waldman, Nanao Sakaki, Michael Horovitz, and other international Beats.

PAUL MESSERSMITH-GLAVIN is a longtime political organizer who helped found the Youth Greens, was a member of the Left Green Network, and is a part of the Parasol Climate Collective. He is a board member of the Institute for Anarchist Studies, and a member of the editorial collective of the journal *Perspectives on Anarchist Theory*. He works as a community acupuncturist in Portland, Oregon.

ERIK MORTENSON is assistant professor in the Department of English and Comparative Literature at Koç University in Istanbul. In addition to developing Koç's literature program, he has published numerous articles on the Beats in journals such as *Chicago Review, Janus Head,* and *College Literature* and has book chapters in *The Emergence of Buddhist American Literature* and *The Beat Generation: Critical Essays.* His book *Capturing the Beat Moment: Cultural Politics and the Poetics of Presence* (2011) examines "the moment" as one of the primary motifs of Beat writing. Currently, he is exploring the trope of the shadow in postwar American literature, photography, and film.

DAVID NEED teaches in the Department of Religion, the Department of Slavic and Eurasian Language and Literature, and the International Comparative Studies Program at Duke University. Recent publications in *Talisman: A Journal of Contemporary Poetry and Poetics* include: "Kerouac's Buddhism" (2006); "Singing at Dawn/Weaving the World: Reading the *Rgveda*" (2006); and "A Man Made of Words" (2007). David's poetry and essays have appeared most recently in *Golden Handcuffs Review* and *Hambone.*

MARC OLMSTED has taught at San Francisco State University, Naropa University, University of California Santa Cruz, and regularly teaches "Writing Kerouac/Sitting Buddha: Spontaneous Poetics and Big Mind" at Writers .com/Writers on the Net. Ginsberg wrote, in his introduction to Olmsted's poetry in New Directions in Prose & Poetry No. 37, that Olmsted "inherited Burroughs' scientific nerve & Kerouac's movie-minded line nailed down with gold eyebeam." Olmsted's work has appeared in *City Lights Journal,* the anthology *Outlaw Bible of American Poetry, Buddhadharma, New York Quarterly,* and a variety of small presses. His own books include *Milky Desire* (1991), *Résumé* (1998), and *What Use Am I a Hungry Ghost?—Poems From 3-Year Retreat* (2001), which also has an introduction by Ginsberg. Olmsted's current book project is a memoir of his relationship with Ginsberg, including their correspondence. As a senior student of Lama Tharchin Rinpoche, he continues to lead meditation from his home in Oakland, California, Last Chance Gonpa.

TOM PYNN is assistant professor of philosophy at Kennesaw State University and coordinator for the Peace Studies program. His poetry has appeared in such publications as *VOX, Interdisciplinary Studies in Literature and Environment,* and *Earth First! Journal.* He has published scholarly essays in *East-West Connections, Humanities in the South, Southeastern*

Review of Asian Studies, and elsewhere, and has contributed cross-cultural essays on phenomenology and Buddhist ontology, ethics, and aesthetics to edited volumes.

ROSEANNE GIANNINI QUINN teaches English, women's studies, and intercultural studies at De Anza College in the San Francisco Bay Area. For the past twenty years, she has researched and published in Italian American literature and culture and multicultural feminist theory. She is very interested in the writing of the San Francisco Beat poets and their contemporary legacy. She has a forthcoming essay on Carole Maso appearing in a volume on Italian American literature and culture, and she is currently writing a monograph on Italian American women narrating the popular and the avant-garde.

F. SCOTT SCRIBNER is associate professor of philosophy at the University of Hartford. He works in nineteenth- and twentieth-century philosophy, with a particular interest in marshaling the conceptual resources of post-Kantian German Idealism for theorizing technology and mass media. He has published numerous articles in this field in journals such as *Idealistic Studies, Journal of Value Inquiry,* and *International Philosophical Quarterly,* as well as the book *Matters of Spirit: J. G. Fichte and the Technological Imagination* (2010). His work with the Nineteenth Jena Circle, his affinity for the surrealist's own uniquely playful approach to technology, and his own irreverent attitude make the Beats inevitable consorts.

ANDREAS ENGH SELAND has taught aesthetics and formal logic at the University of Oslo. In 2010, he won first prize in a short-story competition held by the Norwegian Literary Festival, and his work has since been published in a short-story anthology and in Norway's leading literary magazine, *Bokvennen.* His research interests include the relationship between alienation and ruins in Romantic and post-Romantic literature, German idealism, and Lacanian psychoanalysis.

DAVID STERRITT is chair of the National Society of Film Critics, film professor at Columbia University and the Maryland Institute College of Art, professor emeritus at Long Island University, chief book critic of *Film Quarterly,* and co-chair of the Columbia University Seminar on Cinema and Interdisciplinary Interpretation. His writing on the Beats has appeared in the *Journal of Aesthetics and Art Criticism, Mosaic,* the *New York Times,* the *Christian Science Monitor, The Greenwood Encyclopedia of Poets and Poetry,* and elsewhere. His books include *Mad to Be Saved: The Beats, the '50s, and Film* (1998) and *Screening the Beats: Media Culture and the Beat Sensibility* (2004), and he is currently writing a third book on the Beats.

INDEX

The Philosophy of Popular Culture

The books published in the Philosophy of Popular Culture series will illuminate and explore philosophical themes and ideas that occur in popular culture. The goal of this series is to demonstrate how philosophical inquiry has been reinvigorated by increased scholarly interest in the intersection of popular culture and philosophy, as well as to explore through philosophical analysis beloved modes of entertainment, such as movies, TV shows, and music. Philosophical concepts will be made accessible to the general reader through examples in popular culture. This series seeks to publish both established and emerging scholars who will engage a major area of popular culture for philosophical interpretation and examine the philosophical underpinnings of its themes. Eschewing ephemeral trends of philosophical and cultural theory, authors will establish and elaborate on connections between traditional philosophical ideas from important thinkers and the ever-expanding world of popular culture.

Series Editor

Mark T. Conard, Marymount Manhattan College, NY

Books in the Series

The Philosophy of Stanley Kubrick, edited by Jerold J. Abrams
Football and Philosophy, edited by Michael W. Austin
Tennis and Philosophy, edited by David Baggett
The Philosophy of Film Noir, edited by Mark T. Conard
The Philosophy of Martin Scorsese, edited by Mark T. Conard
The Philosophy of Neo-Noir, edited by Mark T. Conard
The Philosophy of Spike Lee, edited by Mark T. Conard
The Philosophy of the Coen Brothers, edited by Mark T. Conard
The Philosophy of David Lynch, edited by William J. Devlin and Shai Biderman
The Philosophy of Horror, edited by Thomas Fahy
The Philosophy of The X-Files, edited by Dean A. Kowalski
Steven Spielberg and Philosophy, edited by Dean A. Kowalski
The Philosophy of Joss Whedon, edited by Dean A. Kowalski and S. Evan Kreider
The Philosophy of Charlie Kaufman, edited by David LaRocca
The Philosophy of the Western, edited by Jennifer L. McMahon and B. Steve Csaki
The Philosophy of Steven Soderbergh, edited by R. Barton Palmer and Steven M. Sanders
The Olympics and Philosophy, edited by Heather L. Reid and Michael W. Austin
The Philosophy of David Cronenberg, edited by Simon Riches
The Philosophy of Science Fiction Film, edited by Steven M. Sanders

CPSIA information can be obtained at www.ICGtesting.com
Printed in the USA
BVOW072251190312

285229BV00003B/3/P

9 780813 135809